Teaching the Global Dimension

V... ...ng an
i... ...oom.
E... ...ddress
t...

w... ...apters
o... ...actice

-
-
-
- ...more

-
- ...lobal

gl... ...ld of
In... ...ctice.
at... ...chers
to... ...sion
tra... ...cher

D... ...t.

C... ...JK.

Teaching the Global Dimension

Key principles and effective practice

Edited by
David Hicks and Cathie Holden

Routledge
Taylor & Francis Group

LONDON AND NEW YORK

First published 2007
by Routledge
2 Park Square, Milton Park, Abingdon, Oxon OX14 4RN

Simultaneously published in the USA and Canada
by Routledge
270 Madison Ave, New York, NY 10016

*Routledge is an imprint of the Taylor & Francis Group, an informa
business*

Typeset in Garamond by
HWA Text and Data Management, Tunbridge Wells
Printed and bound in Great Britain by
Antony Rowe Ltd, Chippenham, Wiltshire

British Library Cataloguing in Publication Data
A catalogue record for this book is available from the British
Library

Library of Congress Cataloging-in-Publication Data
A catalog record for this book has been requested

ISBN10: 0–415–40448–7 (hbk)
ISBN10: 0–415–40449–5 (pbk)
ISBN10: 0–203–96277–X (ebk)

ISBN13: 978–0–415–40448–8 (hbk)
ISBN13: 978–0–415–40449–5 (pbk)
ISBN13: 978–0–203–96277–0 (ebk)

Contents

Illustrations

Boxes

Figures

Tables

Contributors

Margot Brown is National Coordinator of the Centre for Global Education at York St John University. Having trained in primary education in Edinburgh, she has since taught in Newcastle, London, New Zealand and France. She worked with the Oxfam Education Team in London and then the Centre for Urban Educational Studies. Her work has focused on global issues, including diversity. Since joining the Centre in York she has worked in a range of countries and has developed and published work in human rights education. In addition she has developed work with teachers of modern foreign languages to help them include global issues in their teaching. Address: Centre for Global Education, York St John University, Lord Mayor's Walk, York YO31 7EX (m.brown@yorksj.ac.uk).

Hilary Claire is a freelance writer, lecturer and consultant on history and citizenship. She was brought up and educated in South Africa which has strongly informed her commitment to equality and democracy. She was for many years a primary teacher and deputy head in London, then an advisory teacher in race and gender equality, and then a senior lecturer in history, education and citizenship on primary ITT courses in higher education, most recently at London Metropolitan University. She is the author of several books and articles about equality, teaching history and citizenship in the primary sector, and has edited chapters particularly about equality issues (hilary.claire@dsl.pipex.co.uk).

Lynn Davies is Professor of International Education and Director of the Centre for International Education and Research at the University of Birmingham. Her major teaching, research and consultancy interests are in educational management internationally, particularly concerning democracy, citizenship, gender and human rights. She takes a specific focus on conflict and education, in terms of how education contributes to conflict and/or to peace or civil renewal. She is author of *Education and Conflict: Complexity and Chaos* (2004). Her current research is in the area of pupil participation in decision-making in school and the community. Address: School of Education, University of Birmingham, Birmingham B15 2TT (L.Davies@bham.ac.uk).

Teresa Garlake currently works as a primary school teacher and writer in Oxford. She has previously worked for several development organisations, including Oxfam and Save the Children. Teresa specialises in geography and citizenship education and has written a wide range of educational resources aimed at teachers, and information books for young people. She enjoys working closely with teachers and children to develop materials, trialling new activities and approaches in the classroom. She is also closely involved in her local community and has initiated an intergenerational project which now works in schools across Oxfordshire (tgarlake@onetel.com).

Ange Grunsell is a writer and tutor on the Education for Sustainability programme at London South Bank University. She has taught in both primary and secondary schools and is the author of many learning resources on global issues for children and teachers. Ange has also worked in Initial Teacher Training, with particular focus on developing HE/school partnerships and widening participation in teaching. She was head of Oxfam's Development Education Programme until late 2005 and now undertakes freelance consultancy in global citizenship education. She lives on the Welsh/English border near Hay-on-Wye (ARGrunsell@aol. com).

David Hicks is Professor in the School of Education at Bath Spa University. He is internationally recognised for his work on the need for a global and futures dimension in the curriculum and is particularly interested in ways of helping students and teachers think more critically and creatively about the future. He has published widely in the fields of futures education, global education, geographical education and citizenship education. His most recent books are *Lessons for the Future: the missing dimension in education*, Trafford Publishing (2005) and *Citizenship for the Future: a practical classroom guide*, WWF-UK (2001). Address: School of Education, Bath Spa University, Newton Park, Bath BA2 9BN (d.hicks@ bathspa.ac.uk).

Cathie Holden is Associate Professor in Education at the University of Exeter where she co-ordinates both the PGCE primary humanities and the secondary citizenship programmes. Prior to this she taught in middle schools for 15 years. She is on the QCA working party for citizenship education and co-ordinates regional training for newly qualified teachers of citizenship as part of her work for CitizEd. She is currently researching children's understanding of key local and global issues and the implications of this for the classroom. Books include: *Children as Citizens: Education for Participation* and *Education for Citizenship* (both with Nick Clough). Address: School of Education, University of Exeter, Heavitree Road, Exeter EX1 2LU (c.e.holden@ex.ac.uk).

Harriet Marshall is a lecturer in International Education at the Centre for the Study of Education in an International Context, Bath University. Her interests include: global education and citizenship education; international education; globalisation, education and the curriculum; gender and global citizenship education. She has written on all of these themes, some of which feature in her doctoral thesis *The Sociology of Global Education* (Cambridge 2005). Prior to lecturing, Harriet was a full time teacher of politics, sociology and history at a London comprehensive school. Address: The Centre for Education in an International Context (CEIC), Department of Education, Bath University, BA2 7AY (hm224@bath.ac.uk).

Fran Martin is senior lecturer in the School of Education at Exeter University. She worked as a teacher, advisory teacher and deputy head in Buckinghamshire before moving into higher education. Her research interests are geographical and environmental education with an emphasis on the global dimension and a focus on teacher development at ITE and CPD levels. Recent research has focused on beginning teachers' development as teachers of primary geography, and the impact of study visits to economically developing countries on teacher understanding and practice in the field of sustainable development education. She is editor of *Primary Geographer*. Address: School of Education, University of Exeter, Heavitree Road, Exeter EX1 2LU (f.e.martin@ex.ac.uk).

Robin Richardson is a director of the Insted consultancy and was previously director of the Runnymede Trust and before that chief inspector in Brent and adviser for multicultural education in Berkshire. In recent years he has acted as a consultant for the Commission on the Future of Multi-Ethnic Britain, the Commission on British Muslims and Islamophobia, the British Council and the Churches' Commission for Racial Justice. Recent publications include *Here, There and Everywhere* (2004) and *Education and Race Equality* (2005). For the DfES he has written *Aiming High: Understanding the Needs of Minority Ethnic Pupils in Mainly White Schools* (2004) and compiled the website *Bullying around Racism, Culture and Religion: How to Prevent It and What to Do When It Happens* (2006). Address: Insted Consultancy, 14 High Street, Wembley, HA9 8DD (robin@insted.co.uk).

Julia Tanner is Head of Continuing Professional Development and Educational Enterprise in the Faculty of Education, Community and Leisure at Liverpool John Moores University. She was previously a classroom teacher and then a teacher educator at Leeds Metropolitan University. She has a long-standing interest in primary geography and the emotional aspects of learning. Julia has been involved in global education for more than two decades and is a trustee of the World Studies Trust. Address: Faculty of Education, Community and Leisure, Liverpool John Moores University, Barkhill House, Barkhill Road, Aigburth, Liverpool L17 6BD (j.tanner@livjm.ac.uk).

Ros Wade is Co-director of the first Education for Sustainability programme in the UK, a result of collaboration between London South Bank University and a consortium of environmental and development NGOs. She writes and researches in the field of education for sustainability and global citizenship and has contributed to a number of publications, including *The Sustainability Curriculum* (Earthscan 2004) and *Teaching for a Sustainable Future* (WWF and Centre for Cross-Curriculum Initiatives 2003). She has also written distance learning materials on environmental and development perspectives and helped develop the first education doctorate specialising in equality, diversity and sustainability. Address: London South Bank University, 103 Borough Road, London SE1 0AA (wader@lsbu.ac.uk).

Foreword

Global issues increasingly touch all our lives. We are increasingly aware of them from media coverage, and the twenty-first century child will be greatly influenced by them. Less than 80 years ago no one owned a TV and few people travelled more than 50 miles from their home town in their lives. Today television and the internet bring international news, sport and culture into our homes daily, and international travel is becoming the norm, as is global trade and employment. Our society is enhanced by peoples, cultures and languages originating in many different parts of the world.

If we are to successfully develop a modern, world-class curriculum that prepares all learners for the future we must ensure that it is permeated by a global dimension. A curriculum fit for purpose in the twenty-first century should encourage the development of critically thinking pupils who are not only aware of global issues and events from different points of view but also realise that they can be effective participators in working on challenges, solutions and opportunities.

The Qualifications and Curriculum Authority develops a modern, world-class curriculum that will inspire and challenge all learners and prepare them for the future. Such a curriculum cannot be complete without a global dimension to learning.

The Department for Education and Skills guidance paper, *Developing a Global Dimension in the School Curriculum*, outlines eight key concepts of the global dimension, that underpin understanding of our local–global interdependence.

The new aims for the national curriculum developed by QCA, in consultation with schools, clearly indicate the central importance of the global dimension to the curriculum with a set of aims devised to encourage active and responsible citizenship. Many schools are already embedding a global dimension in their curriculum, actively developing and sustaining global partnerships with schools around the world.

This book will help envision the theory into practice, and is a welcome addition to the debate about what a global dimension will look like in our schools.

Mick Waters
Director of Curriculum
Qualifications and Curriculum Authority
London

Preface

How does a book such as this come about? In the recent sense it began when we were looking at the booklet *Developing the Global Dimension in the School Curriculum* (DfES 2005) and felt that the matter was so important that it warranted a whole book for teachers, student teachers and their tutors. Thanks to the work of all our contributors you are now able to read such a book.

But the book also has a much longer historical gestation reflected in my own (DH) educational journey. As a student in the early 1960s, concerned about a range of global problems, I felt that I needed to know a lot more about what was happening in the world. Whilst a good grammar school education had not covered such matters, I was excited as a young geography teacher, in the late 1960s, to find that my subject was beginning to recognise the importance of studying a range of contemporary global issues. As a young college lecturer in the early 1970s I then became aware of the innovative work of the World Studies Project which focused directly on the need for a global perspective in education. As a post-graduate researcher in the late 1970s I found that a number of issue-based educations were internationally addressing global issues such as poverty, injustice, environment, race, conflict and interdependence. During the 1980s I was able to put these interests into practice through a national Schools Council curriculum project.

In the latter part of the 1980s, however, I witnessed much of this work being attacked and marginalised as the result of a conservative national curriculum being introduced in England and Wales. The innovative work of many educators, organisations, networks and LEAs disappeared or went underground and it felt as if twenty-five years' work on the need for a global dimension in education might have been lost. But in the mid-1990s, as schools became accustomed to the national curriculum, it was clear that something was missing and interest revived in contemporary local–global issues. By the late 1990s citizenship and education for sustainable development were recognised as integral to good education, as also was the need for a global dimension in the curriculum. It seems appropriate that in the twenty-first century we can now build on this good practice from the past in order to teach children about the global challenges of today and tomorrow.

This book is aimed primarily at teachers (both primary and secondary), student teachers and tutors working in Initial Teacher Education and Training. We also hope it will be of interest to educators more widely. The chapters in Part I set out an appropriate educational framework for understanding global concerns. Chapter 1 examines the various ways in which educators have responded to the need for a global dimension in the curriculum. It identifies a number of international initiatives which offer considerable expertise in relation to teaching and learning about world issues. Chapter 2 examines the field of global education and sets out a fourfold model that identifies the key elements required in order to identify good practice. Chapter 3 looks at what is known about young people's concerns for their world and for the future, and Chapter 4 sets out the findings of a research project on the knowledge, understanding and motivation of trainee teachers in relation to a global dimension. Chapter 5 highlights a range of strategies to help teachers handle controversial global issues more confidently in the classroom.

The chapters in Part II take eight key concepts which need to underpin appropriate learning experiences in the classroom – conflict, social justice, values and perceptions, sustainability, interdependence, human rights, diversity and citizenship. Each is explored here in detail for the first time. Taken together these chapters provide a conceptual framework for developing, teaching and evaluating a global dimension across the curriculum. Each follows the same format: i) a brief introduction to the issue; ii) reference to positive action for change that is being taken to address the issue; and iii) examples of current good practice in the classroom. The final two chapters in Part III demonstrate the different ways in which a global dimension can be developed in the curriculum, both in primary and secondary schools.

Finally, our thanks must go to all those, both past and present, who have worked tirelessly in so many ways to help establish a global dimension in the curriculum.

David Hicks
Bath Spa University

Cathie Holden
Exeter University

Acknowledgements

Figure 2.1 – Copyright One World Trust.

Figures 2.2 and 2.4 and Box 2.1 are reprinted with the permission of Pearson Education Ltd from Fisher, S. and Hicks, D. (1985) *World Studies 8–13: A Teacher's Handbook*, Edinburgh: Oliver & Boyd.

Table 2.1 and Box 2.2 are reprinted with the permission of Pippin Publishing Corporation from Pike, G. and Selby, D. (2000) *In the Global Classroom 2*, Toronto: Pippin Publishing. All rights reserved.

Figure 2.3 is reproduced with permission of Oxfam GB from *A Curriculum for Global Citizenship* (1997) Oxford: Oxfam GB. Oxfam GB does not necessarily endorse any text or activities that accompany the materials.

Figure 7.1 is reproduced with permission of Oxfam GB from The coffee chain game (online 2006) Oxford: Oxfam GB. Oxfam GB does not necessarily endorse any text or activities that accompany the materials.

Figures 10.1, 10.2 and 10.3, and Boxes 10.1 and 10.2 are adapted by the author from Garlake, T. (2003) *The Challenge of Globalisation*, Oxford: Oxfam GB, with the permission of Oxfam GB. Oxfam GB does not necessarily endorse any text or activities that accompany the materials, nor has it approved the adapted text.

Figures 11.1 and 11.2 reproduced with thanks to Viv Isotta.

Figure 14.2 is reproduced with the permission of Shelly School.

Parts of Chapter 2 first appeared in *Educational Review*, 55 (3), 2003.

Part I
The global dimension

Chapter 1

Responding to the world

David Hicks

How can and should education respond to world events in the early twenty-first century? This chapter begins by noting the long-standing interest which teachers and others have had in helping young people become more world-minded. It then considers some of the educational responses to global issues that have emerged over recent decades and, through a series of thumbnail sketches, indicates both their variety and their relevance to schools today.

Introduction

What is it that teachers need to know if they are to help young people make sense of the world in the early twenty-first century? Long-standing global issues – those to do with poverty, environment, conflict and social justice – constantly take on new forms, whether in relation to the complexities of globalisation, the 'war against terrorism' or global climate change. Some of the global trends reported in recent Worldwatch Institute reports (2005, 2006) include: a) a decrease in the number of wars worldwide; b) severe weather events on the rise; c) wind power as the fastest growing energy source; d) the gap between the poorest and richest countries continuing to grow; e) world population growth slowing down. Clearly some global trends are positive whilst others are a cause for concern. In trying to assess the current state of the world some commentators have argued that we may be on the edge of a major transition.

> The western economic model – the fossil-fuel based, automobile centred, throw away economy – that so dramatically raised living standards for part of humanity during [the last] century is in trouble ... The shift towards an environmentally sustainable economy may be as profound a transition as the Industrial Revolution that led to the current dilemma was.
>
> (Worldwatch Institute 1999: 4)

Global issues, trends and events are so called because they are ones that have a major impact across the planet. It would be wrong, however, to see them as issues that only occur 'elsewhere' and thus perhaps not of relevance to young people in our own communities today. Every global issue has a local impact, though its form may vary from place to place – local and global have become two sides of the same coin.

These are not, of course, matters which educators are unaware of. Indeed a concern that education should help young people become more world-minded dates back to the work of progressive teachers in the early twentieth century. As this chapter will show, there is thus a long tradition of teaching about global issues, trends and events and a growing consensus has emerged that such matters have a major part to play in educational debates.

Eight out of ten 11–16-year-olds, for example, feel that it is important to learn about global issues at school so that they can make more informed choices about their lives (MORI 1998). Official support for this in England, Scotland and Wales is given respectively in *Developing a Global Dimension in the School Curriculum* (DfES 2005), *The Global Dimension in the Curriculum* (Scottish Executive 2001) and *Education for Sustainable Development and Global Citizenship* (ACCAC 2002). The Department for International Development (2006a) provides a website for teachers which identifies a wide range of resources that help young people develop a global perspective. Subject bodies, such as the Geographical Association, have similarly responded with detailed advice for teachers on the global dimension in geography (Lambert *et al.* 2004).

The argument that lies behind initiatives such as these is that we cannot fully understand life today in our own communities unless we set this in the wider global context. What happens elsewhere in the world constantly impacts on our daily lives whether this is international finance, food, fashion, crime, the weather or popular music. Education thus has a central role to play in helping create citizens who can think and act globally as well as locally. This is no easy task for at heart this is about how we help young people understand their interconnections with others and how we help them make sense of the human condition. On the one hand humans are capable of great compassion, altruism and vision and on the other great cruelty, selfishness and destruction. On the day after September 11, 2001 I had to talk on the global dimension to over a hundred new PGCE students. I struggled all morning with what I might say in the light of the events in New York. In the end all I could say was:

> As you will be only too well aware the world is both a good place and a bad place. This will also be true of your own communities and the schools you are about to teach in. One of the key tasks for you as a teacher is to find a way of being present to that tension, both in your own life and those of your pupils.

Given the history of the twentieth century it is not surprising that in the 1990s many people looked forward to the new century with some ambivalence (Real World Coalition 1996). The future was seen as a place for concern rather than as a source of hope. Hope, however, has to be central to the human condition. This means that any classroom investigation of an issue must look not only at the nature of the problem but also at the range of possible solutions. Not to do so would be an educational crime for the result is to disempower pupils (surely not one of our learning outcomes) rather than empowering them to take part in responsible action for change. 'One of the tasks of the progressive educator …', says Paulo Freire, 'is to unveil opportunities for hope, no matter what the obstacles might be' (1994: 9).

Educational responses

Teachers who wish to encourage greater understanding of local-global issues amongst their students have a long educational tradition to draw on. From the 1960s onwards a growing number of new educational movements emerged internationally. This was because an increasing number of educators began to question whether education did actually help young people understand the contemporary world. Each movement had as its focus an issue that was not only national but also global. I collectively refer to these fields as 'issue-based educations'.

Some observed that the curriculum took a national rather than a global perspective on the world. They therefore felt it was vital for young people to understand the notion of global *interdependence*. Others observed that people were increasingly concerned about environmental matters and felt that the *environment* should be highlighted more in schools. Others looked at issues to do with global inequality and argued that issues of *development* needed to be more deeply understood. Others looked at the local and global community and observed that pupils needed a deeper understanding of issues to do with *peace and conflict*. Others looked at British society and saw widespread *racism* as the major concern. They felt that the curriculum needed not only to reflect the cultural diversity found in society but that it should also challenge issues of racism. Others looked at education and observed that it did not prepare children for a future that would be very different from today. They argued that schools should help pupils develop a more *future* orientated perspective on the world. More recently educators and others have drawn attention to the need for schools to address issues of *citizenship* and also of *sustainable development*.

Issue-based educations

Because these issue-based educations each had their own particular focus they each developed different areas of expertise. Internationally these fields are known as global education, environmental education, development education, peace education, anti-racist education, futures education, citizenship education and education for sustainable development. Whilst some of these labels may not be widely used by teachers they are nevertheless useful shorthand for alerting the educational community to particular global concerns. Gradually a range of organisations, networks, newsletters, publications and classroom resources have emerged, all of which offer specific expertise in teaching and learning about global issues. In many cases educators were also able to draw on the insights of scholars working in corresponding academic fields.

During the 1980s there was much debate about whether and how these issue-based educations might relate to each other. Lister (1987) argued that these 'new movements in education' shared various features in common and thus represented a major historical shift in education that warranted particular attention.

[Their] twin stresses on human-centred education and global perspectives constitute a radical shift away from the dominant tradition of schooling (which is knowledge centred and ethnocentric). Thus, the new vanguard educators seek to give to education a new process and a new perspective on the world.

(Lister 1987: 54)

In contemplating the differences between these issue-based educations and their contribution to the wider educational scene Richardson (1990) argued that they could each be seen as parts of a greater whole and highlighted the danger of each field trying to achieve its goals without reference to the others. Some educators like to see these initiatives as all being part of a wider 'movement' (Marshall 2005b) whilst other proponents put more stress on the distinctive features of each.

Since these initiatives are central to the concerns of this book seven exemplars, drawn from the experience of the UK, will be outlined here. As noted above, some like to see them as distinctly different fields of enquiry, whilst others see them as closely related. In the context of this book it is useful to see them as each highlighting a particular concept or perspective that is integral to the global dimension in the curriculum.

Global education

In the UK early interest in global matters was found amongst the progressive teachers who set up the World Education Fellowship and its journal *The New Era* in the 1920s and those educators who set up the Council for Education in World Citizenship in the late 1930s (Heater 1980). Such initiatives contributed to what was known in the post-war years as 'education for international understanding'. In the 1960s James Henderson and colleagues at the University of London Institute of Education coined the term 'world studies' as shorthand for recognition of this need for a global dimension in the curriculum. Henderson was also involved in an important curriculum initiative called the World Studies Project.

It was this influential project, under the directorship of Robin Richardson (1976), that identified the core ideas informing global education in the UK. At the same time American educators were also beginning to develop a series of important conceptual frameworks. Anderson (1968) was one of the first to argue that a systems view was needed in order to understand the nature of global interdependence and that this needed to be reflected in the curriculum. Other ground-breaking work on learning objectives and classroom materials came from the Mid-America Program for Global Perspectives in Education at Indiana University (Becker 1975). Tye's (1999) international research shows such initiatives to be part of a worldwide movement.

Other important initiatives in the 1980s were the World Studies 8–13 Project based at the University College of St Martin's in Lancaster and the Centre for Global Education then at the University of York. Both are described in more detail in Chapter 2. The World Studies Trust continued this tradition through its work with teacher educators on local–global issues. Such issues can usefully be seen as falling into four broad categories: wealth and poverty, peace and conflict, rights and responsibilities, and environmental concerns (see Chapter 2). A key document for educators is *Developing a Global Dimension in the School Curriculum* (DfES 2005), whilst amongst the many excellent resources available for teachers are *In the Global Classroom* by Pike and Selby (1999/2000) and *Global Citizenship: The Handbook for Primary Teaching* (Young and Commins 2002).

Development education

In the late 1960s and early 1970s a number of NGOs concerned with issues of global poverty, such as Oxfam and Christian Aid, felt they needed to develop an education programme in addition to their main fund-raising function. This was partly as a result of opinion surveys at that time which showed there was a general lack of public awareness about issues of development. The purpose of such programmes was not to fund-raise but rather to look at the ways in which issues of development could be taught about in schools. A number of ex-teachers brought their classroom expertise to such initiatives and developed both courses and materials for teachers.

Initially the focus of development education was on the causes of poverty in less developed countries but this soon broadened to look at different definitions of development and the notion that 'underdevelopment' was an on-going process rather than a state some countries found themselves in. The cause of such problems was seen to lie in the process of unequal development that began as a result of European imperialism and colonialism in the late nineteenth century. Issues of trade and aid were also examined and the ways in which these could perpetuate such inequalities. Global notions of the rich North and the poor South added to this analysis, together with an understanding that cultural imperialism often marginalised the voices of those living in the global South.

A comprehensive definition of development education is provided by the Development Education Association (DEA website). The DEA defines development education as lifelong learning that:

- explores the links between people living in the 'developed' countries of the North and those of the 'developing' South, enabling people to understand the links between their own lives and those of people throughout the world
- increases understanding of the economic, social, political and environmental forces which shape our lives
- develops the skills, attitudes and values which enable people to work together to take action to bring about change and take control of their own lives
- works towards achieving a more just and sustainable world in which power and resources are more equitably shared.

The DEA is one of the main coordinating bodies for development education in the UK. It is linked to a national network of Development Education Centres (DECs) which in different ways support teachers and other educators who wish to explore the nature of current global issues. Some centres, such as TIDE (2006a) in Birmingham and Manchester DEP (2006a), work closely with schools and LEAs in providing continuing professional development and a wide range of excellent teaching materials. *The Development Education Journal* provides a valuable forum for international debate. Some NGOs, such as Oxfam (2006a), have chosen to operate under the heading of 'global citizenship', in some ways possibly a clearer label than development education. An exciting range of classroom materials is available from organisations such as Oxfam (2006b) and also from Teachers in Development Education (2006a).

Education for sustainable development

One of the crucial precursors to education for sustainable development (ESD) (QCA 2006a) was environmental education which emerged in the late 1960s. Since then the emphasis in environmental education has shifted, from conservation of the countryside in the 1960s–1970s (plants, trees, hedgerows, wildlife), to national and global problems in the 1970s–1980s (pollution, resource depletion, global warming), to issues of sustainability in the 1990s and today. International developments in environmental education were very much influenced by UNESCO (United Nations Educational, Scientific and Cultural Organisation) and UNEP (United Nations Environment Programme) at milestone international conferences in the 1970s and 1980s when definitions of its nature and scope were agreed on (Palmer 1998).

Three different but interrelated forms of environmental education have frequently been noted (Palmer 1998). Education *about* the environment focuses on the need for factual information but may say less about the changes needed in social and political systems to resolve environmental problems. In education *through* the environment, students' experiences of various environments are used as a medium for education. This adds reality and such experiential learning can engender feelings of environmental concern. Education *for* the environment engages students in exploration and resolution of real issues and highlights the importance of human agency in creating a better world.

The Earth Summit at Rio in 1992 and Johannesburg in 2002 crucially drew together the twin global concerns of development and environment. The welfare of both people and planet were now seen as two sides of the same coin, and the terms education for sustainable development or education for sustainability are now used to embrace these twin concerns. Development education is thus also a major influence on education for sustainable development. The first report of the Sustainable Development Education Panel (1998: 30) offered this definition of ESD:

> Education for sustainable development is about the learning needed to maintain and improve our quality of life and the quality of life of generations to come. It is about equipping individuals, communities, groups, businesses and government to live and act sustainably; as well as giving them an understanding of the environmental, social and economic issues involved. It is about preparing for

the world in which we will live in the next century, and making sure that we are not found wanting.

Perhaps the greatest body of experience in education for sustainable development in the UK lies with NGOs such as the World Wide Fund for Nature UK (2006a) and the Development Education Association (2006) and also in higher education with courses such as the Masters in Education for Sustainability at London South Bank University. Such bodies provide invaluable resources for teachers as well as exciting possibilities for continuing professional development.

During and since the 1990s there has been an on-going debate about the similarities and differences between environmental education and education for sustainable development. Some see the latter as a new version of the former, but now incorporating notions of sustainable development (McKeown and Hopkins 2003). Others (e.g. Sterling 2001) argue that ESD is something much more radical altogether warranting nothing less that a paradigm shift in education.

Peace education

During the 1950s the academic field of peace research began to emerge, partly prompted by the Cold War between the USA, the Soviet Union and their allies, but also by other conflicts around the world. The initial interest in peace research was on direct (personal) violence, i.e. violence directed by one person against another as in the case of assault, torture, terrorism or war. This emphasis meant that peace was at first defined negatively as the absence of war (negative peace). By the late 1960s and early 1970s researchers' attention was shifting from direct to indirect (structural) violence, i.e. the ways in which people also suffer as a result of social, political and economic systems. Such structural violence may equally lead to death or the diminishing of human well-being, for example as a consequence of sexism or racism. This shift of emphasis led to a broader definition of peace (Hicks 1988). Instead of being just the absence of violent conflict it was now seen as involving non-violent social change, aimed at creating more equitable and just structures in society (positive peace).

Peace education is thus concerned with non-violent conflict resolution and ways of creating positive peace in situations ranging from the personal to the global. The International Peace Research Association (IPRA) is the main academic body concerned with these matters, and its Peace Education Commission (PEC) (see website) provides a forum for educators working in both formal and informal contexts and at all levels of education. The new international *Journal of Peace Education* (2006) publishes articles that advance understanding and develop good practice in educating for peace.

During the 1980s peace educators were particularly concerned about the nuclear arms race and ways in which such a difficult issue could be dealt with in schools. However, the concerns of peace education, as indicated above, also embrace issues to do with conflict resolution, global events, disarmament, human rights and intercultural understanding. A wealth of good practice from around the world in relation to such issues is available for teachers to draw on (Burns and Aspeslagh 1996;

Harris and Morrison 2003). With the current increase in bullying and racism in schools there are many valuable insights that can be drawn on from peace education. In particular this relates to expertise on conflict resolution (Isenhart and Spangle 2000) and appreciating the ways in which violence is often part of the educational endeavour itself (Davies 2004).

Race and education

Educational responses to cultural diversity have changed over the last thirty years and Gaine (1995) has highlighted the ideological shifts that have occurred in Britain in relation to this. The initial educational response to Black and Asian immigration to the UK in the 1950s/1960s was one of laissez-faire. The assumption was that nothing extra needed to be done as everyone was equal before the law. However, Britain's imperial and colonial past underpinned widespread racism and during the 1960s there was a call for assimilation based on the notion that minorities should accept the norms of dominant White culture. In the 1970s and early 1980s the emphasis shifted to multiculturalism with its stress on pluralism highlighting the need for racial equality and the valuing of cultural diversity. Black and Asian educators, however, saw multicultural education as avoidance of the crucial issue of racism and thus argued for a clearer anti-racist approach.

In the mid- and late 1980s a right-wing backlash lead to a sensationalisation of 'race' issues in the media. The Conservatives' Education Reform Act in 1988 effectively marginalized both multicultural and anti-racist initiatives. In the revised national curriculum, issues of cultural diversity have been subsumed under the notion of opportunities for all. There is now, however, a clearer focus on the need to confront racism as a result of events such as the Stephen Lawrence Inquiry (Macpherson 1999), the Race Relations (Amendment) Act, which outlines the specific duties of educational institutions (Commission for Racial Equality 2002), and the growing prejudice against Muslims since 9/11 (Commission on British Muslims and Islamophobia 2004).

Organisations such as the Runnymede Trust (2006) have played an important role in clarifying these matters and the major issues are well set out in *The Future of Multi-ethnic Britain* (Commission on the Future of Multi-ethnic Britain 2000). The tension between valuing cultural diversity on the one hand and the need to oppose personal, cultural and institutional racism on the other continues in relation to debates about immigration and asylum seeking (Ouseley 2004). The journal *Race Equality Teaching* regularly covers a variety of issues relating to race and education, as do many other publications from Trentham Books. The difficulties that teachers from all-White areas have in understanding the significance of race and racism in Britain today is well charted in *Still No Problem Here* (Gaine 1995). Some of the many positive ways in which schools set about raising awareness of these issues are described in *Equality Stories: Recognition, Respect and Raising Achievement* by Richardson and Miles (2003). Current debates on race and education are explored in *The RoutledgeFalmer Reader in Multicultural Education* (Ladson-Billings and Gillborn 2004).

Futures education

Futures education is amongst the most recent of the issue-based educations although the scholarship and research that it draws on has a much longer pedigree. This is the international field of futures studies which emerged in the 1960s. Inayatullah (1993: 236) observes that futures studies encompasses two dominant modes of knowledge – 'the technical concerned with predicting the future and the humanist concerned with developing a good society'. The scope of this field of enquiry is well set out in Bell's (1997) scholarly two-volume work *Foundations of Futures Studies* and in Slaughter's (2005) *The Knowledge Base of Futures Studies*. Broadly the concern of futurists is to propose and explore a range of possible, probable and preferable futures, on scales from the local to the global. These may be in relation to a wide range of issues, such as community planning, the future of education, environmental issues, conflict resolution and life planning.

It was Toffler (1974: xxii) who noted that 'All education springs from images of the future and all education creates images of the future. Thus all education, whether so intended or not, is a preparation for the future'. Whilst the need to help young people think more creatively and critically about the future would seem to be at the heart of the educational endeavour this seldom explicitly occurs. Research into young people's hopes and fears for the future shows that their concerns are not only for their personal lives and their community but also global in scope. Page (2000) has thus examined how children in the early years conceptualise the future. Hicks and Holden (1995) have looked at both primary and secondary pupils' concerns (updated in Chapter 3) and Hutchinson (1996) has focused on secondary pupils. He notes, in particular, that western society offers only a narrow view of possible futures to young people.

Some subject areas, e.g. geography, design and technology, and science are already dealing with issues of change and the ways in which present actions may influence the future. Many activities fade out at this point, however, often merely suggesting that the future will be some high-tech version of today. Any issue, from the personal to the global, can benefit from considering what both probable and preferable alternative futures may be (Hicks 2001, 2006).

The World Futures Studies Federation is one of the main international bodies for those involved in the futures field. A number of its members have a particular interest in schools and education. The 1998 *World Yearbook of Education* took futures education as its focus and contains case studies from all levels of education (Hicks and Slaughter 1998). Case studies from Australia can be found in Gidley *et al.* (2004) and articles of interest to educators are also sometimes found in the *Journal of Futures Studies*. It would be true to say, however, that the nature of, and need for, a clear futures perspective in education has yet to be fully understood by many educators (Hicks 2003).

Citizenship education

Whilst the notion of citizenship predates all of the other issue-based educations referred to in this chapter (Heater 2004), debates about the need for citizenship education in English schools did not begin to attract serious interest until the 1990s. Kerr (1999: 1), in his review of citizenship education, pointed out that there was 'no great tradition of explicit teaching of citizenship education in English schools or of voluntary and community service for young people'. Whilst various groups had supported the notion of citizenship education, discussion was often characterised by lack of clarity and there was little strong support for a separate subject called citizenship. In 1988 the Speaker of the House of Commons set up a Commission on Citizenship which in its report (1990: ix, 101–5) made recommendations for the teaching of citizenship in schools and provision was made for this in the national curriculum. New Labour set up the Advisory Group on Citizenship (1998) under the chairmanship of Professor Bernard Crick and it was this report that argued for the inclusion of citizenship education in the revised national curriculum.

Whilst some teachers felt that this was merely a political initiative on the part of the UK government it was in fact only one of many international initiatives that educators were involved in at that time. These included *Becoming Political: Comparative Perspectives on Citizenship Education* (Hahn 1998), *Citizenship for the 21st Century: An International Perspective on Education* (Cogan and Derricott 2000) and *Civic Education Across Countries: Twenty-Four National Case Studies* (Torney-Purta *et al.* 1999). In part such studies were prompted by concerns about low voter turn-out and the suggestion that there might be a general lack of interest in social and political matters amongst younger people.

Prompted by the inclusion of citizenship in the national curriculum a number of organisations now exist that give support to educators and teachers, e.g. CitizEd (2006), the Centre for Citizenship and Human Rights Education and the Citizenship Foundation. A range of useful classroom activities can be found in sources such as *Education for Citizenship: A Practical Guide for Teachers of Pupils Aged 7–14* (Clough and Holden 2002). The global dimension of citizenship is also explored in Osler and Vincent (2002) and by Young and Commins (2002).

Overview

These thumbnail sketches of differing issue-based educations provide an interesting snapshot of the numerous ways in which educators internationally have responded to global issues, events and trends. They are a reminder that such matters have been on the educational agenda for at least thirty years and that, over this period, a wealth of professional expertise has been accrued in relation to teaching and learning about such matters (Goldstein and Selby 2000). Within each of these issue-based fields it is possible to identify, with some variations, relevant academic scholarship and research, academic and professional organisations, journals, guidance for tutors and teachers, and practical classroom resources.

Some educators like to stress the similarities between these fields since they each relate, in different ways, to contemporary social and global issues. There is clearly a value in alliances between these initiatives and there are some excellent examples of this in practice, for example the work of the West Midlands Commission on Global Citizenship in the UK (2002). An undue stress on similarities, however, can be used to disguise the essential separateness of many of these fields. Each has developed in its own way and many practitioners are not particularly conversant with the other fields, although a number are aware of overlapping concerns and the potential for forging alliances. There is also the question of where such a list of issue-based educations should end. This chapter could also have looked, for example, at human rights education, education for gender equity and humane education (Selby 1995).

The purpose of these seven sketches is threefold. First, it is a reminder that there is a wealth of educational expertise on global issues that teachers can draw on. Second, it is a reminder that educational interest in global issues and events has a long history. Third, it is a reminder that the global dimension requires knowledge and understanding of a number of key issues and concepts.

Four of the main documents mentioned in this chapter identify concepts that can be used in curriculum planning. These are *Developing a Global Dimension in the School Curriculum* (DfES 2005), *Education for Sustainable Development and Global Citizenship* (ACCAC 2002), the QCA (2006a) website on education for sustainable development and *Education for Global Citizenship: A Guide for Schools* (Oxfam 2006a). In this book we have chosen to focus on the eight key concepts proposed by the DfES, each of which is explored in a separate chapter in Part II. Each chapter follows the same format with sections on: i) understanding the issue; ii) action for change; and iii) examples of good practice from primary or secondary school.

Chapter 2

Principles and precedents

David Hicks

This chapter explores the specific field of global education through examples of its evolution taken mainly from the UK. In particular it looks at three curriculum initiatives that have been influential in developing awareness of the need for a global dimension in the curriculum. It goes on to support a fourfold model of global education which identifies the interrelated elements that need to be present to constitute good practice in the classroom.

Introduction

It was noted in Chapter 1 that the term global education may be used in two different ways – to refer to a specific educational field and, more broadly, as an umbrella term to embrace all of the issue-based educations. This chapter is concerned with the specific field of global education. Whilst its origins lie in the work of progressive educators in the second decade of the twentieth century, it began to take on its current form in the early 1970s. In 1973 the One World Trust set up the World Studies Project and, in so doing, gave birth to the UK variant of global education. Some of the key milestones in the development of the field are considered below in order to understand the nature of current debates about what properly constitutes global education.

Three projects

The World Studies Project

This project, directed by Robin Richardson, ran a series of inspiring and innovative conferences in the 1970s attended mainly by secondary teachers, tutors in initial teacher education and educators from NGOs. It was Richardson (1976) who provided the first conceptual map of world society that many educators went on to use in their work. As a result, by the end of the 1970s, there was a loose national network of educators in the UK committed to promoting world studies in school and teacher education. At the time his model for exploring global issues (Figure 2.1) was an important innovation as was his thesis that such issues fell into four broad categories:

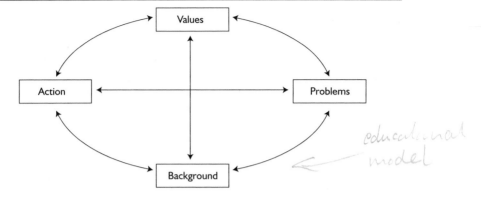

To understand the causes of any global problem it is important to explore
the political and economic background, values relating to how society
should be organised, and the action needed to resolve the problem and its
causes

Figure 2.1 Richardson's framework for exploring global issues

poverty, oppression, conflict and environment. Both the conceptual framework and
participatory pedagogy developed by Richardson owed much to the work of radical
educators such as Johan Galtung (peace research), Paulo Freire (political education)
and Carl Rogers (humanistic psychology) (Hicks 1983/4). The Project's influential
publication, *Learning for Change in World Society* (Richardson 1976), instantly
became a benchmark for all those interested in developing a global dimension in the
curriculum.

The pedagogical importance of Richardson's framework lies in the widening of
focus that it brought to the study of global issues. Previously teaching materials had
often tended to focus narrowly on the nature of different global problems. Little
wonder that pupils often lost interest when fed such a diet of global issues for they
were unable to develop any sense of their own agency in such matters.

To explore the political and economic background to an issue is to begin to
understand some of its causes. Similarly, to understand that the values people hold
will affect how an issue is seen and also what is considered appropriate action to
resolve it leads to greater clarification of the matter. Looking at examples of positive
action for change can in turn lead to a greater sense of hope and empowerment.

Richardson's work in the 1970s was seminal in its insight and innovative and
inspiring in its practice. Events run by the World Studies Project pioneered active and
participatory ways of working with educators that were quite different from those
of conventional conferences. Similarly the Project's classroom materials encouraged
active debate and engagement both amongst students and teachers. Many of the
young teachers influenced by this radical pedagogy went on to work in the fields
of teacher education, development education, multicultural education and global
education in the 1980s and beyond.

World Studies 8–13

In 1980, as a direct successor to Richardson's work, the World Studies 8–13 Project was set up in order to work with pupils in the middle years of schooling. World studies was defined as an approach to education which 'promoted the knowledge, attitudes and skills needed to live responsibly in a multicultural society and an interdependent world' (Fisher and Hicks 1985: 8). The project built on Richardson's earlier work and also developed its own framework for curriculum planning in the middle years of schooling (see Figure 2.2).

The project was one of the first to identify a number of key concepts that could be used as focusing ideas in global education. Such concepts provide a powerful tool both for learning and for making sense of the world. Those used by the project are shown in more detail in Box 2.1.

The project's two publications for teachers, *World Studies 8–13: A Teacher's Handbook* (Fisher and Hicks 1985) and *Making Global Connections: A World Studies Workbook* (Hicks and Steiner 1989), were widely used by educators in the UK and also in a number of other countries. By the end of the 1980s this national curriculum project, originally part-funded by the Schools Council, was involved with in-service work in 50 LEAs, i.e. half those in England and Wales (Hicks 1990). In 1989 the project, now under the auspices of the World Studies Trust, initiated a new phase of work on active learning (Steiner 1992) and then on initial teacher education. This

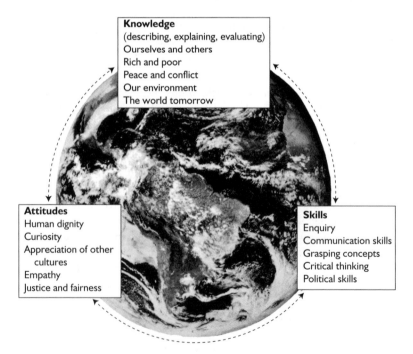

Figure 2.2 World Studies 8–13: a framework for planning

Box 2.1 World Studies 8–13: key concepts

Concepts for use in world studies

Causes and consequences
Our actions and also events in the wider world have different sorts of causes. Similarly, actions and decisions, whether ours, other people's or those of governments or big business, have different sorts of consequences, often unintended or unforeseen. Understanding causes and consequences can give us more control over our own lives and also make events in the wider world more comprehensible.

Communication
People exchange information, views and feelings in a variety of different ways and languages, both with and without words. Clear communication is essential if we are to understand the motives and actions of others and if we are to be understood by others. The mass media are primary communicators of information about the wider world and, inevitably, of bias and distortion also.

Conflict
We live in a world of conflict. Human beings continually disagree with each other, and often fight with each other. This happens in our own society, in other societies and between our society and others. Conflicts can be analysed and resolved in a variety of ways. Understanding how conflicts occur can make it easier to resolve them constructively.

Co-operation
Individuals, groups and countries often work together, or at least wish to appear to be doing so, in order to tackle common problems. Co-operation enables tasks to be performed which would not otherwise be possible. It is essential if conflicts are to be resolved peacefully. Co-operation can be as stimulating and rewarding as many forms of competition, requiring as it does a high level of communication and sensitivity to others.

Distribution of power
People and groups are able to influence what happens in the world. In most groups, countries, and in the world as a whole, power and wealth are distributed unequally. This affects people's life chances, their freedom and welfare. An awareness of this inequality raises important questions about fairness and justice.

Fairness
Fairness involves respecting the rights of other people and seeking solutions to conflict which take into account the interests of all parties. Some laws are an attempt to institutionalise fairness at national and international levels. For

the world to be a fairer place, priority needs to be placed on the fulfilment of essential human needs through patterns of living which are equitable and in harmony with the planet

Interdependence
People depend on each other in a variety of ways, ranging from caring and emotional support to the exchange of goods and services. This interdependence pervades every aspect of life, at individual, group and international level. It can have both positive and negative effects. The most urgent problems facing humankind need to be tackled at the global level and across national boundaries, as well as at the local level.

Similarities and differences
There are many different ways of doing things and not all human beings do the same as we do. But everyone has a similar nature deep down, the same physical needs and similar wishes and hopes, for example, for friendship, love, happiness, enjoyment. It is important to find out about and understand both the differences between people, and those things which we all have in common.

Social change
Change is a constant feature of world society. It is brought about by people, whether deliberalely or by accident. The best place to begin changing things for the better is where each individual happens to be, each with their own background, needs and aspirations. In order to do this people need to be free to take maximum control over their own lives.

Values and beliefs
People have different views about what is important. Ways of life, behaviour and traditions vary. Our values and beliefs, our sex, social and cultural background, affect the way we perceive people and events, and the way other people see us. Finding out about the values and beliefs of other people can help us to understand them, and ourselves, better.

is described in *Developing the Global Teacher: Theory and Practice in Initial Teacher Education* (Steiner 1996). From 1996–2005 the Trust continued this work with the Global Teacher Project (2006) which worked nationally with tutors and students in Initial Teacher Education.

Centre for Global Education

Equally influential nationally in the 1980s was the work of David Selby and Graham Pike at the Centre for Global Education based at the University of York. They had also been inspired by Richardson and focused mainly on work with secondary schools. Like the 8–13 project they produced innovative materials for teachers and ran regional and national in-service courses. At that time these two ventures together worked with probably two-thirds of the LEAs in England and Wales. In *Global Teacher, Global Learner* Pike and Selby (1988) further developed the conceptual map of the field. In particular they highlighted what they called 'the four dimensions of globality'. These were: i) the spatial dimension; ii) the temporal dimension; iii) the issues dimension; and iv) the inner dimension. Influenced by the work of Hanvey (1976), they also set out five aims for global education which they considered to be the 'irreducible minimum' for a global perspective (see Box 2.2).

Further developments

Attacks from the Right

The growth of interest in global education in the 1980s did not go unnoticed by Conservative politicians. World studies, along with initiatives such as peace education and multicultural education, increasingly found themselves under attack from the political Right which saw these concerns as forms of indoctrination. Indeed Scruton (1985) argued that education was being used for 'political' ends and that world studies was guilty of: indoctrination (giving one-sided views of the world); politicisation (bringing politics into the classroom); improper teaching methods

---

Box 2.2 Five aims of global education (Pike and Selby 1988)

1 *Systems consciousness* – Students should: i) acquire the ability to think in a systems mode; ii) acquire an understanding of the systemic nature of the world; iii) acquire an holistic conception of their capacities and potential

2 *Perspective consciousness* – Students should: i) recognise that their worldview is not universally shared; ii) develop receptivity to other perspectives

3 *Health of planet awareness* – Students should: i) acquire an understanding of the global condition; ii) develop an informed understanding of the concepts of justice, human rights and responsibilities and be able to apply that to the global condition; iii) develop a future orientation in their reflection upon the health of the planet

4 *Involvement consciousness and preparedness* – Students should: i) become aware that the choices they make and the actions they take individually and collectively have repercussions for the global present and the global future; iii) develop the social and political action skills necessary for becoming effective participants in democratic decision making at a variety of levels

5 *Process mindedness* – Students should: i) learn that learning and personal development are continuous journeys with no fixed or final destination; ii) learn that new ways of seeing the world are revitalising but risky.

(using simulation games and role-play); and lowering educational standards (world studies was not a proper subject).

This attack was the harbinger of a Conservative national curriculum in the late 1980s and a broader assault on the professionalism of teachers in the 1990s. It reflected a wider international shift towards neoconservative and neoliberal forms of education which opposed and marginalised progressive initiatives such as global education (Apple 2001). In a sense Richardson had foreseen this when, influenced by the work of Freire, he drew up a 'map of the tensions' which highlighted the ideological differences between conservative, liberal and radical views of education (Hicks and Townley 1982: 15). These attacks, together with the 1988 Education Reform Act and the introduction of a national curriculum, effectively marginalised global education and related fields in England until the mid-1990s. Similar right-wing attacks were also launched against global education in Australia, Canada and the USA.

North America

In the early 1990s Selby and Pike set up the International Institute for Global Education at the University of Toronto where they felt there was greater freedom to develop their ideas. The Institute had a significant impact on the Canadian scene and, as a result of their outreach work, on the form of global education in a number of countries including Syria, Brazil and Japan. Selby (2000) has continued to develop a systems view of global education in particular through drawing on the insights of quantum research. During the 1990s many Canadian provinces set up global education projects as a result of funding from the Canadian International Development Agency and these carried out much good work. These too, however, were eventually subject to the vagaries of political change. More recently Pike and Selby (1999/2000) have continued to elaborate on their model of global education (see Table 2.1) and have provided an excellent range of classroom activities that contribute to the development of a global perspective.

Amongst important long-standing American initiatives are the American Forum for Global Education and Global Education Associates, both of which provide valuable resources and professional newsletters for teachers. The American Forum has produced detailed guidelines on the different key aspects of global education focusing in particular on: i) global issues, problems and challenges; ii) culture and world areas; iii) the United States and the world. Detailed knowledge, skill and participation objectives are available for each of the three areas. Key works on global education in the American context include Merryfield et al. (1997), Tye (1999) and Gaudelli (2003), all of which offer interesting comparisons with approaches developed in Europe.

Global citizenship

Another useful framework available in the UK for planning is Oxfam's (2006) *Education for Global Citizenship: A Guide for Schools*. Its proposed framework for

Table 2.1 A four-dimensional model of global education

	Key ideas	Knowledge	Skills	Attitudes
Spatial dimension	• interdependence • local–global • systems	• of local–global connections and dependencies • of global systems • of the nature and function of a system • of connections between areas of knowledge • of the common needs of all humans and other species • of oneself as a whole person	• relational thinking (seeing patterns and connections) • systems thinking (understanding the impact of change in a system) • interpersonal relationships • co-operation	• flexibility in adaptation to change • willingness to learn from and teach others • willingness to work as a team member • consideration of the common good • sense of solidarity with other people and their problems
Issues dimension	• local–global issues • interconnections between issues • perspectives	• of critical issues, at interpersonal through global levels • of interconnections between issues, events and trends • of a range of perspectives on issues • of how perspectives are shaped	• research and enquiry • evaluating, organising and presenting information • analysing trends • personal judgement and decision making	• curiosity about issues, trends and the global condition • receptivity to, and critical examination of, other perspectives and points of view • empathy with/respect for other people and cultures
Temporal dimension	• phases of time as interactive • alternative futures • action	• of the relationship between past, present and future • of a range of futures, including possible, probable and preferred • of sustainable development • of potential for action, at personal to global levels	• coping with change and uncertainty • extrapolation and prediction • creative and lateral thinking • problem solving • taking personal action	• tolerance of ambiguity and uncertainty • preparedness to consider long-term consequences • preparedness to utilise imagination and intuition • commitment to personal and social action
Inner dimension	• journey inwards • teaching/learning processes • medium and message	• of oneself – identity, strengths, weaknesses and potential • of one's perspectives, values and worldview • of incongruities between professed beliefs and personal actions	• personal reflection and analysis • personal growth – emotional, intellectual, physical, spiritual • learning flexibility (learning within a variety of contexts and a variety of ways)	• belief in own abilities and potential • recognising learning as a life-long process • genuineness – presenting the real person • preparedness to take risks • trust

planning provides a valuable 'map' of the knowledge, attitudes and skills required to develop a global dimension in the curriculum (see Figure 2.3). The choice of title appears to be an attempt to move beyond the term development education (not always clear to teachers) hitherto used by Oxfam and other development orientated NGOs. It also highlights its relationship to citizenship education, now statutory at secondary level and non-statutory at primary in England. The official guidelines on citizenship refer to pupils learning:

> … about the wider world and the interdependence of communities within it. They develop their sense of social justice and moral responsibility and begin to understand that their own choices and behaviour can affect local, national or global issues and political and social institutions.
>
> (Qualifications and Curriculum Authority 1999: 139)

In the accompanying resource book by Young and Commins (2002: 1), *Global Citizenship: The Handbook for Primary Teaching*, the notion of global citizenship is discussed further with much practical detail.

> At Oxfam Education, we believe that Global Citizenship is more than the sum of its parts. It goes beyond simply knowing that we are citizens of the globe to an acknowledgement of our responsibilities both to each other and to the Earth itself. Global Citizenship is about understanding the need to tackle injustice and inequality, and having the desire and ability to work actively to do so. It is about valuing the Earth as precious and unique, and safeguarding the future for those coming after us.

Issues arising

What then are some of the wider observations that have been made about the field of global education? Tye (1999), in his exploration of global education in more than 50 countries, found that both acceptance of, and the form of, such education varied considerably. The most common issues identified (in order of frequency) were: ecology/environment, development, intercultural relations, peace, economics, technology, human rights. What is clear is that global education is largely a 'rich world' initiative and thus, not surprisingly, some of Tye's respondents were suspicious of this endeavour. He also refers to a major dilemma faced by global education, namely the existence of related fields which, whilst 'part of' global education, also have their own separate identities, e.g. peace education, development education, environmental education (see above and Chapter 1).

Also of interest is Pike's analysis of some of the similarities and differences between global education in the UK, Canada and the USA. At the broadest level, he argues, 'the big ideas of global education and its overall purpose as an educational reform movement are largely consistent' (Pike 2000: 3). Common key concepts in all three countries are interdependence, connections and multiple perspectives. American

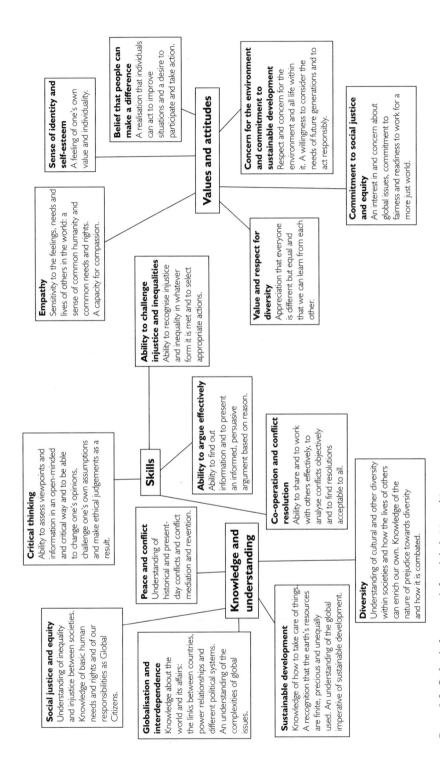

Knowledge and understanding

Social justice and equity
Understanding of inequality and injustice between societies. Knowledge of basic human needs and rights and of our responsibilities as Global Citizens.

Globalisation and interdependence
Knowledge about the world and its affairs: the links between countries, power relationships and different political systems. An understanding of the complexities of global issues.

Sustainable development
Knowledge of how to take care of things. A recognition that the earth's resources are finite, precious and unequally used. An understanding of the global imperative of sustainable development.

Diversity
Understanding of cultural and other diversity within societies and how the lives of others can enrich our own. Knowledge of the nature of prejudice towards diversity and how it is combated.

Peace and conflict
Understanding of historical and present-day conflicts and conflict mediation and prevention.

Skills

Critical thinking
Ability to assess viewpoints and information in an open-minded and critical way and to be able to change one's opinions, challenge one's own assumptions and make ethical judgements as a result.

Ability to argue effectively
Ability to find out information and to present an informed, persuasive argument based on reason.

Ability to challenge injustice and inequalities
Ability to recognise injustice and inequality in whatever form it is met and to select appropriate actions.

Co-operation and conflict resolution
Ability to share and to work with others effectively, to analyse conflicts objectively and to find resolutions acceptable to all.

Values and attitudes

Sense of identity and self-esteem
A feeling of one's own value and individuality.

Belief that people can make a difference
A realisation that individuals can act to improve situations and a desire to participate and take action.

Empathy
Sensitivity to the feelings, needs and lives of others in the world: a sense of common humanity and common needs and rights. A capacity for compassion.

Value and respect for diversity
Appreciation that everyone is different but equal and that we can learn from each other.

Concern for the environment and commitment to sustainable development
Respect and concern for the environment and all life within it. A willingness to consider the needs of future generations and to act responsibly.

Commitment to social justice and equity
An interest in and concern about global issues, commitment to fairness and readiness to work for a more just world.

Figure 2.3 Oxfam's framework for global citizenship

educators, he notes, tend to focus on discrete countries and cultures and reformist goals which do not call for the reshaping of the world. Canadian and UK educators are more likely to focus on the common interests of people and planet and personal growth rather than national development. Whilst Americans emphasise harmony and similarity, British and Canadian practitioners tend to highlight differences in relation to wealth, power and rights. Global education in the UK is marked by a particular emphasis on the process of teaching and learning.

A global dimension

Core elements

It is clear that a significant amount of work has been carried out internationally over the last thirty years which directly relates to the development of a global dimension in the curriculum. Recent initiatives in the UK funded by the Department for International Development (2006b) are thus part of a long educational tradition which can build on long-standing theoretical and practical expertise. What is not clear, however, is whether current initiatives by NGOs and schools are actually drawing on that expertise since much of it was marginalised with the introduction of a national curriculum. As this chapter shows, a number of conceptual frameworks have been developed for global education and for some this diversity may seem confusing. However, Case (1993: 318) argues, 'We should not automatically assume that greater clarity about the goals of global education is necessary. Loosely defined coalitions…often permit otherwise disparate factions to ally in pursuit of common, or at least compatible, goals'.

If we look at what these frameworks have in common I believe it is possible to identify the core elements that are required for any endeavour to be labelled as global education. My own 'minimum' for any such initiative would follow the same fourfold model as Pike and Selby (2000), but with their 'inner dimension' being replaced by a 'process dimension' that highlights issues of pedagogy, i.e. teaching and learning (see Figure 2.4). The brief elaboration that follows on each of these dimensions is my own.

Issues dimension

There are four broad problem areas that need to be explored. These are issues of wealth and poverty, human rights, peace and conflict, and the environment. Not only do pupils need to learn about specific examples from each of these problem areas they also importantly need to study a range of solutions to such problems.

Spatial dimension

This involves exploration of the innumerable interconnections that exist between the local and the global. It focuses on the concept of interdependence between issues,

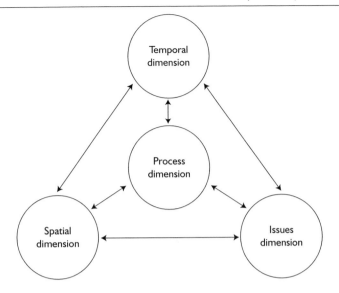

Figure 2.4 The global dimension: core elements (adapted from Pile and Selby 2000)

people, places and countries, whilst also exploring the nature of dependency, i.e. the fact that many such connections are inequitable ones.

Temporal dimension

This involves exploration of the innumerable connections that exist between past, present and future. In particular it focuses on the need to think more critically and creatively about the future impact of local–global issues and thus investigates the nature of possible, probable and preferable futures.

Process dimension

This is about the personal and social skills that are needed in order to work co-operatively with others. It is also about the form of teaching and learning that is most appropriate for the exploration of global issues, events and trends. In particular this requires a holistic and participatory approach that focuses on exploration of differing values perspectives and which leads to politically aware local and global citizenship.

Each of these four elements needs to be present, I believe, before one can claim to be promoting a global dimension in the curriculum. Anything less than this fails to address adequately the global condition. It is the minimum that is required for a framework because it draws together: i) relevant contemporary global issues; ii) ways in which they are spatially interrelated; iii) ways in which they are connected over time; iv) the pedagogy that is most appropriate for investigating such matters. Having a French pen-friend, doing a project on an Indian village or setting up a school linking project are therefore not on their own examples of good 'global education'. This is not to say they are not worthwhile educational activities in their own right.

There is some debate about what should be included under the heading of global issues and how they should be categorised. The simpler and more elegant the categorisation the better, I believe. The four categories I have identified above go back to the work of Richardson referred to at the beginning of this chapter. They come originally from the work of Johan Galtung (1976) who argued that most global issues fall under these four broad headings. Importantly he pointed out that reversing each of these problems indicates the goal that educators and others should be trying to achieve. Thus if inequality is the problem then equality is the goal. If injustice is the problem, justice is the goal. If conflict is the problem, peace is the goal. If damage to the environment is the problem then care of the environment is the goal. Whilst, in some ways, this may seem a simplistic formulation, what it draws attention to is the need for pupils to spend as much time exploring solutions to problems as the problems themselves.

In the classroom context these four categories would more likely be referred to as the need to learn about wealth and poverty, rights and responsibilities, conflict resolution and environmental matters. Some people have reservations about such a categorisation because it does not refer to their own particular concern, e.g. issues of race and gender, or notions such as sustainable development. However, if one wanted to identify particular examples of inequality or injustice, to look then at issues of race and gender would be most appropriate. One might also look at homelessness, migration, poverty, human rights, discrimination or debates about the nature of development. Education for sustainable development (ESD) is now part of the national curriculum in England so it is imperative that young people understand this concept. Much of the literature on this, however, still errs either towards environment or development, rather than giving equal attention to both welfare of people and planet.

There is an argument that people fail to understand their part in creating global issues because they do not understand the complex web of local–national–global interrelationships that govern life today. By taking a systems view of the world we are reminded that everything is connected literally to everything else. It is thus not enough to do a project simply on growing bananas and where they come from, whatever geographical insights this may develop. The only connection that might be made is that we like eating bananas. To explore the living conditions for banana growers, to look at what they earn, the costs of shipping, the cut the retailer takes, and the price we pay for bananas in the shops, begins to expose webs of interconnection that may also relate to issues of inequality and dependency. My breakfast, my clothes, the classroom, all so personal and local, connect us to the rest of the global village (Garlake 2003). Understanding these connections highlights the role we all play in different systems, we are not separate (despite the Western illusion that we are) but inextricably bound together, and with this should come some sense of shared responsibility for the 'other'.

Such interconnections also exist over time. Clearly history helps us understand the connections between past and present, although what we consider the 'lessons of history' to be will vary depending on our ideological values and beliefs. What is often missing from the curriculum is consideration of how actions in the present will affect future time and the lives of future generations (Hicks 2006). Exploring different scenarios for the future when looking at a particular issue, whether traffic, climate change or economic migration, makes clearer the different options that are available. There is also an important difference between probable futures (those which are most likely to come about) and preferable futures (those we would choose to come about). If we are concerned about issues of social justice or sustainable development then we need to be able to envision futures, both local and global, in which such goals have been achieved. Temporal connections are thus not just with the past but should equally be seen as with the future.

And how is all this best taught about in the classroom? What sort of pedagogy is most suited to global education? Global education has long recognised that any understanding of the contemporary world needs to be based on participatory and experiential ways of teaching and learning. It needs to involve both head and heart (the cognitive and affective) and the personal and political (values clarification and political literacy). It needs to draw on the learner's direct or simulated experience and it requires the development of interpersonal, discussion and critical thinking skills, as well as skills of participation and action. One good place to start is with the free web-based courses on the Open University website TeachGlobal.

Terminology

Some of the terms found in official and NGO documentation relating to the global dimension are used as if they were interchangeable. However, different terms each have their own distinct meanings so this can lead to a conceptual fuzziness that does not assist clear thinking about global education. My own clarification of these terms is shown below in Box 2.3.

Box 2.3 'Global' terminology

Global education
The term used internationally to designate the academic field concerned with teaching and learning about global issues, events and perspectives. NB During the 1970s–1980s this field was known as world studies in the UK.

Development education
Originated with the work of NGOs that were concerned about issues of development and North–South relationships. Focus of concern has widened to embrace other global issues but development remains the core concept.

Global dimension
Refers to the curriculum taken as a whole and the ethos of a school; those subject elements and cross-curricular concerns that focus on global inter-dependence, issues and events.

Global perspective
What we want students to achieve as a result of having a global dimension in the curriculum; in the plural refers to the fact that there are different cultural and political perspectives on global matters.

International dimension
Literally 'between countries' – as in international relationships; also refers to the study of a particular concern, e.g. education, as it manifests in different countries. NB International refers to the 'parts' and 'global' to the whole.

Global citizenship
That part of the Citizenship curriculum which refers to global issues, events and perspectives; sometimes also used as an umbrella term to embrace all of the issue-based educations.

Globalisation
The innumerable interconnections – economic, cultural, technological, political – which bind the local and national into the global community; the consequence of neo-liberal economic policies which see everything, including education, as a commodity to be sold in the global market place.

It is important to recall that many of the issues referred to in this chapter relate to concerns that began to crystallise amongst progressive educators in the 1920s (Heater 1980). Richardson (1990: 6–7) highlights two long-standing traditions which have influenced global education.

> The one tradition is concerned with learner-centred education, and the development and fulfilment of individuals. This tradition is humanistic and optimistic, and has a basic trust in the capacity and will of human beings to create healthy and empowering systems and structures ... The second tradition is concerned with building equality, and with resisting the trend for education merely to reflect and replicate inequalities in wider society of race, gender and class; it is broadly pessimistic in its assumption that inequalities are the norm wherever and whenever they are not consciously and strenuously resisted.
>
> Both traditions are concerned with wholeness and holistic thinking, but neither, arguably, is complete without the other. There cannot be wholeness in individuals independently of strenuous attempts to heal rifts and contradictions in wider society and in the education system. Conversely, political struggle to create wholeness in society – that is, equality and justice in dealings and relationships between social classes, between countries, between ethnic groups,

between women and men – is doomed to no more than a partial success and hollow victories, at best, if it is not accompanied by, and if it does not in its turn strengthen and sustain, the search for wholeness and integration in individuals.

Four scenarios

So what might the future for global education look like? Traditionally when attempting to consider different alternative futures, a minimum of three scenarios is used each of which deliberately highlights a contrasting possible future. What I have tried to summarise in these thumb-nail scenarios (Table 2.2) are four different ways in which global education might develop.

Uncritical scenario

The first scenario is a 'fuzzy' form of global education that lacks any conceptual clarity and is only generally to do with learning about the world. It is uncritical both about social and political formations and appropriate pedagogical procedures for exploring the world. This is a 'popular' form of global education where any reference whatsoever to the wider world is somehow taken to be a good thing.

Critical scenario (self)

The second is a form of global education which focuses on personal growth and understanding as its main outcome. This is often found amongst educators who want to explore the world today but particularly in a child-centred way. Whilst it stresses

Table 2.2 Four scenarios for global education

	1. Uncritical	2. Critical (self)	3. Critical (society)	4. Critical (holistic)
Purpose	Learning about the world and what is happening in it	Wholeness in the individual – personal and social development	Wholeness in society – working for a more just, equitable and sustainable society	Wholeness in self and society – each interrelated sides of the same coin
Pedagogy	Descriptive and transmissive; no analysis of global issues	Active, participatory and experiential learning	Socially critical with a focus on differing value perspectives and political literacy	Both student-centred and world-minded, participatory and socially critical
Politics	Conservative – focus on the world as it is	Progressive – focus on changing of self	Radical – focus on changing society	Radical/holistic – focus on changing both self and society

the importance of developing self-esteem and co-operative skills, it often pays much less attention to the use of critical thinking skills in a local and global context.

Critical scenario (society)

The third is a form of global education which focuses on critical understanding of social and political issues and the development of a pedagogy which challenges dominant neoliberal ideology and market driven forms of education. However it may fail to pay attention to the personal and social skills needed for the development of self-esteem and empathy.

Critical scenario (holistic)

The fourth scenario is a form of global education which draws on the previous two critical traditions in arguing that education needs to be about changing both self and society. In doing so it embraces personal and political change equally, aiming at the self-actualisation of the individual but embedded within the context of a socially and environmentally responsible local and global citizenship.

The second and third scenarios relate, of course, to the two traditions identified by Richardson above – the child-centred and the world-minded. For at least the last thirty years, however, a number of global educators have attempted to demonstrate why and how these two traditions belong *together*, that they are two sides of the same coin and that education is necessarily about changing both self and society. It is the fourth scenario, I believe, that offers the most critical and creative way forward. This scenario embraces the four core elements of global education (as set out in this chapter) and should thus be the one to underpin the global dimension in the curriculum.

Chapter 3

Young people's concerns

Cathie Holden

This chapter provides further evidence of the need for a global dimension in the curriculum by looking at the concerns young people have for the local and global community. This is based on research into young people's hopes and fears for the future including a study undertaken specifically for this chapter.

Listening to young people

This chapter acknowledges what young people themselves have to say and reflects two principles: a belief in children's rights (including the right to be heard and to participate) and a belief in children's competence. It builds on the work of Wood (2005: 65) who maintains that young children have much to offer as 'expert informers and witnesses' and Rudduck and Flutter (2000) who have worked extensively with secondary pupils to understand their experiences of home and school. Gidley and Inayatullah (2002), writing about Australian youth aged 15–25, also argue the need to engage young people in dialogue about matters of crucial importance to them, i.e. the future of the local and global community.

Primary level

The majority of work around young people's concerns for the future has related to pupils in secondary schools. Less has been done on the views of younger children and yet their voices deserve to be heard. Research in the mid-1990s (Hicks and Holden 1995) was the first to explore the hopes and fears of UK pupils (aged 7, 11, 14 and 18), making it possible to trace the development of children's thinking. A decade later, in 2004/5, part of that survey was repeated for this chapter drawing on the views of over 500 primary and secondary children.

Concerns of primary children in 1994

In the earlier research, 7- and 11-year-olds were asked about their hopes and fears for their personal futures, their local area and the world. They were asked about: specific issues (environment, poverty, unemployment, violence, prejudice and racism), what they had learnt in school about such issues and the extent to which they felt they wanted to work for change themselves.

The majority of both the 7- and 11-year-olds aspired to a conventional personal future. They wanted material success, to do well at school, get a good job, get a partner and have children. Their concerns centred on health, family and relationships and the possibility of being poor because unemployed. They were optimistic that the future for people in their local community would be good but wanted more amenities for young people and an improved environment. Their fears focused on dangers from crime, violence and terrorism, traffic and the effects of poverty, e.g. homelessness. Some of these concerns reflected issues in the news at the time, for example a few children thought IRA violence and conflict in Bosnia might spread to their own community.

The hopes and fears of primary children for the world mirrored what they said about their own communities. They were concerned about poverty and pollution – but this time on a global scale – and many were worried about the possibility of more wars. For the 7-year-olds there was a concern about 'global disasters' which they thought might occur in Britain too.

In summary it appeared that by the end of primary school children were increasingly aware of social, economic and environmental issues and of their complexity. Whilst they were fairly optimistic that the quality of life would improve for those in their local area, they were less optimistic that specific issues would be resolved and even less optimistic about the global situation improving (as indicated in Tables 3.1 and 3.2). They felt they had learnt little about these issues at school but thought opportunities would arise in secondary school.

Concerns of primary children in 2004

Ten years on, we wished to ascertain in what ways children's views might have changed. In the UK unemployment was half what it had been in 1994 and both homelessness and reported crime were down on the previous decade. Whilst debates about institutional racism were still in the headlines, there was also concern about immigration in relation to asylum seekers and refugees. Environmental issues were frequently in the news and Britain was engaged in an unpopular war in Iraq. Would these issues be mirrored in the hopes and fears of children? And would the advent of citizenship in schools have made a difference to children's perceptions of what they felt they had learnt at school?

In order to investigate children's concerns a new survey was undertaken with 425 children aged 9–11 from twelve different English primary schools in 2004. Four of the schools were those used in the original study whilst the others were selected to represent schools across a range of settings: urban, rural, inner city, affluent and economically deprived. As in 1994 children were asked to write freely about their hopes and fears for their personal future, the future of the local area and of the world. They were asked for their views on the same issues, about their own possible interest in working for change and also what they felt they had learnt about such issues at school.

PERSONAL FUTURES

As in 1994, the majority of the children in 2004 thought their life would be the same or better in the future. Well over three-quarters had aspirations to a good job (boys focusing particularly on sport) and over half talked about the material possessions they aspired to. The importance of good relationships was also evident from their comments about having a partner, children and good friends. Their fears related to failure in relationships (divorce, friendship problems), being a victim (mugged, raped) and ill health. Compared with 1994, these children placed more emphasis on getting a good job, but otherwise their hopes and fears were similar.

LOCAL FUTURES

Children's hopes and fears for their local community reflected the adult world but were informed by their own needs and perspectives. The following areas emerged as being of greatest concern: crime and violence, local amenities, environmental issues, poverty, jobs and housing, community relations and traffic.

Crime and violence was a concern for three-quarters of the children. They wanted a community with less violence, less crime and fewer drunks, drug dealers, addicts and gangs. They worried about mugging, rape, paedophiles, people with knives and guns and those who commit vandalism or 'do graffiti'. Some feared that the violence they had witnessed on TV would spread to their local area, with one boy being worried about 'terrorists' while another hoped 'that Bin Laden don't bomb Bristol'.

Linked to this were concerns about poverty and homelessness. Many understood the relationship between employment and housing and wanted more or cheaper housing along with 'enough jobs' as otherwise in the future it might be that only 'rich people could afford houses'. Over half of the children also wanted improved amenities – in particular more or better shops, sports facilities and parks and places to play. The vulnerability of children as pedestrians and cyclists was evident in their concerns about traffic. It was not just less or slower traffic that the children wanted, but better transport and roads, safer drivers, more cycling and more pedestrian crossings. Along with improvements to the built environment were hopes for an improved natural environment. 'There needs to be grass; it needs to be more quiet,' said a girl from an inner city area. There were concerns about increased pollution, trees being cut down, litter, loss of wildlife and 'more factories'.

Improved community relations were mentioned by both girls and boys, but more often by the former. They wanted 'friendly neighbours' and 'kinder people', while children living in the inner city hoped for 'no racism'. In general their comments indicate a real desire for a better quality of life in their community and they also reflect the concerns of the adult world about house prices and increasing urbanisation.

A series of closed questions allowed comparison to be made between the 11-year-olds in 1994 and 2004. Children were presented with five issues and asked if they thought that in the future there would be more, the same, or less poverty etc. in their local area. Table 3.1 indicates the perceptions of the 11-year-olds about each issue, with data from 1994 in brackets as a comparison.

NB. The results of the 11-year-olds only are given, as in 2004 both 9- and 11-year-olds were surveyed, whereas in 1994 7- and 11-year-olds were surveyed. Using the data from the 11-year-olds in both 2004 and 1994 thus allows for a more accurate comparison.

Table 3.1 indicates that whilst most children in 2004 thought levels of poverty, prejudice/racism and violence would stay the same, they were more optimistic that there would be solutions to poverty than to crime and violence. Opinion was evenly divided over whether unemployment and racism/prejudice would become more of a problem or not. The notable exception is the environment, where over two-thirds thought there would be more problems. There are some interesting differences between the 1994 and 2004 cohorts, notably the greater optimism of the latter about employment prospects and the eradication of racism and prejudice, possibly reflecting the greater economic prosperity of the mid-2000s and the increasingly diverse nature of British society. However, the children in 2004 were notably less optimistic than those a decade before about environmental progress.

Table 3.1 Perceived importance of local issues in the future: 11-year-olds (as %) (2004 n=217; 1994 n=125)

Issues	Poverty		Prejudice and racism		Violence		Environmental problems		Unemployment	
	2004	(1994)	2004	(1994)	2004	(1994)	2004	(1994)	2004	(1994)
More	19	(41)	27	(48)	32	(41)	68	(53)	30	(51)
The same	50	(44)	47	(32)	53	(44)	23	(32)	34	(28)
Less	30	(15)	26	(20)	15	(15)	8	(16)	35	(21)

Table 3.2 Perceived importance of global issues in the future: 11-year-olds (as %) (2004 n=217; 1994 n=125)

Issues	Poverty		Prejudice and racism		Violence (incl. war)		Environmental problems	
	2004	(1994)	2004	(1994)	2004	(1994)	2004	(1994)
More	35	(48)	38	(54)	61	(64)	68	(64)
The same	35	(34)	33	(28)	25	(15)	19	(17)
Less	30	(18)	29	(18)	13	(21)	12	(19)

GLOBAL FUTURES

The concerns of children about the global future in 2004 centred around: violence and war, environmental issues, disasters, poverty, health, politics and government. Two-thirds of children wanted peace or an end to wars. In most cases this was a general plea, but there were some specific references to wanting an end to the war in Iraq or the war on terrorism. This was linked to a desire for less violence and crime in general, with children wanting 'less unrestricted gun use especially in America' and 'no harming of children'. Others were concerned about an increase in natural disasters, such as earthquakes, tornados, flooding and meteorites. Their awareness of major events in the news was evident.

A third hoped for a solution to poverty in the developing world, linking this with an end to homelessness, hunger, lack of jobs, overpopulation and overcrowding. An 11-year-old boy, for example, wanted to see people 'putting the world's money together and giving Africa water'. The older children also made political references. They talked about 'better governments' which could eradicate poverty and wars and expressed concerns about what Tony Blair or George Bush 'might do next'.

As with the local area, environmental issues emerged as a concern. The children wanted less pollution, more recycling and an end to global warming. There were also fears about the destruction of trees, the extinction of animals and the disappearance of the countryside. An 11-year-old girl worried that 'the whole world will become a series of never ending cities' and another feared that 'there won't be any land to grow crops'. Comments relating to health mirrored those made about the local community. They wanted less smoking, fewer drugs and healthier people along with 'more cures' for diseases, including cancer, and 'better medicines'.

Again a comparison between the 11-year-olds in 1994 and 2004 shows the extent to which they felt optimistic or pessimistic about solutions to key global concerns and how perceptions have shifted (see Table 3.2).

A comparison with Table 3.1 indicates that in both 1994 and 2004 children were generally less optimistic about the global future than they were about the local. This is particularly true of their concerns around increased violence and poverty. However, as with the local area, the children in 2004 were more optimistic than those in 1994 that poverty and prejudice/racism might be alleviated. The belief of two-thirds of the group that both violence/war and environmental problems will get worse may reflect events at that time (Iraq war; terrorism) and a high profile in the media for environmental issues especially in relation to climate change.

ACTION FOR CHANGE

In spite of the concerns reported above, the majority of children thought they could do something to bring about positive change. The environment was most frequently mentioned with children saying they didn't drop litter, they recycled, saved energy or walked to school. Two cited 'sharing lifts to school' and 'buying stuff with less packaging' as examples. One in three mentioned their involvement in campaigns or fundraising, usually linked to work at school. They talked about Oxfam, Christian Aid, Comic Relief, Blue Peter, Children in Need and cancer charities. It is noteworthy that in 1994 only one in ten children mentioned such involvement. This difference might be a reflection of the new citizenship curriculum where pupils are encouraged to participate actively in community projects.

When asked how much they felt they had actually learnt at school about such issues, the most common response was that they had learnt 'a little' rather than 'a lot'. However, all thought it was important that they did learn about these things, as summed up by two boys:

> It's important 'cause otherwise you can't do anything about it.

> And like say we didn't know anything about wars and everything, then, like, as Josh said, it's your future and you wouldn't know what to do or how to handle it.

In summary, primary children in the mid-2000s appear to be well aware of current local and global issues. They have taken on adult concerns about poverty, employment and housing and wish for communities where there are good relationships and where the built and natural environment is respected. They are more optimistic than their 1994 counterparts about employment prospects and improved race relations but less optimistic about environmental progress. Their concerns for the global future mirror current events and they appear committed to increased social and economic justice. They are more politically aware than children a decade ago. Whilst the majority of children in both cohorts claimed to have only learnt 'a little' about such issues in school, more children in 2004 say they have been taught about such issues and more are involved in campaigning.

Secondary level

Research into secondary pupils' hopes and fears for the future has been gradually increasing, for example Oscarsson in Sweden (1996), Hutchinson in Australia (1996) and Rubin in Finland (2002). Reference is also made again to the 1994 and 2004/5 surveys. It should be noted, however, that most of this research has been carried out in Western countries. More work is needed on the views of young people in non-Western contexts and also on how class, ethnicity and gender may affect such responses.

Concerns of pupils in the 1990s

In reviewing research from the 1990s a picture emerges in which secondary pupils appear to have been optimistic about their personal futures and, like the primary pupils, desiring a future based on the family and fulfilling work. They were much less optimistic about the future for their community or the world – in fact there is a marked dissonance between what they expected in their personal lives and what they expected for the wider world. They were also generally more cynical than primary children about their ability to effect change.

Research from Finland in the mid-1990s epitomises the above: young people hoped for bright, conventional futures, with family, house and successful career but, when asked about the future of the wider community, there was a different story. They saw their country descending into 'a society of corruption, unemployment, growing environmental problems, drugs and dirty urban centres full of poor people struggling for their livelihood' (Rubin 2002: 103). There were also concerns about the arrival of refugees and the impact this might have on the welfare state. Their concerns for the global community centred on poverty and hunger, wars, overpopulation and environmental pollution. Rubin points out that this research was done in a time of recession in Finland which may have influenced young people's responses.

Similar findings are reported by Oscarsson (1996) who worked with teenagers in Sweden. The majority of his students held positive views about their own future, with any concerns that they had centring on unemployment. They were less optimistic about the future for Sweden, where economic conditions were seen as uncertain. Like their Finnish counterparts they were even less optimistic about the global future and cited fears about environmental issues and global conflict.

Hutchinson (1996) reports on the views of secondary pupils in Australia. Working with nearly 650 upper secondary school students he found that many felt a sense of helplessness and despondency about the problems they thought society would have to face in the near future. When asked what they thought the probable future for Australia would look like, Hutchinson identified six major scenarios which are listed in Box 3.1.

Box 3.1 Australian secondary pupils' probable futures

1 *An uncompassionate world* – in which competitive pressures in schools would increase and unemployment rise leading to increasing alienation and a lack of caring relationships.
2 *A physically violent world* – in which there would be increased direct and psychological violence with a high likelihood of conflict and war.
3 *A divided world* – in which there would be an increasing divide between the 'haves' and the 'have nots' and consequently increasing economic instability, both locally and globally.
4 *A mechanised world* – in which daily life would be increasingly dominated by technology and rapid technological change.
5 *An environmentally unsustainable world* – in which little real progress would have been made in addressing problems of environmental degradation.
6 *A politically corrupt and deceitful world* – in which there would be widespread cynicism about the value of voting and traditional party politics.

These teenagers' hopes for their preferable futures indicate that while some thought there might be 'high-tech' solutions to their concerns, others were keen for a more equitable and sustainable world where conflicts would be dealt with constructively rather than destructively. Many said that little time was given to such issues in their schooling – an omission which they regretted.

Our earlier research (Hicks and Holden 1995) resonates with the above. We found that secondary school students (aged 14 and 18) in the UK were fairly optimistic about their personal future, but less so about the quality of life for people in their community or around the world. They were concerned that poverty, unemployment and environmental problems would increase but had little idea of what role they could play as active citizens, either now or in the future.

Concerns of pupils in 2004/5

In 2004/5 100 14-year-olds were surveyed in four schools from a range of rural/ urban and socio-economic backgrounds in the south-west of England. The responses indicate that in 2004/5 secondary pupils were still optimistic about their personal futures, hoping for material success, good relationships and a good job. They were more optimistic than their 1994 counterparts about the future of their local area with just under half thinking it would be better or a bit better in the future, and one-third thinking it would be about the same. They had clear views about the areas which needed addressing and were concerned in particular about: facilities for young people, violence and crime, community issues, environmental issues and poverty.

They talked of wanting 'more things for teenagers to do' including sports facilities, entertainment and places to play. They wanted 'less drunks', 'less addicts and dealers' and feared an increase in vandalism, gangs, murder and paedophiles. Concerns about community issues related to racism, unrest and the area becoming overcrowded or 'run down' whilst concerns about poverty related to a lack of jobs or homelessness.

When asked to consider the future of the world, they were particularly concerned about the alleviation of world poverty. Two-thirds cited this as a hope for the future, followed by an end to war (mentioned by half the pupils) and a solution to environmental problems. The importance placed on an end to world poverty may reflect the emphasis given to this by the Make Poverty History campaign and Live 8 concert at the time.

When asked about specific issues, these teenagers thought that violence, unemployment and in particular environmental problems would increase both in their local area and globally. They were more optimistic about the alleviation of racism/prejudice and poverty where they thought the situation would either improve or stay the same. With the exception of the environment, the teenagers in 2004/5 were more optimistic than their 1994 counterparts. This was particularly marked in their views on world poverty: in 1994 over 80 per cent of 14-year-olds thought poverty would get worse or stay the same; in 2004/5 only half thought this, with the other half hoping things would improve.

Two-thirds of the 14-year-olds thought it was important or very important to learn about such issues at school. However, only 14 per cent claimed to have learnt a lot, with half saying they had learnt 'a little'. They gave as examples learning about the developing world, global warming and issues current at the time such as the Asian tsunami. Whereas one in three primary pupils in 2004 said they were involved in fundraising or campaigns of some kind, the vast majority of these teenagers claimed not to be involved in any national or local organisations working for change, and a few went so far as to say that such involvement would be 'sad'. This is interesting given the introduction of citizenship in 2002 with its emphasis on action in the community. It appears that secondary pupils in 2004/5 felt they had learnt less about global issues than their primary counterparts and that either they had fewer opportunities to work for change or that fewer wished to be thus involved.

National surveys

A different kind of approach was taken by Save the Children, an NGO based in the UK, to identify the concerns of 11–18-year-olds. In a survey designed and implemented by young people, this age group was asked about their opinions on local and global issues, community participation and human rights issues. Responses were received from over 4,000 pupils some of whom were subsequently interviewed.

The teenagers' concerns about local issues indicate significant interest in the wellbeing of their community (see Table 3.3). Whilst the majority were concerned about crime, it is interesting that half of the respondents named the provision of youth and leisure facilities as a matter of concern. This resonates with the concerns of the UK secondary students in 2004/5.

When presented with a list of key global issues, the teenagers overwhelmingly saw war and conflict as of greatest concern, which may well reflect the situation in Iraq at that time (see Table 3.4). Although politics was a matter of concern for fewer

Table 3.3 Teenagers' concerns about local issues (n=4,137)

Crime	71%
Youth and leisure	50%
Education	39%
Local government	33%
Health facilities	32%
Transport	29%
Employment	18%
Other	4%

Source: Wicks 2004: 2.

Table 3.4 Teenagers' concerns about global issues (n=4,129)

War and conflict	90%
Health	45%
The environment	41%
Poverty	33%
HIV/Aids	24%
Access to water and sanitation	20%
Fair trade/worker rights	12%
Politics	12%
Other	7%

Source: Wicks 2004: 2.

than one in eight, this did not necessarily indicate political apathy. When asked if they intended to vote, over 60 per cent said they would do so when they were able to and the same proportion said they would consider writing to their member of parliament if they felt strongly about something. Wicks (2004: 12) adds a note of caution, pointing out that only 39 per cent of 18–24-year-olds voted in the 2001 General Election which may reflect 'a gap between intention and action'.

Wicks argues (2004: 18) that

> the results challenge the idea, often recorded in the press, that the UK's young people are uninvolved, uncaring and uninterested in society. In fact the survey respondents come across as reasonably well informed people, aware of key social issues, eager to know about their rights and prepared to involve themselves in their community.

More recently Davies *et al.* (2005) have investigated both primary and secondary pupils' understanding of global citizenship education and found a strong desire to learn more about contemporary issues at school. In particular secondary pupils were concerned about poverty, drought, famine, disease and environmental issues and wanted to know more about war and its causes. The authors conclude that there 'was a strongly expressed need for contemporary global political and social issues to be dealt with in more depth and to have more background provided, particularly in relation to issues concerning war and the environment' (2005: 50). Garner (2005) notes that an increasing interest in conflict has resulted in more pupils taking A-level politics and religion which would seem to endorse these findings.

Young adults

The views of young adults are equally interesting. One study from Australia (Eckersley 1999) gathered data from 950 young people aged 15–25. The study sought to understand what young Australians expected and wanted of their country in 2010 with particular reference to social, economic and environmental issues.

As with the research into school-aged students' hopes and fears, Eckersley found a dissonance between what young people wanted and what they expected. Most wanted a society where the emphasis was on community, family, the environment and co-operation, but most feared the opposite.

> Major concerns included: pollution and environmental destruction, including the impact of growing populations; the gulf between rich and poor; high unemployment, including the effect of automation and immigration; conflict, crime and alienation; family problems and breakdown; discrimination and prejudice; and economic difficulties, including the level of foreign debt.
>
> (Eckersley 1999: 77)

Eckersley compared findings between the 15–18, 18–22 and 22–25 age groups and found that the older the person the more pessimistic they became about the possibility of positive change. It would appear that 'young people become less optimistic as they leave the relative security of school and home to venture out into the wider world of adulthood and independence' (1999: 80). Thus an increasing ability to act in society does not necessarily create a more positive and hopeful outlook on life.

Two studies from Japan and Norway add to this picture. Wright (2002) warns that a subculture of Japanese youth is emerging which feels increasingly disempowered. Many are challenging current Japanese social conventions and the assumption that economic growth will continue at its present rate. There is a need to listen to these people's concerns, he says, as otherwise youth vitality will be lost and there will be increasing cynicism and intergenerational division.

A similar story about disaffected youth comes from Norway. Brunstad listened to students aged 18–20 and found a prevailing attitude of 'don't care' and 'live for today'. Because they felt powerless to make any kind of change these young people focused on immediate gratification symbolised by the importance of body image and clothes. They held negative views towards public life and public institutions, exhibiting

> a kind of post modern melancholy, irony or boredom. ... A lot of dark shadows loom above their small, intimate and privatised world. Failing at school, divorce, loneliness, illness, unemployment, boredom, violence, crime and gangs are all threatening clouds on the horizon.
>
> (Brunstad 2002: 148)

Conclusions

The 2004/5 research suggests that primary children in England are more involved as active citizens than they were ten years ago and that they have a commitment to social justice and environmental progress. Secondary pupils also showed an understanding of the complexity of current issues and a commitment to the alleviation of world poverty but were not as actively involved. Some international studies endorse this picture of young people concerned about local and global issues but unsure about their own role in acting for change, whilst other research paints a more negative picture of disaffected youth. The level of optimism/pessimism and willingness to act for change seems to reflect both the current socio-economic conditions of the student's country and their age. It would appear that the younger the student the more optimistic and active they are and the older the student the more pessimistic and disempowered they feel. It is important though to be mindful of Eckersley's (1999) observation that having concerns for the future is not the same as being fearful, nor does it necessarily indicate that students are immersed on a day-to-day basis in anxiety and pessimism.

However, the message from this research seems clear. If we are to have an informed and participative electorate committed to social and economic justice, then the challenge of global education must be addressed at an early age. The enthusiasm and energy of primary pupils needs to be harnessed, addressing their concerns and ensuring that such commitment is not dampened when they arrive in secondary school. There needs to be time in the secondary curriculum for pupils to talk about their concerns and to take action in a way that is relevant to their interests and age. Involvement in community action and interest in political and global issues needs to increase, not decrease, as pupils grow older so that as young adults they feel motivated to make a difference. A first step towards a curriculum where global issues and action for change are central is to ensure that teachers themselves understand the need for a global dimension.

Chapter 4

Student teachers' views

Cathie Holden

This chapter focuses on the perceptions that trainee teachers have of the world. What are their concerns and do they feel that there should be a global dimension in the curriculum? The knowledge, understanding and motivation of student teachers to teach about global issues are explored through a recent research project involving students in south-west England.

Introduction

The previous chapter showed that many young people today are concerned about issues of wealth and poverty, war and peace, technological change and environmental damage both in their local communities and in the wider world. Some pupils said they had learnt about such issues at school, but many also said they wanted to know more and felt they needed this understanding to help them in the future. Research into the views of young adults showed that they were still concerned about the same local and global issues but that they were more pessimistic about the possibilities of change and the outlook for the future.

Whilst we know about the concerns of many young people, less is known about the views of student teachers who will have the responsibility for educating children about global issues. Do they share some of the pessimism of other young adults, or does their choice of career mean that they feel more pro-active about change? What do student teachers themselves know about global issues and, most importantly, to what extent do they feel motivated to teach about them?

The global dimension in ITET

Partly as a result of funding from the Department for International Development a number of initial teacher education and training (ITET) institutions in the UK have developed aspects of the global dimension in teacher training. A recent report, entitled *Global Perspectives in Teacher Training*, contains eight case studies documenting emerging good practice. In considering the way forward this report notes:

> It is clear from the case studies that a richness of practice already exists within teacher training institutions on ways in which the global dimension can be

incorporated within ITET. Whilst some of the case studies describe and offer innovative teaching and learning techniques, others ... highlight and present the need for further research and investigations into the process and issues of mainstreaming this agenda.

(Symons 2004: 51)

This chapter reports on some of the 'further research' that is needed in relation to ITET. The importance of such work is highlighted by Robbins et al. (2003) at the University of Wales, Bangor, who analyse a project concerned with embedding education for global citizenship into initial teacher education and training courses (World Education Centre 2004). Such courses, they write:

... have a key role in equipping teachers with the necessary competence to contribute effectively to cross-curricular and whole-school approaches which promote progress towards concern and action for equal opportunities, social justice and sustainable development from the local to the global scale.

(Robbins *et al.* 2003: 94)

At the end of the course under discussion 76 per cent of the secondary student teachers and 59 per cent of the primary students felt that global citizenship should have a high priority in the curriculum although there were significant differences in attitude depending on the student's main subject area. However, only 35 per cent felt confident that they could contribute to a whole-school approach to this in school.

The south-west study

In order to investigate further the knowledge and understanding that student teachers have of global issues and their motivation to include a global dimension in their teaching, an inter-university research team in the south-west investigated the following questions (Holden and Hicks 2006):

*   How knowledgeable do student teachers feel they are about different global issues?
*   What are the influences on students' knowledge and understanding of such issues?
*   What prior experience of global issues/matters do students bring to their studies?
*   To what extent do students feel motivated to teach about global issues?

How the research was carried out

Both questionnaires and interviews were used in this study, the former in order to obtain responses from a large sample and the latter to enable more in-depth exploration of student understanding. Student teachers from four universities in the south-west of England were recruited to provide data for three cohorts which reflect the training routes taken by most prospective teachers:

- Cohort 1: 313 primary PGCE
- Cohort 2: 442 secondary PGCE
- Cohort 3: 101 primary undergraduate (total 856).

The sample was divided more or less equally between secondary and primary students. Within the primary sample almost a quarter of the students were first year undergraduates. Half of the total sample was in the 18–23 age range, with just over a third being in the 24–34 age range and 15 per cent over 35. Three-quarters of the sample was female; the majority of the men were secondary students.

The questionnaire design was based on that used by MORI (1998) to investigate pupils' knowledge of global issues so that some comparison could also be made with this survey. New questions were added to elicit information about students' prior experience as it was felt this could have a bearing on their knowledge and understanding. This is in line with Thomas (2001) who found that teachers with experience of Voluntary Service Overseas (VSO), for example, were more committed to introducing global perspectives into their teaching.

The in-depth interviews provided the qualitative data. Over 200 students volunteered to be interviewed, from which a sample of 41 was selected reflecting the balance of the three cohorts. The themes in the questionnaire provided the basis for the interviews and the responses helped the team gain insight into students' understanding, prior experience and motivation.

Questionnaire findings

Knowledge of global issues

From Table 4.1 we can see that the majority of students claimed to either know 'something' or 'a lot' about many of today's global issues. They appeared to know most about the reasons for war and famine and least about the reasons for economic

Table 4.1 Student teachers' knowledge of global issues (n=856)

Knowledge of global issues	Know a lot	Know something	Know nothing
Reasons for war in the world	17%	81%	2%
Reasons for famine in the world	17%	79%	4%
Reasons for environmental problems	20%	74%	6%
Reasons for overpopulation	20%	74%	6%
Reasons for the Third World's economic problems	15%	74%	11%
Reasons for human rights abuses	11%	75%	14%

problems in less economically developed countries and human rights abuses. We wished to find out if levels of knowledge and understanding were evenly distributed across all students. For example, were those who said they knew a lot about the reasons for war mainly from one training route or were they evenly spread across all three? Were secondary PGCE students more likely to 'know something' about the reasons for environmental problems than the undergraduates? An analysis of the responses to two of the global issues listed – 'reasons for war' and 'reasons for environmental problems' – was carried out and some interesting differences found.

Tables 4.2 and 4.3 show that students' perceived levels of knowledge varied according to the age they were training to teach and whether they were undergraduates or postgraduates. Figures in italics indicate statistically significant differences. Secondary postgraduates were the most confident in their knowledge of both of these issues and primary undergraduates the least. While the majority of the undergraduates 'knew something' they were much less likely to 'know a lot' and one in ten of them claimed to 'know nothing' about the reasons for global environmental issues.

When the figures were analysed further by gender, other significant differences were found. It was male students (secondary and primary) who were the most confident in their knowledge of both issues. Men were three times as likely as women to say they 'knew a lot' about the reasons for war, and twice as likely to say they 'knew a lot' about reasons for environmental problems. This may be a result of greater confidence among male students or it may be that they were indeed more interested and more knowledgeable about such issues. Either way there are implications for increasing the confidence of female students with regard to their perceived or actual knowledge base.

Table 4.2 Student teachers' knowledge of reasons for war by cohort (*n*=856)

War	PGCE primary	PGCE secondary	Undergraduate	Total
I know a lot about this	11%	24%	5%	17%
I know something about this	86%	75%	91%	81%
I know nothing about this	3%	1%	4%	2%
Total	100%	100%	100%	100%

Table 4.3 Student teachers' knowledge of reasons for environmental problems by cohort (*n*=856)

Environmental problems	PGCE primary	PGCE secondary	Undergraduate	Total
I know a lot about this	17%	24%	10%	20%
I know something about this	77%	72%	79%	74%
I know nothing about this	6%	4%	11%	6%
Total	100%	100%	100%	100%

Looking at the subject specialism of the students revealed further differences. Just over a third of secondary history students and over half of citizenship students said they knew a lot about reasons for war (compared with 17 per cent of students overall), and citizenship, geography and science students were most likely to say they knew a lot about reasons for environmental problems. Early years students were the most likely to say they 'knew nothing' about either of these issues.

Sources of information

It is interesting that the majority of students felt that they got most of their information on global issues from the media (television and newspapers) rather than from school or university (see Table 4.4). This was true for students on all three training routes and raises questions about the nature of this claimed knowledge and their ability to critically evaluate this information. Undergraduates appeared less likely to look to their peers as sources of information and more likely to cite their work in school than postgraduates. They were understandably less likely to refer to university as a source of information as this group were only in the first year of their degree.

Prior experience

Questions on prior experience of global issues as well as exposure to cultures other than their own were included in the study as it seemed likely this might be a significant factor in determining both students' knowledge and their motivation to teach about global issues.

Overall, a considerable number of students (40 per cent) had lived or worked abroad and over half had friends or family from cultures other than their own or were interested in global issues (see Table 4.5). However, a sizeable minority – nearly

Table 4.4 Student teachers' sources of information about global issues by cohort (n=856)

Sources of information	PGCE primary	PGCE secondary	Undergraduate	Total
Television	94%	96%	97%	95%
Newspapers	90%	92%	86%	90%
Friends	65%	60%	37%	59%
Family	58%	52%	58%	55%
Internet	47%	58%	47%	53%
University	48%	48%	11%	44%
School	30%	35%	47%	34%

Note
Responses total more than 100% as students could tick more than one source.

Table 4.5 Student teachers' experience of and interest in global issues by cohort (*n*=856)

Prior experience of global matters	PGCE primary	PGCE secondary	Undergraduate	Total
Have lived and worked abroad	45%	45%	5%	40%
Have family/friends from other cultural backgrounds	64%	56%	28%	55%
Am particularly interested in global issues	59%	58%	17%	53%
Not applicable	11%	12%	59%	18%

Note
Responses total more than 100% as students could tick more than one source.

one-fifth – had no particular interest in global issues and no connections with other places or peoples.

Analysis by cohort indicates that the PGCE students were most likely to have lived or worked abroad and there was a direct correlation between this and their interest in global issues. Primary and secondary PGCE students appeared to have had the same level of experience abroad and claimed the same level of interest, but secondary students claimed greater knowledge (see Tables 4.2 and 4.3). This greater confidence amongst secondary students may warrant further research. Does this relate to gender (the majority of men were secondary students) or are secondary students generally more knowledgeable about world issues? Also of note is the statistically significant number of undergraduates who said these areas were 'not applicable' – well over half claimed to have no particular interest in global issues and no experience of other cultures or countries. This correlates with their expressed lack of knowledge on such issues and raises a vital question for undergraduate programmes: if a knowledge and understanding of global issues is important to prospective teachers, how can we broaden the experiences, both direct and mediated, that undergraduates have?

Student motivation

The above findings referred to students' claimed knowledge and experience. In order to understand their motivation as learners, they were asked to indicate which of the global issues listed in Table 4.6 they would like to know more about.

Table 4.6 indicates a strong desire on the part of most students to know more about global issues. A comparison with Table 4.1 indicates that students felt least confident in their knowledge of reasons for human rights abuses, and this appears in Table 4.6 as the area they most wished to know more about. Whilst knowledge of the reasons for war came first in Table 4.1, the fact that over two-thirds of trainees still wished to have more knowledge of this area may signify its importance to them.

In a final question students were asked whether they felt they could make a difference to pupils' understanding of global issues when they became teachers. Over

Table 4.6 Student teachers' desire for more knowledge of global issues (*n*=856)

More knowledge of global issues	Total
Reasons for human rights abuses	74%
Reasons for war in the world	69%
Reasons for the Third World's economic problems	65%
Reasons for famine in the world	63%
Reasons for environmental problems	61%
Reasons for overpopulation	54%

Note
Responses total more than 100% as students could tick more than one source.

half of the students 'strongly agreed' that they could make a difference to pupils' understanding with a further 40 per cent 'tending to agree'. PGCE students were more likely to feel they could make a difference than the undergraduates who, having less experience of these issues, were more ambivalent in their response.

Taking these last two questions together, it appeared that the majority of students were both motivated to learn more about global issues themselves and felt that they could make a difference to pupils' understanding of these issues. What was not clear was the extent to which they felt confident and prepared to teach about such issues in the classroom. It was hoped that the in-depth interviews would provide some answers.

Comparison with the MORI survey

The questionnaire was partly designed to reflect the MORI poll (1998) which mapped over 1,000 11–16-year-olds' knowledge of global issues. Comparison indicates that while student teachers (and particularly postgraduates) knew more, both pupils and student teachers felt most confident in their knowledge of reasons for war and least confident in their knowledge of human rights abuses. A notable minority of both undergraduates and pupils knew nothing about (or did not understand) the topics under discussion.

Both pupils and students cited television and newspapers as their primary sources of information about global issues. Other important sources for the pupils were school and parents – also mentioned by the undergraduates. Three out of five of the pupils either agreed or tended to agree that they should be taught at school 'about issues affecting the world' and the majority of student teachers felt they could make a difference to pupils' understanding of such issues. There appeared to be much common ground between the groups: both felt global issues were important and should be part of the curriculum and both seemed motivated to learn more.

Findings from the interviews

The purpose of the interviews was to shed more light on the above data and to illuminate the thinking behind students' responses. Understandably, since the students had volunteered to be interviewed, they were generally very positive about the inclusion of a global dimension in the curriculum and seemed representative of the majority who stated that such issues were important. None of the significant minority (see Table 4.5) who had few connections with other cultures or who said they were not particularly interested in global issues volunteered to be interviewed. Further research is needed into the perceptions of such students.

Prior experience

In the interviews students who had lived and/or worked abroad were asked to say more about the nature of this and its effect on their own knowledge and understanding. A wide range of experiences was revealed. Some had taught English in other countries, e.g. India, Nepal and Morocco. Others had done voluntary work abroad, such as working for VSO, for the Raleigh International Project in Ghana and for Aids Awareness in Zimbabwe. Some had lived abroad with their families (in India, Australia, Nigeria) or travelled extensively (in Nepal, Pakistan, China, Spain). All spoke of the importance of experiencing difference. They spoke in terms of cultural difference, ideological difference and the difference in terms of wealth and privilege. For many their time abroad had raised issues of justice and equality and had given them greater knowledge and new insights. One student explained:

> It opens up your eyes to how other people live and the problems they face and how like you they are ... I feel that everyone is similar to each other ... we live in different places but we're fundamentally the same.

A student who had been going to India since she was young because her father worked there, described the experience as 'forming who I am'.

Those who had not had experience of living or working abroad were asked what had helped form their opinions about global issues. Some said that though they did not have this first-hand experience they were nonetheless aware of and interested in such issues. Some were involved with campaigning organisations or charities in the UK, such as Amnesty, Greenpeace, Traidcraft and local action groups. Interest in and commitment to environmental and sustainability issues was high, particularly among the undergraduates. One spoke of her group of friends where a lot of emphasis was put on recycling; another said she was not 'politically active' but tried to buy eco-friendly products, dolphin-friendly tuna and Fairtrade coffee.

When asked to talk more generally about influences on their thinking, many cited the importance of parents, friends or religious beliefs. Six students spoke about coming from a family which 'discusses a lot' or was politically aware. Others mentioned parents who encouraged social responsibility or were involved in campaigning of some sort. Seven spoke of their personal values and belief systems, referring to the influence of their religion (Quaker, Christian, Buddhist) or of being vegetarian, for example. One said: 'I feel a responsibility to live a certain way [but] I don't actively tell other people about it'.

For some their undergraduate degree had made the biggest difference. Five referred specifically to their degree having made them 'better informed'. Two cited their degrees in European studies where they felt they had gained 'a broad view on different issues', whilst another talked about his degree in economics which included a global perspective. The experience of students in the workplace was also important. Many mentioned this as 'opening their eyes' and one talked of her work with a company writing an environmental management plan which taught her about pollution, land use and conflicting needs.

Many wanted to point out that while they themselves were interested in global issues and committed to working for change they did not feel other students necessarily shared their concerns. A mature student commented:

> I live in a flat with people who are ... 22, they honestly just don't give a damn, they don't think about it, they're not involved with any charities, they don't give a toss about environmental concerns, they just want to go out, get pissed on Friday night and watch the footy on Saturday and have fun – there's this whole kind of Hollyoaks youth culture which wasn't [around in] my adolescence and I find that really scary.

This perception reinforces the need for further research into the views of those trainees with no apparent interest in global issues.

Students' motivation

The data from the questionnaires indicated that the majority of students wished to know more about global issues and felt they could make a difference to pupils' understanding. This was reflected in the interviews. Students said it was 'essential' that pupils learnt about such issues, that they had broad horizons, were able to 'live internationally' and could see beyond their own 'small world'. One argued that teachers who did not think globally were 'short-changing the children'. For another there was an important link between 'active citizenship and global awareness. You need to be aware of your actions ... that your actions have consequences'. The enthusiasm of one student for such an approach came from a placement school where she saw that the whole-school ethos reflected a commitment to cultural diversity and global citizenship.

A common perception among these students was that teaching literacy and numeracy was only part of a bigger picture. Several commented that the skills of reading and writing were only important in terms of how they were used. One felt that while 'learning tables and handwriting are valid skills that you need in life ... if you're not exposed to all those other issues, you're not going to be a fully formed person'. Many felt it was imperative for environmental issues to be addressed and sustainable lifestyles developed. Another felt that education was too often 'geared toward economic production' or restricted by the political regime, whereas true education was about 'freedom in your mind ... it's what we should be striving for' and it was here that she saw the links to global education. What was common to all was a view that education needed to be about widening horizons and about preparing children for the challenges of life in an increasingly global society.

Whilst the majority of those interviewed were committed and enthusiastic about including global perspectives in their teaching, this was tempered by concerns about how best to teach what seemed to be complex and sensitive issues. An undergraduate had been on her first school placement in a Year 1 class at the time of the 9/11 attack. In interview she recalled:

> [Children] came up to me and said 'Did you see what happened and how many people died?' but the teacher wouldn't discuss it. I think they should have had a moment, a few minutes just to discuss it briefly, get it off their chests, try to understand it in their own way without just going [straight] into the numeracy hour.

The student felt she was not allowed to talk about what had happened with the children and was left feeling frustrated by her inability to address their needs. Another primary teacher worried about being 'vested with this huge authority as a teacher' which might, she thought, lead her to influence children without letting them make up their own minds. Concerns voiced by others throughout the interviews were:

- The fear factor, i.e. children's reactions to war and violence
- Knowing how to judge what is/isn't appropriate, especially with young children
- Their own role – should they try to be neutral or give their opinion
- The reaction of parents to teachers dealing with controversial issues
- Finding time to teach about global issues along with everything else
- A lack of confidence in dealing with sensitive issues, e.g. Iraq, immigration
- Knowing how to facilitate meaningful discussion
- Having sufficient knowledge themselves of current issues.

While the findings from the questionnaires indicated a desire to know more about global issues and a belief in their ability to help children understand such topics, the concerns raised in the interviews revealed some of the barriers to effective delivery in the classroom. Students felt they needed more guidance and more knowledge themselves if they were to feel competent to teach about global issues.

Summary

Findings from the questionnaires indicate that these student teachers appeared well motivated to teach about global issues and confident in their own knowledge, with the majority 'knowing something' about the issues under discussion. However there were considerable differences in levels of assumed knowledge and motivation among students. Secondary students were more confident in their knowledge than their primary counterparts, with their subject specialism having a bearing on this. History and citizenship students were most confident in their knowledge about reasons for war; geography, science and citizenship students were most confident in their knowledge about reasons for environmental problems. Men were significantly more likely to say they 'knew a lot' about reasons for both these issues than women, with undergraduates as a whole being significantly less confident in their knowledge. Early years students, whether undergraduate or postgraduate, were also less confident in their knowledge of such issues, with one in five saying they 'knew nothing' about the reasons for environmental problems.

Sources of information were primarily TV and newspapers, followed by friends, family and the internet. Prior experience (living/working abroad) and contact with other cultures appeared to directly influence students' interest in and knowledge of global matters. The undergraduate students who had the least experience of other cultures and who were least likely to have lived or worked abroad were much less motivated to teach about global issues.

The interviews endorsed the wealth of prior experience brought by many to their PGCE courses and reflected their level of commitment to global issues. They indicated that even though many expressed doubts about some elements of their own knowledge, they nonetheless felt committed to addressing young people's concerns about these issues. The interviews also shed light on the reasons for many students' expressed lack of confidence: global issues were seen as sensitive, controversial and complex and they felt they needed specific guidance on appropriate teaching methods and better subject knowledge.

Some implications

Schools are being encouraged to introduce a global dimension into the curriculum (DfES 2005a) and there is a renewed emphasis in English primary schools on creativity and going beyond the confines of the classroom (DfES 2003). Using new teachers' experiences of and commitment to global issues could be one way into a broader curriculum and more relevant and innovative teaching. The introduction of citizenship education as a statutory subject in secondary schools also provides opportunities for active learning about global issues. Its effective delivery in schools, however, will in part depend on the understanding, ability and motivation of student teachers to help young people make such 'global connections'. What happens in ITET is therefore of crucial importance.

Our research suggests that the majority of student teachers are interested in and motivated to teach about global issues but are concerned about their own subject knowledge and appropriate pedagogy. The increasing popularity of 'gap' years and the diverse nature of British society mean that many students arrive with a wealth of knowledge and experience of other countries and cultures. Work experience also provides many postgraduates with knowledge of equality issues and economics. ITET programmes thus need to broaden their remit so that they recognise the experiences and commitment such students bring and build upon these interests. This would include time for trainee teachers to learn strategies for teaching about global and controversial issues and time for them to improve their own knowledge and understanding. It is worth noting that the majority of student teachers appear much more optimistic about their role in making a difference than the young adults of similar age reported in the previous chapter. Such optimism needs to be nurtured if we are to retain a young workforce committed to change.

A significant minority of the students in this study appeared to be disinterested in global issues and to lack knowledge and experience of other cultures. This was particularly true for undergraduates, which raises the question of how such students can be given the kind of experiences which helped develop the knowledge and understanding of their postgraduate counterparts. There may be implications here for the content of undergraduate courses and the types of cultural experiences students have. The latter might be fostered through student exchange (with other parts of the UK or with other countries) or through work experience or placements where students have opportunities to engage first-hand with issues of social justice and equality. Embedding knowledge about global issues in undergraduate courses seems equally important. Some Education Studies courses have begun to show what is possible here (Ward 2004) and a report on *Global Perspectives and Teachers in Training* (Development Education Association 2003a) shows how some undergraduate courses are changing. Students can take modules such as Global Citizenship and Civic Society, Globalisation and Ethics in the Workplace and Global Responsibility and Sustainable Business Practice. Should such students then wish to train as teachers they would come with considerable global insight.

As this chapter has highlighted, those working in ITET have a crucial role to play in ensuring that efforts by policy makers to include a global dimension in the curriculum are supported by globally literate new teachers. Effective delivery of a global dimension in schools over the next decade will largely depend on the understanding, ability and motivation of student teachers to help young people make local–global connections. Young people want to know more (as evidenced in Chapter 3) and the majority of student teachers are motivated to teach about such issues but need help with their own subject knowledge, and with teaching what they see as complex and controversial issues. The following chapters in this book specifically aim to help teachers in schools and ITET start on this journey.

Chapter 5

Teaching controversial issues

Cathie Holden

Many of the issues that young people need to learn about today are controversial in nature. This does not mean that they should be avoided in the curriculum for, as this chapter explains, there is a range of appropriate procedures that can be used when discussing such issues in the classroom.

Introduction

> I do circle time, I covered it in my training, but I wouldn't discuss anything controversial, partly because I think it would be contentious and … you worry about parents.
>
> (Year 4 newly qualified teacher)

> We've looked at the Anne Frank story, we made ID cards, and discussed arguments for and against them and considered which people might feel most vulnerable and threatened by such a system. This led to a discussion about Britain's refugees. We tried to consider what it would be like to be a refugee, being displaced and disempowered and often the focus of people's hatred. We've also discussed Damilola Taylor and Stephen Lawrence – looking at prejudice, policing, fear, trust and the courage it takes to speak up.
>
> (Year 4 teacher)

Controversial issues are part and parcel of everyday life. Whilst some would argue that the school's role is to protect children from encountering issues which might be sensitive or difficult, others would argue that learning how to handle controversy is an essential element of life in a democratic society. Young people themselves tend towards the latter view. The young people in Chapter 3 wanted to know more about global issues. They realised these were complex and controversial and wished to be better informed so they could make up their own minds about such issues. The student teachers in Chapter 4 also acknowledged that learning about such issues was important but they were concerned about how best to approach them and about what was appropriate in the classroom.

The student teachers' concerns echo those of serving teachers. Research into primary teachers' views about the teaching of citizenship found some teachers argued explicitly that school was not the place for discussing contentious or 'distressing issues' as it should provide children with a 'safe haven' from the outside world and its problems. Newly qualified teachers felt particularly vulnerable and were concerned about what parents might say. Other teachers acknowledged the importance of teaching about topical and controversial issues and said they dealt with questions from children as and when they arose. While few planned any teaching specifically on such issues, there were some who took sensitive matters in their stride. The two teachers talking at the beginning of this chapter exemplify these two perspectives (Holden 2000: 122).

Whilst much of the early work on teaching about controversial issues dates from the 1980s (Stradling *et al.* 1984; Carrington and Troyna 1988) a renewed interest in how to teach about such issues is marked by the work of Wellington (2003), Oulton *et al.* (2004a, 2004b) and Fiehn (2005). This chapter thus argues that controversial issues are too important to be left to chance questions that might arise at any time or perhaps not at all. Operating a 'safe haven' approach may deny children the opportunities to explore relevant topical and political issues and leave them unprepared to cope with controversial issues that they see on the television or meet in the community. Instead, what is required is an approach where controversial issues are planned for and taught about within a structured framework, so that when difficult matters arise both children and teachers are equipped to deal with them.

The chapter looks first at definitions of controversial issues and then in more depth at why they should be taught. It then discusses the role of the teacher, strategies for the classroom and examples of good practice.

What are controversial issues?

There is, unsurprisingly, no one definition of 'controversial issue' although that offered by Wellington (1986: 3) is still widely used. He states that a controversial issue is one which a) is considered important by an appreciable number of people and b) involves value judgements, so that the issue cannot be settled by facts, evidence or experiment alone. Similarly, Stradling *et al.* (1984:2) point out that whilst some issues are controversial because there is not enough evidence on which to make a judgement, others are:

> controversial precisely because they are not capable of being settled by appeal to the evidence. These are issues where the disagreement centres on matters of value judgement. The major political, social and economic issues of our time or of any previous era tend to be of this type.

Richardson (1986: 27) elaborates on this in more detail when he writes:

... controversy is not to do with different levels of knowledge and information but with different opinions, values and priorities, and, basically and essentially, with different material interests. A controversial issue, in brief, is one on which society is divided. The difference of opinion may be about the very definition and the naming of the problem to be solved; and/or about its causes in history, in society, in human nature; and/or about the actions which should be taken, ... to remove or manage the problem; and/or about the structure and contours of the ideal situation, state or society towards which action is taken ...

This kind of account of controversy is not unproblematic however. It envisages that the definition of an issue as controversial, as distinct from one arising only from differences of knowledge and information, is a straightforward empirical question – 'people agree or they don't, society is divided or it isn't'. The reality, however, is that certain interests are served by maintaining that there is no controversy, no difference of opinion, no protest or discontent, that we're all one happy family; conversely certain other interests are served through the recognition that such and such an issue should be debated, should be on the agenda.

Controversial issues are thus those that deeply divide a society and that generate conflicting explanations and solutions based on alternative value systems (Stradling *et al.* 1984). They might be local issues, e.g. decisions made about youth and leisure facilities or global issues such as damage to the environment or international conflict. Teachers on an MEd module on Citizenship Education (at Exeter University) said that for them the most sensitive and difficult topics were where the global became local, e.g. the arrival of asylum seekers, the rise of the British National Party or anti-European Union feelings amongst local farming children. Fiehn (2005: 11), writing for a post-16 audience, gives 'war, immigration, abortion, gay rights, the European Union' as examples of relevant controversial issues.

It is important to recall, as Richardson indicates above, that people's value perspectives derive from deep-seated ideological beliefs or worldviews about politics, economics, society and environment. The term ideology, as Meighan and Siraj-Blatchford (2003: 186) explain, thus refers to a 'broad interlocked set of ideas and beliefs about the world held by a group of people that they demonstrate in both behaviour and conversation to various audiences'. Such belief systems or worldviews act as the lens for a group to make sense of the world, becoming the taken-for-granted way of explaining why things are as they are. Thus an ecocentric view of society is very different from a technocentric one. Western ideology is very different from an Islamic worldview. In exploring controversial issues it is thus important to remember that it is not just about weighing up facts or evidence but about understanding differing belief systems.

In general terms a controversial issue is therefore one in which:

- the subject/area is of topical interest
- there are conflicting values and opinions

- there are conflicting priorities and material interests
- emotions may become strongly aroused
- the subject/area is complex.

(Adapted from Perry 1999)

Not all controversial issues are global but one could argue that all global issues are controversial. If we take long-standing global issues to do with human rights, the environment, peace and conflict, equality and social justice, they meet all the above criteria; they are complex, of topical interest and involve competing values and interests. Of course it would be possible to teach about such issues in a way that denies their controversial nature. One could deal simply with the 'facts' without acknowledging that such facts will be interpreted differently by different parties. But such an approach denies children the opportunity to learn how to deal with topical, controversial issues in a structured classroom environment.

Why teach about controversial issues?

If we are to enable young people to think critically and work co-operatively with others to evaluate problems in the wider community then education must have at its core the open and democratic discussion of controversial, topical and political issues. Such discussion often has positive outcomes in terms of increased tolerance and understanding of democratic processes. Frazer (1999: 11) thus argues that 'the evidence for a link between a democratic, discussion and deliberation based classroom practice, and anti-authoritarian or pro-democratic attitudes and value commitments is strong'.

Bernard Crick, writing about the principles underpinning the introduction of education for citizenship in England, also put the case for such an approach. He argues that young people are interested in particular political and controversial issues (e.g. animal rights, environmental issues, improving their local community), and therefore we need to equip them with 'the political skills needed to change laws in a peaceful and responsible manner' (QCA 1998: 10). Teaching about controversial issues is at the heart of this:

> Controversial issues are important in themselves and to omit informing about and discussing them is to leave a wide and significant gap in the educational experience of young people.
>
> (QCA 1998: 56)

This approach is endorsed by Huckle, a long-standing advocate of the need for a political education that includes discussion of controversial issues. He cites protests over road constructions and live animal exports as examples of 'the appeal of cultural politics amongst the young and its power to build new alliances in changed times' (Huckle 1996: 34). Teaching about such matters may be the key to gaining pupils' interest in topical, political and global issues.

Teaching about controversial issues, however, is more than a way into the teaching of politics or global issues. It also provides opportunities for involving both 'head and heart', and for teaching knowledge, critical thinking skills and emotional literacy. There follow six further learning opportunities which can occur as a result of teaching about controversial issues.

Multiple perspectives

People hold different views, according to their value system, e.g. in how they define a situation, judge an action or solve a problem. Multiple perspectives exist because humans view the world differently depending on, for example, ethnicity, age, gender, class and culture. See, for example, Kawagley and Barnhardt's (1999) exploration of Western and indigenous worldviews. That there are multiple views of reality can be brought home to pupils through discussion of controversial issues. A central focus is understanding the complexity of such issues and that compromise between different value positions is not always possible.

Critical thinking

In the discussion of controversial issues, basic assumptions need to be revealed and claims need to be reasoned, with judgements based on knowledge and opinions based on evidence (Fisher 2001). Thus the discussion of controversial issues provides opportunities for pupils to learn the skills of critical thinking, realising the importance of presenting decisions as 'reasonable' on the grounds of fairness, evidence and compromise. The aim is to move away from 'winning' arguments and to find creative resolutions to apparent conflicts.

Participation

Controversial issues are an invitation to everybody to participate in the discussion. Where the atmosphere in the classroom is positive and controversies are welcomed, there is an opportunity for all pupils, regardless of ability, to express their own point of view and to feel able to contribute and find their voice (Antidote 2003).

Speaking and listening

Classroom talk is still dominated by teachers. English *et al.* (2002) report that nine out of ten pupil contributions to the literacy hour are of less than three words and that teachers feel pressed to move through materials at a pace which does not allow for deliberation. Discussion of controversial issues provides opportunities for open-ended debate where the objective is not necessarily to find the 'best' solution, but to let pupils listen to each other and try to find a solution which feels appropriate to them.

Communication skills

Children have to learn to deal with difference and controversy. They are not born knowing how to do this and need to practise skills of listening, stating their case and being prepared to change their minds or re-think their values if necessary. Learning how to deal with sensitive, controversial issues in a structured setting, i.e. through topics introduced into the classroom, can be a rehearsal for dealing with more immediate controversy in the playground, home or community.

Real-life contexts

One can teach about controversial issues using fictitious moral dilemmas, stories and myths, as Fisher (2001) has effectively demonstrated. However the same skills can be taught using current local and global issues as scenarios, thus providing children with authentic or 'real-life' learning contexts. These can, indeed should, include issues raised by young people themselves.

Teachers often express a concern about what parents may say if they introduce controversial issues into their teaching. Yet research into the views of parents of both primary and secondary children shows that parents are not opposed to such teaching if they know that teachers have clear guidelines and boundaries (Holden 2004). Indeed many parents welcome the support that teachers can give in helping children understand the complex issues seen on TV which they find difficult to explain. Parents of secondary pupils are well aware that getting teenagers to listen to each other and weigh up information dispassionately can be a difficult task, and thus welcome the teaching of these skills at school. However, they want to be better informed about what kind of topics will be covered and reassured about the role of the teacher in handling sensitive issues with their children.

The role of the teacher

The teaching of controversial issues requires that the school provides opportunities for open discussion about points of conflict and agreement that are found in the local and global community. It follows that there will be an increased role for the child to express opinions, discuss, debate and develop ideas during lessons. However, this can bring its own problems, and many teachers express concern that their own contributions or those of pupils in their class may be biased or reflect strongly held opinions which may be difficult to manage in the classroom.

For this reason the Crick Report (QCA 1998) includes clear guidance to teachers on strategies for managing controversial issues in classrooms. It recognises the need for balanced and careful measures of neutrality on the part of the teacher, whilst acknowledging that there may be some occasions when the teacher needs to assert a commitment to a value position. At other times the teacher may need to intervene if class discussion has not been sufficient to counter the expression of an anti-social viewpoint (for example a racist opinion) with the effect that individuals in the class are left exposed and vulnerable. The three approaches recommended are:

- *The neutral chair*
  This requires the teacher not to express any personal views, as these may be given undue weight by pupils, but to act only as a facilitator. It can mean, however, that children hear only what they want to hear and it denies pupils the opportunity to hear the teacher's views.
- *The balanced approach*
  In this, teachers ensure that all aspects of an issue are covered. The teacher expresses his/her view in order to encourage the students to present theirs. The teacher ensures that a range of opinions is expressed. This approach can run the risk of giving equal weight to all arguments and leaving students confused as to those of real merit.
- *Stated commitment approach*
  In this the teacher openly expresses his/her view as a means of encouraging discussion, but it can run the risk of indoctrinating students.

A fourth position, *Challenging consensus approach*, suggested by Fiehn (2005), is that the teacher consciously and openly takes up an opposite position to that expressed by participants or resource material.

Teachers may, of course, use a combination of these approaches as the need arises. Whatever role the teacher adopts, it is important that pupils are 'offered the experience of a genuinely free consideration of difficult issues' (QCA 1998: 60) and that issues are analysed 'according to an established set of criteria, which are open to scrutiny and publicly defensible' (QCA 1998: 61). These criteria or guidelines need to be established with the class in advance of any work on controversial issues. They should include the establishment of 'ground rules' (see below). Pupils should be encouraged to 'cultivate tentativeness' and explore the many sides to an argument as 'often the goal of teaching a topic is not "clearer ideas" but "greater confusion". This has to be tolerated as a stage in moving towards an independent opinion' (Stradling *et al.* 1984: 116).

A good example of guidelines is given by Claire (2004). These are written for teachers in primary schools but would work equally well at secondary level.

1   *You may not be abusive, derogatory or put people down – this includes both child and teacher.*
    Encourage children to think carefully and not to say anything that they would not be prepared to say directly to someone for whom the issue was important. Encourage positive responses and politeness even in disagreements. Model this for children with words like 'I hear/understand what you're saying, but wonder if you have considered …'.

2   *You must be able to back up statements with evidence which can be evaluated.*
    Children will need help in distinguishing between opinion and evidence. 'My
    Dad says ...' is not evidence and one example is not sufficient to back up an
    argument. This may also require discussion of stereotyping and recognition of
    the fact that it is wrong to attribute the same characteristics to a whole group of
    people. You can help children decide on criteria for evaluating evidence and do
    this in a 'neutral space' so that you have already established what's acceptable and
    can call on earlier agreements.

3   *Help children to think tentatively and to problematise the issue.*
    Help them reserve judgement and be prepared to wait to hear a variety of points
    of view before they articulate a definite position. They can learn to use words like
    'it may be that, but I'm not sure till I've found out more, I need to think about
    this, or see what happens if ...'.

4   *Help children break free from 'closed' or 'black and white' thinking.*
    Model different perspectives; invite them to think of and represent the position
    of someone who might feel differently. Acknowledge that you have changed
    your mind about something and encourage them to see changing your mind and
    open-mindedness as a strength, not a weakness.

(Adapted from Claire 2004)

Strategies and opportunities

In order to educate students to think and to participate one needs to use interactive
participatory methods of teaching which model democratic processes. Fiehn
acknowledges that, in discussing controversial issues, it is inevitable that there will
be situations where differences of opinion and strong views are expressed, and that
therefore, 'it is important that facilitators are armed with a number of strategies'
(2005: 21). These approaches are offered for teachers of post-16 students but would
work equally well with younger pupils.

Distancing procedures

When an issue is sensitive, students can look at an analogous situation, e.g. if looking
at the situation in Palestine, an analogy could be Northern Ireland. The analogy can
be examined and students then asked how similar or different one situation is from
another.

Compensatory procedures

If students are expressing strongly held views based on ignorance, teachers can
introduce more information through card sorts, games and 'for and against' lists,
which require students to sift the information to make judgements. They can also be
asked to use the information to make a strong case for an opinion other than their
own (e.g. attitudes towards asylum seekers).

Empathetic procedures

If students do not have any experience of the views under discussion and their responses are fairly simplistic, perhaps based on the media, they can be introduced to role play and simulations, in which they take on the role of people with different viewpoints. Through this they can be introduced to facts as well as people's responses to issues (e.g. the criminal justice system).

Exploratory procedures

When the issue is not at all clear and teachers would like to develop students' investigative skills, they can carry out fieldwork and interviews in the local community, or research a topic on the internet. Making a presentation of their findings can sharpen students' thinking on the key issues.

With all these approaches many students will still need help to move from dualistic thinking (right/wrong) to a more deliberative approach. Clarke (2001) suggests a framework for discussion which can be used in a variety of contexts. He refers to it as a 'demystification strategy', a way of making sense of a complex issue, considering the merits of an argument and forming an opinion on the basis of critical analysis. He suggests the following framework.

1   *What is the issue about?*
    The point here is to identify the key question about which there is controversy. Is it to do with values (what is best?) or information (what is the truth here?) or concepts (what does this mean?). Such an initial question allows pupils a chance to analyse the case dispassionately before deciding on the merits of the case.
2   *What are the arguments?*
    This question encourages pupils to consider the various positions on the issue. What are the values stated? What criteria are being used to make a judgement? Are the claims in the information accurate? Are the arguments clear? Are they consistent? Such questions will help pupils judge the validity of certain claims.
3   *What is assumed?*
    Once pupils have considered the arguments in an issue, the critical questions centre around the assumptions behind these. Not every point of view is acceptable as the assumptions underpinning it may be ethnocentric, racist or parochial. Thus pupils need to ask, are the assumptions based on prejudice or some other attitude contrary to universally held human rights? Who is saying this? Is it an informed opinion from someone with knowledge of the situation or is it an outsider, with little first-hand experience?
4   *How are the arguments manipulated?*
    This question helps pupils judge the quality of the information they are receiving and understand how information can be used to influence opinion. Questions which can help are: Who is involved? What are their particular interests in this issue? What are their reasons for taking this particular stance? Such questions

can help pupils to see how information can be selected, emphasised or ignored according to its value to various positions on an issue.

(Adapted from Clarke 2001)

The above framework will be suitable for older pupils. Teachers of younger children will find the same principles underpinning thinking skills programmes and may find the introduction of a thinking circle, as devised by Fisher (2001), useful. The thinking circle enables the teacher to present a story or moral issue, after which children reflect individually on a number of key questions, discuss in small groups and then as a class. Children are taught to look for evidence to back up their statements, to question others and to review their thinking. If teachers introduce their pupils to this framework with stories from the past or contemporary moral dilemmas, then when an event happens in the news or a controversial issue arises, the children (and the teacher) will know how to approach the discussion. Children can also be encouraged to bring to the thinking circle their own concerns to discuss and to formulate their own questions. The skills learnt in a thinking circle can then be transferred to role-play and to discussions in other curriculum areas.

Whilst the thinking circle provides an opportunity for teachers to introduce topical or controversial dilemmas, there are many other opportunities within the formal curriculum. Environmental issues in science and geography provide opportunities for such discussions (e.g. the use of wind farms, GM crops, pollution), and children studying the Romans, or Britain since the 1930s, can relate migration in the past to the issue of refugees today.

The example in Box 5.1, from a Devon primary school, is an interesting example of how one Year 4 teacher helped children to understand both the global and controversial nature of energy. In many ways this could be taken as an example of good practice: the teacher encouraged the class to explore many aspects of the debate and acted as a neutral chair. However, one could also argue that this was insufficient as it suggests that there are no 'right' or 'wrong' answers to such issues. The key issue in relation to energy futures is that some fuel sources cause climate change and others do not – some fuel sources are thus clearly more environmentally-friendly than others.

A number of starting points identified by secondary teachers at an in-service course (see Box 5.2) show how controversial issues can be explored in most subject

---

Box 5.1 Discussing energy issues

I wanted to teach about the many ways of generating power at the same time as helping children understand that methods of obtaining energy are controversial and that there are no 'right' answers. I also wanted them to understand the global dimension to the energy debate.

We did work on different sources of power and energy conservation: e.g. fossil fuels, hydroelectric, nuclear, geothermal, solar and wind powered electricity. I then staged a 'great debate' where the children were put in groups, with an energy source each, and had to argue the case for their source. They were given time prior to the actual debate (filmed) to prepare as many arguments for and against their source as they could and to come up with a question or criticism of the other sources. They also had to produce visual aids to strengthen their case.

The children had quite firm preferences at the start of the topic and there was some resistance to adopting and arguing for the obviously 'unpopular' options. We discussed this and emphasised that exploring all the energy sources equally was important as in their role as scientists they needed to be able to make informed decisions.

The actual debate had a chairperson, a camera person and reporter (drawn from the children) and followed a clear structure with three minutes for each group to make their case, tabled questions from other groups and an open session to allow for extra questioning and answers that has arisen during the debate. After the debate we discussed the following:

* How did it feel having to defend your particular energy source?
* Were you persuaded by others' arguments? Why or why not?
* Which source of energy is most expensive? Why?
* Which sources of energy have negative effects, e.g. cause pollution?
* Which sources of energy affect people in other countries?
* How can we conserve energy?

It emerged in the end that those with a source of energy that was 'difficult' to promote or defend were the best prepared.

We followed up this work with a residential trip to North Wales, visiting a decommissioned nuclear power station where the children were able to put their questioning skills to the test. They asked why Greenpeace objected to the outfall from Sellafield and heard the representative argue that there were also objections to wind farms. We had visited an anti-wind farm website earlier to understand the nature of their protest and had visited the Greenpeace website to find out about their support. The children were thus able to look at the various arguments, considering all points of view. While in Wales we also visited a hydroelectric power station and the Centre for Alternative Technology where the children began to understand how different power sources are useful in different circumstances: a useful lead in to the use of energy in different parts of the world.

areas and that these often provide the links between citizenship education and that subject. In identifying the controversial, one is often also identifying what is current, involves value judgements and has resource implications, either for the local or global communities.

Pupils who learn how to take part in discussions on controversial issues will be better able to understand the values of others and to respect those who may have

---

Box 5.2 Opportunities for teaching about controversial issues

Mathematics
Use and abuse of statistics
Interest rates, the role of the World Bank
Working with authentic data (e.g. about global health and demographics)

Dance
Appreciating dance from other cultures
Stereotyping and respect, e.g. gender and homophobic issues
Funding for the arts

Art and design
Responses of artists to controversial and political events
Dead white men or living artists as a focus? Gender and race issues
Issues around what and how art is valued

Design and technology
Gender issues
Co-operation and problem solving
Technology for sustainable development

ICT
Who has access? The North/South global internet divide
Moral, ethical and environmental impact of ICT
Legal and human rights issues of access to information

English
Use of texts which deal with controversial issues
Learning to campaign and be persuasive: are all topics OK?
Critically evaluating information in the media

Science
Controversial issues, e.g. cloning, GM crops
Environmental issues, e.g. energy
Experiments and the law, e.g. animal testing and protests

Modern foreign languages
Challenging stereotypes, e.g. understanding different cultures
English as a world language: is this right?
Texts from other countries about controversial issues

Geography
Global topical and environmental issues, e.g. budget airlines, global warming
Less economically developed countries: issues of justice and equality
Involvement in local controversial issues, e.g. new housing, new arrivals

History
People who came, e.g. colonialism, refugees
Conflicts in the past: what were the arguments for and against? Who was right?
Acquisition of artefacts: should they be returned? e.g. Elgin Marbles

Religious education
Different beliefs within Christianity, e.g. about creation
Challenging stereotypes about world religions, e.g. Islam
Church schools: should they be encouraged?

Physical education
Should everyone have to do PE in school? Rights versus health
Issues around football, e.g. racism, violence and nationalism
Gender issues: is there equality in sport?

opinions different from their own. Pupils used to looking at current events from a number of points of view, or indeed to exploring different versions of events in the past, are learning how to weigh evidence and make informed judgements. Pupils whose geography or science lessons, for example, go beyond facts and figures to look at current topical issues are learning about the nature of controversy in real-life contexts. Teaching about controversial issues, both local and global, helps young people gain the knowledge and skills that citizens need for effective participation in a democratic society.

Part II
Key concepts

Chapter 6

Conflict resolution

Lynn Davies

Understanding the nature of conflicts, their impact on development and why there is a need for their resolution and the promotion of harmony.

(DfES 2005a)

Understanding the issue

Conflict is clearly one of the major issues of our time and there is little evidence that the world is becoming less conflictive. Conflict occurs of course not just at the global level, but at regional, national, institutional and family levels and any resolution is complicated by the fact that certain types of conflict are inevitable and indeed necessary. Conflict is an essential element of the human condition since people will – and should – disagree on matters as a result of their differing beliefs, values and access to resources. The dilemmas therefore are twofold: first, how one resolves conflict, whether violently or peacefully, competitively or cooperatively, and second, at what point should one generate conflict in order to surface a perceived wrong. An interesting question throughout this chapter is whether the same analyses can be applied at the school level as can be applied at international level.

A summary of definitions (Davies 2004; Isenhart and Spangle 2000) would be that conflict is:

- a real or apparent incompatibility of interests or goals
- a belief that parties' current aspirations cannot be achieved simultaneously
- a struggle over values and/or claims to status, power and scarce resources.

Much analysis and terminology revolves around the stage of a struggle – when does a difference of opinion become a conflict, and when does a conflict become a crisis? A crisis implies that a radical change is necessary, a transition when disaster threatens, with disaster defined as 'the situation that occurs when crisis outstrips the capacity of a society to cope with it' (Roche 1996: 23). An important concept here is that of the frozen struggle – where resolution is unlikely and de-escalation difficult because of rigid perceptions or the conviction that the conflict arises from centuries of intractable difference. Frozen struggles in schools on the other hand often revolve around issues of what are seen as non-negotiables, such as teacher–student relationships or even uniform.

There is an important distinction between negative and positive conflict. Negative conflict is where one or both parties are seeking a win–lose situation, destruction of the other party, revenge and even escalation of violence, whilst positive conflict aims to surface a problem or an injustice and to make an active challenge to seek some sort of new and more peaceful order. I have equated positive conflict with 'interruptive democracy' (Davies 2004), the process whereby people are enabled to intervene in practices which continue injustice. Democracy by definition contains the seeds of conflict, as it is not an end-state but a process whereby people hold leaders accountable and argue for rights for themselves and others.

As with democracy, Fisher *et al.* (2000:10) see peace as a process, 'a many sided, never-ending struggle to transform violence'. As they point out, peace is often compared to health, in that it is more easily recognised by its absence. Yet they contrast negative or cold peace, i.e. the absence of war, with positive or warm peace which encompasses all the aspects of a good society. The classic definition remains that of the United Nations:

> Peace includes not only the absence of war, violence and hostilities ... but also the enjoyment of economic and social justice, equality and the entire range of human rights and fundamental freedoms within society.
>
> (United Nations 1993: 8)

In the context of school these complex definitions or nuances imply the need for:

- An understanding of the causes of conflict, the links to poverty and the links to education
- Recognition of the difference between negative and positive conflict, and promotion of the latter
- Finding ways to teach about conflict and controversial issues
- Exploring parallels between international conflict and conflict at the school or classroom level
- Skills in conflict resolution by both teachers and students
- Identifying ways to prepare young people to take action around global conflicts.

Action for change

Change in this sense means attempts at peace-making and transformation of conflict to create a more stable society or community. Whilst the protagonists in the war in Iraq would argue that their intervention was to create a freer, more democratic and stable society, I do not put this into the category of positive action for change, as events have borne out. Here I explore action for sustainable peace at local, national and international levels and how these may intersect.

At the international level the major players would be the United Nations and a range of international non-governmental organisations (INGOs). The UN distinguishes between several types of intervention in addition to humanitarian aid or emergency assistance. The categories are:

Peace-making – interventions designed to end hostilities and bring about an agreement using diplomatic, political and military means as necessary

Peace-keeping – monitoring and enforcing an agreement, using force if necessary. This includes verifying whether agreements are being kept and supervising agreed confidence-building activities

Peace-building – undertaking programmes designed to address the causes of conflict and the grievances of the past and to promote long-term stability and justice.

(Fisher *et al.* 2000: 49)

Education initiatives cut across all these phases (and it has to be remembered that there are often no clear-cut conflict and post-conflict divisions). In the midst of a conflict zone, efforts may simply be to try to keep schools open, to keep students and teachers safe and to try to prevent children being abducted to become child soldiers. In the immediate aftermath of a conflict stress is on the provision of schooling as part of a return to some sense of normality, and on trauma counselling, play and other healing activities. There is the rebuilding of schools and providing education materials such as Teacher in a Box kits, which provide basic necessities for teaching such as pens, chalk, paper and basic activities for literacy and numeracy. Long term, however, an education that seeks to question previous 'normality' might be needed, with education used for social renewal and building a strong civil society. Here, as well as the usual emphasis on literacy, may be international assistance in legal education, citizenship education, human rights, culture, communication and media analysis – to enable people to have the tools and skills to avoid or challenge conflict, authoritarianism or violence in the future (Davies 2005). Specific concerns would relate to the education of refugees, whether as host country or in terms of what happens when refugees return to their own countries and education systems. The reintegration of child soldiers into a conventional education system has proved a particular problem of acceptance on both sides.

For change at national level there are the civil society questions in the paragraph above. As well as education strategies to renew civil society and promote social cohesion, interventions at state level would focus on a range of strategies to lessen or prevent ethnic or religious tensions. These include legislation and equal opportunities bodies, inter-ethnic and inter-faith forums, and training of government employees, such as the police, in human rights and anti-racist work. There are currently debates about some of the national strategies used to counter terrorism – ID cards, and what are seen as inroads into freedom of speech such as prohibition of incitement to racial hatred or glorification of terrorism.

At local level there are similar efforts to bring dialogue between different groups and examples of young people trying to promote less violent communities, perhaps working with community police. Making local–global connections in relation to action for change and positive conflict could mean going on demonstrations about war and joining campaigns such as those against the arms trade. There is also contributing to the work of charities and NGOs which are working in conflict zones, whose work may include both humanitarian assistance as well as an advocacy role with governments.

While I have distinguished different levels, it is often difficult to differentiate them – ethnic tension in a society could lead to young people being radicalised, which may in turn contribute to international conflict. It is to be hoped that the converse is also true, that young people who learn to question absolutism will want to work for a more plural and more tolerant world.

Good practice

Good practice in learning about conflict resolution raises issues of context and coherence within the school – as in UNICEF's (2006a) Rights Respecting School – in that there may be little point in learning about conflict resolution in Liberia if one's own school is authoritarian and violent. Thus the activities mentioned in this section cut across both local and global conflict. The aims of work in schools in relatively stable or pre-conflict societies would include:

- Providing knowledge and understanding about conflict
- Wanting to promote outrage against injustice but equally wanting to prevent students joining fundamentalist groups or voting for racist parties
- Giving a sense of agency and the skills to challenge negative conflict now and in the future, locally and nationally, including holding governments accountable for conflict and violence.

Mention the war

In our research study on the needs of teachers and learners in global citizenship (Davies *et al.* 2005), we found that the most outstanding need of learners was to understand about war – in the current context and not just historically. Both primary and secondary students wanted to understand the war in Iraq, the reasons for hate, the real reasons for the invasion and why people have weapons. Many felt concerned because these issues were not covered sufficiently or teachers felt uncomfortable about dealing with them. We found nonetheless good examples of tackling the war in Iraq and other contemporary conflicts. In 2003, one teacher used the notion of The News in Numbers each week, with a chart giving numbers on one side and the 'fact' on the other, for example: 871,000 – the number of Iraqi refugees that it is estimated will be created if there is a war; £15 million – the amount that Gordon Brown has set aside to cover the cost of military action against Iraq. This was used in tutorial time with students having to match the numbers and the facts (not all were about the war). This multicultural school also created a war bulletin board so students could write their opinions on a card, stick it on the board and thus share their views with friends and staff.

Another school followed the QCA (2002) Scheme of Work *Unit 11: Why is it so difficult to keep the peace in the world today?*. Students researched issues related to war, producing timelines on The Road to Conflict and using the internet and newspapers to research the views of British people in order to complete a two-way chart on 'Should Britain go to war?'. A Coventry school became involved in Coventry Peace Month and teachers looked for ways to cover the traumatic experiences their refugee children had had. Schools made good use of materials on the Holocaust and, at primary level, used books such as *Zlata's Diary* (Filipovic 1993), the account of a girl caught up in the Balkan conflict. All these initiatives show that war and conflict can be tackled across different areas of the curriculum and that young people respond positively to them. Any work in citizenship education on media and language analysis also gives pupils skills to look at both government rhetoric and at the way different communities and nations portray each other.

Identity and agency

One theory about why people are prone to ethnic hatred, violence or joining fundamentalist groups is that they lack a secure sense of self. They need to feel that they belong to a collective and part of an important movement for change. Essential work thus needs to be done on identity, in terms both of enabling young people to analyse their own and others' multiple identities and of giving them confidence and self-esteem. The former is possibly easier to do – there are many exercises in conflict manuals on identity and 'Who am I?'. The latter is more difficult in a selective education system which has winners and losers, constant tests and means to differentiate between people. It is also difficult with young people who have suffered abuse and loss and hence a bereavement of self (Davies and Leoni 2006). Schools have the task of making every child feel valued – a phrase which all schools will say they buy into, but in practice does not always happen. My favourite head teacher was one who said 'I try to give every child in the school a job to do and then no-one can be absent without being missed'. The new UK citizenship initiatives, with the emphasis on active citizenship, give the opportunity for agency and a sense of having accomplished something which is at the heart of self-esteem.

A review for the Carnegie Young People's Initiative of the impact of pupil participation in decision-making found one of the key benefits mentioned by both teachers and students was self-confidence (Davies *et al.* 2006). An action research study by Hudson (2005) is illustrative here. Her GCSE Citizenship coursework invited all students to engage in a 'change activity' in the school or local community.

In the follow-up questionnaire 28 students wrote about the difference they could make to crime, mentioning working with the police as partners. Previously they had expressed scepticism about how trustworthy and reliable the police were. They were researching issues such as mobile phone theft and presenting their findings to their local MP. The students on this course as well as in the School Council and the local Council of Champions moved from a passive to an active 'politicised identity'.

Inclusive schools

The question then arises as to the context in which young people are gaining a secure identity and feeling a sense of agency. This, in part, relates to the debate about faith schools versus integrated schools. The proponents of faith schools argue that these provide a sense of secure identity and that it's possible to have a school based on religious values which also value others. However, the central dilemma is that if one does genuinely and equally value all faith positions, why is there a need for separation or the 'badging' of one? The key message from any faith school (or ethnically divided school) is that this religion/ethnicity and its values are of central importance and define the naming and ethos of the school. It is difficult for those wanting secular schools to see how this promotes valuing and respect, except in a patronising way which 'tolerates' other faiths or humanist positions just as one might tolerate weaknesses and frailties in others. It has to be acknowledged that in the UK there may be Church of England or Catholic schools which have 90 per cent Muslim children, but the issue is more about those schools which actively promote one set of values to the exclusion of others (as in creationist schools).

Good practice is exemplified by schools that are trying to work 'across the divide', whether as fully integrated schools or as schools located in one community which is genuinely trying to reach out to others. A classic example is the Neve Shalom-Wahat Al-Salam school in Israel, which translated means 'Oasis of Peace' (Feurverger 2001). This village school is committed to educating its students in a full Arabic-Hebrew bilingual, bicultural, binational setting. It is set in a village of Arabs and Jews who do not share the same religious and cultural values and norms but do subscribe to similar underlying beliefs in equality, justice, respect and peaceful coexistence. This does not mean the village is without moral conflict and the Gulf War has 'opened up some deep splits'. But in the school, teachers are 'border crossers', able to listen critically to the voices of their students and to each other. The unique feature is that each class has an Arab and a Jewish teacher, and children are exposed to two points of view. Critical pedagogy is stressed – not just using both languages, but reflecting critically on language practices. Language conditions how the world is seen, for as a Palestinian teacher explained, 'learning the history of Israel in Hebrew is totally different from learning it in Arabic!' (Feuerverger 2001: 61).

Such schools (and there are other examples and workshops in Israel/Palestine) work on the principle of 'the encounter' – that it is crucial to meet and talk, and if necessary share experiences of pain. A second excellent example of the value of dialogue and encounter for young people is the Let's Talk 80:20 project (2001).

Since 1997 this has brought together young people in Ireland, Northern Ireland, Birmingham and Australia to talk about conflict and how best to live together. It is based on three core assumptions:

- Conflict, peace and reconciliation in Northern Ireland are not just issues for people living there. They also directly involve people throughout the islands of Ireland and Britain and elsewhere. These communities have a right and a responsibility to contribute to the peace process in its broadest sense.
- Young people have not been given enough opportunity to learn about, debate and discuss local, national and international issues of conflict, peace and justice and to contribute to resolving problems and challenges.
- We can all learn something from each other. Sharing ideas and experiences in an international arena helps everyone.

One Australian student participant in Belfast commented:

> The introductory session was typical of the level of debate throughout the conference – a 'getting to know you session' with two ex-paramilitary soldiers. These men belonged to opposing sides of the Northern Ireland conflict, the UVF and the IRA. Both men had killed and the amount of emotion generated in the room was incredible … The very fact that two men with such differing opinions, to the point where they had taken lives to highlight these, agreed to talk together to the group and encourage reconciliation efforts was a very positive beginning to 'Let's Talk Belfast' and a personally inspiring event.
>
> (Let's Talk 80:20 2001: 9)

While schools may invite the army in to talk to pupils about careers, it is less likely that they invite the soldiers of two opposing sides. Yet a school with the courage to do this may well generate the personal inspiration which is at the heart of agency.

The Independent (2005) reported on an interesting experiment in which two rival gangs from London went to Belfast to live together in a house for a week and talk to local youth – the organiser said they would either kill each other or learn to get on. The London gangs could not understand the tension in Northern Ireland when they were all the same colour; the Belfast youth could not understand why the Londoners were fighting when they were the same religion. Encounters are also about having others see your conflict, not just seeing the opposition's views. Of course, one should not be too romantic about 'encounter' and there have been critiques of this, particularly in Israel, as a process which does not reach those in power who make the decisions about aggression. Smith and Robinson (1996) found that there had been an assumption that prejudice and hatred in Northern Ireland was based on ignorance and misunderstanding, yet increased contact and improved understanding did not necessarily improve relations. Research on the integrated schools in Northern Ireland found, however, that friendship networks did cut across religious boundaries. A study of the second oldest integrated school found staff using the opportunity provided by an integrated setting to address issues related to social division and conflict (Gallagher 2004).

Positive conflict

A mechanism for inclusion, active citizenship and conflict prevention within the school is the promotion of 'interruptive democracy', mentioned in the introduction. This is more than just the democracy of voting or even of participation, it is a democracy based on the disposition to challenge. It is founded on the principle of positive conflict. There are many good examples of the interruptive school as described below.

First, there are a wide range of forums for positive conflict, e.g. school councils, circle time, representation on governing bodies, representation on teaching and learning committees, going to young parliaments, support for school student unions. It is obviously important that as many students as possible are involved in some form of representative democracy and hence 'good practice' schools will ensure that every child is in a class council or circle time or is on some sort of committee. In terms of conflict prevention there is an obvious role for school councils and class councils in drawing up the 'rules of engagement'. Learning contracts can be drawn up by children working out what in others' behaviour helps or hinders their learning (including the behaviour of the teacher). This avoids meaningless school rules which have nothing to do with learning and everything to do with teacher control.

Second, there is the provision of organised and frequent ways to generate dialogue, encounter, deliberation, argument, information exchange, empathy and feedback between learners, and between teachers and learners as encounters between equals. Students as researchers, systematically researching their teachers and lessons, in a project on London School Councils (*The Times* 2006), is an example of positive conflict in different ways, e.g. overcoming teacher resistance to being 'researched', as well as the assumption that a teacher will change his/her behaviour if research shows it is needed. International youth networks on the internet also provide a forum for exchange and even activism.

Third, there is the modelling by teachers of protest and resistance to injustice, e.g. being part of pressure groups or campaigns, going on demonstrations or at least writing letters or signing petitions. In our research on global citizenship (Davies *et al.* 2005) we found that whilst some schools banned pupils from demonstrating about the Iraq war, and even punished them if they did, other schools were there marching with a banner. One cannot model active citizenship if teachers and heads are not prepared to lead the way and show that agency works.

Making peace

Part of interruptive democracy is providing the skills for engagement, and a particular skill, which should be a compulsory part of any curriculum, is that of conflict resolution. Materials on global conflict often show how conflicts in different parts of the world are resolved whilst some of the conflict resolution material in more stable societies relates to interpersonal conflict, emphasising the individual, with increasing concern about behaviour and disruption in school. However, it is important to stress that conflict resolution does not rely on a pathological approach to a 'culprit' or 'offender', but is based in the acknowledgement that any conflict is about a transaction – in schools between students or between a student and a teacher. Current approaches to anger management, for example, are not to see anger management as a way to control children but to ask the question 'how can we help them heal so that they don't need to continue and escalate their violence?' (Bemak and Keys 2000). A link to more global conflict is that of using the techniques used in emergency and humanitarian work with traumatised children and adults which centre round healing, play and creativity. Whilst it would be wrong to equate the experiences of a child in a refugee camp in Darfur with those living in a family 'war zone', it is interesting that the techniques used are similar.

Mediation is another technique which is used at international levels as well as institutional ones. A UNICEF (1995) pack usefully goes through the four classic stages of mediation: introduction and ground rules; story-telling, summary and clarification; problem-solving options; agreement and congratulations. The last, agreement, stage includes telling friends about the outcome to stop rumours from spreading. 'Other groups of friends keep a conflict going and growing and will not let go. Informing them that it is over lets them forget about it' (UNICEF 1995: 87).

Stewart (1998) describes the work of peer mediation in UK schools which has quite a long history. Much of this springs from the Quakers and the Quaker Peace Education Project (see website) which has been influential in Northern Ireland as part of the Education for Mutual Understanding project. The advantages of one mediation scheme were found to be: better and quicker understanding of the conflict by participants, a greater sense of fairness, and skills that could be used outside the school. At the same time some serious disputes had to be taken to a teacher and some children even made up disputes just for the fun of being mediated (Stewart 1998: 84–5)!

A final concept borrowed from global conflict is that of restorative justice. This is the opposite to retributive justice which demands revenge, with the severity of the penalty matching the seriousness of the crime and justified by its advocates as a deterrent. The theory of restorative justice was developed from utilitarianism which seeks the greatest good or greatest happiness for the greatest number. More suffering should therefore not be inflicted, instead the emphasis is on reforming the offender so that he will not reoffend. It seeks to move forward in a collaborative way in order to repair damage, giving the offender an opportunity to express remorse and make amends. It is often part of truth and reconciliation programmes, as in South Africa and Rwanda.

If we attempt to apply this to education there can be some difficulties. In school it is not always easy to identify victim and offender. If a pupil attacks a teacher with a knife then this seems a clear case of offence. Yet in this, and certainly in more minor confrontations, the pupil may claim a series of 'offences' by the teacher which have led to this reaction. The '3Rs' of restorative justice outlined by Alexander (2001) in his work on the 'citizenship school' are: recognition of the *reasons* behind the action and the needs driving the behaviour; the perpetrator takes *responsibility* for their actions and accepts they have done wrong; the perpetrator makes *reparations*, which might include restitution, restoration and reconciliation to settle differences. So identification and acceptance of a 'perpetrator' is a central issue here. Using a model suggested by prison abolitionists, Lees (2000) suggests a participatory or 'conference' approach to dispute resolution within citizenship education, whereby a victim can have representatives to argue their view of events. So, for example, if a pupil has been bullied, the victim's definition of harm or threat would be at the centre of proceedings. She is thus transformed from a humiliated victim to an active claimant, identifying her own requirements and drawing her own lines in future contacts with the perpetrator.

Restorative justice, unlike 'no blame' approaches, does not mean that wrongdoers evade responsibility. The key is that amends are not the same as revenge. Much global conflict and terrorism centres round revenge, with spirals of hurt and escalations of violence. The Chinese proverb says that 'those who seek revenge must remember to dig two graves'. Particularly problematic is the perception of an insult to a God which has to be avenged through violence. Schools too condone and use revenge in their punishment regimes – actions unrelated to the offence, such as detentions for rudeness or in some countries beating a child for lateness or a wrong answer. The message is that it is alright for the powerful to exact swift retribution. One task of a school for peace would be to question the efficacy of revenge in and out of school settings and to explore alternatives.

This chapter has tried to show that understanding conflict within global settings is intricately bound up with understanding conflict in personal and institutional settings. If the dictators and warmongers of history and today had experienced this in their schooling would the world be a different place?

Starting points

Citizenship Pieces (www.citizenship-pieces.org.uk) is based in Tower Hamlets in London, and their *Possible War Against Iraq: Advice and Guidance for Teachers* (2003) is still a very useful guide. It has advice on teaching about war and terrorism, how to deal with controversial issues and has lesson ideas as well as INSET ideas for teachers.

Dealing With War is a Citizenship Project for 14–18-year-olds based on ideas developed at the School for Peace in the Arab/Jewish village of Neve Shalom–Wahat Al-Salam. As well as information about the school and the Arab–Israeli conflict, there are student activities on dealing with conflict, conflict mapping, building trust, identity and mediation. See: www.cjap.com/nswas/index.htm.

'Iraq: war and peace' (Oxfam 2006c) is a resource for teachers which includes a fact file on Iraq, arguments for and against the war, the poles of influence and power and the aftermath of the war, with classroom activities including media analysis. It can be accessed online at www.oxfam.org.uk/coolplanet/teachers/iraq/index.htm.

Making Sense of World Conflicts: Activities and Source Materials for Teaching English, Citizenship and PSHE (Oxfam 2005a). Explains cause and effect of global conflicts, but also what young people can do in the UK and elsewhere. It is hard hitting, with a section on gun culture and the arms trade and how to challenge it. There is a useful appendix on how to teach controversial issues and an excellent resources section.

Peace Child International (www.peacechild.org) is an educational charity which aims to empower young people to take responsibility for peace, human rights and the environment through various volunteer and ambassador programmes, materials production and showcase activities. On the website is a section called 'Get Involved' and a section on 'Educational Materials' which contains books and lesson plans created by young people.

UNICEF UK (www.unicef.org.uk) produces a number of information sheets about armed conflict, for example on small arms, child soldiers, impact on women and girls, children, HIV/AIDS and conflict. *How Do We Make Peace?* (UNICEF 2004) is a book of six case studies with photos which contains activities to build awareness of peace and conflict, using initiatives involving young people in Burundi, Cambodia, Northern Ireland and Scotland.

Chapter 7

Social justice

Ange Grunsell

Understanding the importance of social justice as an element in both sustainable development and the improved welfare of all people.

(DfES 2005a)

Understanding the issue

Young people today are growing up in a world where prosperity and technological progress exist alongside mass poverty and an environment under threat. Children and young adults deserve to know that their fate is inextricably linked to and affected by, the lives and decisions of others across the world. They have a right to understand the crucial issues facing the planet and know they can personally play a part in helping shape the future.

(ACCAC 2002: 5)

We live in a world in which there are huge gaps between the rich and the poor and the conditions in which people live locally and globally. Worldwide some 1.3 billion people live on less than a dollar a day, whilst 103 million children receive no schooling at all, 57 per cent of them girls. Across the world it is the poor who die younger, who lack vital access to drugs and healthcare, who die of hunger when crops fail or wars disrupt their lives.

The World Bank defines poverty as having less than $1 a day of purchasing power but poverty is also related to the cost of purchasing necessities in whatever society you live in. In the US this is estimated as $11 a day. So it is the gap between the rich and the poor at all scales – local, national, global – that is crucial. Whilst children in China work as many as 16 hours a day for less than 10 pence an hour to make the free toys McDonalds gives away in the UK, their young staff in the UK are also amongst the most poorly paid in the country (*The Guardian* 2006). The activities of transnational corporations put both Welsh and Jamaican dairy farmers in the same precarious position, although the scale of the financial difficulties each faces is different (Oxfam 2006d). At a global level progress towards achieving the UN Millennium Development Goals (see website), which were agreed in 2000 to bring countries out of poverty, is painfully slow.

All of these issues raise questions about the nature of equality, justice and fairness in both the local and global community. The issue of social justice and its relationship to poverty is complex. Where does the teacher begin when young people ask the question 'How can I make a difference to such a problem?' or how does one reply to the statement 'It isn't fair' or, alternatively, that 'The poor are always with us'?

The starting point has to be that this is a question that everyone grapples with at some time. A sense of fairness is a powerful driver for even the youngest children in the classroom and issues of social justice crop up daily in parental conversations, in every community and in national and international politics. So the challenge is how to equip young people to grapple with these questions for themselves in such a way that they also develop an understanding of the entitlement that they and others have to justice.

All education for social justice has an ethical basis, from young children's strong sense of fairness and unfairness as applied to themselves to the recognition that all people are as real as they themselves are. All learners need to understand that the adage 'Do as you would be done by' can be applied from personal behaviour to the causes of international terrorism. Issues of social justice range from not bullying and exploiting others in one's immediate environment to supporting equality of opportunity and recognising the collective responsibility that we always have to challenge injustice and inequality. If the humanity of all people is recognised then justice is also owed across national borders and the condition of the globally worst-off must be a central concern. Defining what social justice means at a global scale is not a simple matter. Global justice is not a reality – it is an ideal. Experiences of solidarity between people, nations and organisations are increasingly supranational in a globalised world.

There are some difficult questions to examine when exploring the exercise of social responsibility at a global level. For example, when and how is it legitimate for rich nations to make interventions, either humanitarian or military, in states other than their own? And further, when thinking about privilege or deprivation within or across societies, what should be the limits of 'permissible inequality' between people? Here is a creative space in which teacher and learner can engage in delineating and problem solving the 'unknown' from a basis of personal ethical issues with which they are familiar. One of the most useful ways of exploring the concerns of this chapter is through the notions of teaching about, for and through social justice.

Education *about* social justice involves learning about historical and contemporary struggles for freedom, whether in relation to colonisation and enslavement or sweat shops and child workers today. It makes use of the experiences of others from the fictional (The Lorax's Save the Trees Game (see website)) to the real (*The Diary of Anne Frank*, Anne Frank Center website). Young people become familiar with the Millennium Development Goals through informational case studies of other people's lives around the world and of action to improve these. Older pupils can also learn about both the potential and dilemmas associated with different national and international systems of justice.

Education *for* social justice requires the development and practice of the ethics of inclusion and fairness in the classroom and wider society. Role-plays and simulation games can be used to explore trade rules and realities and to illustrate how globalisation operates. Skills of critical thinking and participation in decision making are developed and visions of more sustainable patterns of resource use and consumption are developed.

Education *through* social justice involves students planning and taking action for change in their own school and community, for example, introducing Fair Trade products, challenging racism or setting up peer counselling against bullying. Students come to understand that through even small actions they can make a difference and have a positive personal impact. They come to understand that everyone's impact on others is considerable and that this can be both positive and negative.

Action for change

The gap between rich and poor globally has never been wider and through television and the internet it is increasingly visible to young people throughout the world. The issue of how to solve world poverty and to move towards greater social equity has become an urgent and major theme of international and media discourse in recent years. The early twenty-first century is a period of major opportunity in which increasing numbers of people, young and old, are becoming involved in action for social justice.

At the global level a significant move forward was made in 2000 when the 189 member states of the United Nations General Assembly unanimously adopted the Millennium Declaration commitment to working towards a more just, peaceful and equal world. In the UK, behind education policies which affirm social justice as a key concept within the global dimension, lies the government's policy commitment to social justice at local and global levels. This commitment is expressed both in targets for child poverty reduction in the UK and in support of poverty reduction targets in the poorest regions of the world (DfID 2006c).

The British presidency of the G8 group of countries in 2005 provided an opportunity to create real impetus to anti-poverty action and to respond to the challenge of the Make Poverty History alliance in Britain. Make Poverty History provided a broad backdrop of non-governmental organisations in over 80 countries, North and South, aiming to mobilise action for social justice, which was made accessible and attractive to young people by join-up white wrist bands and messaged actions and concerts. A global movement of over 500 NGOs worked together to demand trade justice, more and better aid and debt cancellation for the world's poorest countries. In the UK 250,000 people went to Edinburgh during the G8 conference, 40,000 people e-mailed the prime minister and many schools and colleges took part in campaigning activities and action. School students made 3.5 million 'buddies' as part of the global campaign Send my Friend to School (see website). This campaign exemplified both education for and through social justice and developed the passion of many young people for such matters.

Another example of successful education and campaigning for greater social justice is that of fair trade. In a free market world and consumerist economy, exercising one's rights and choices as a buyer can have a major impact (Ethical Consumer website). Whilst fair trade cannot solve the problem of trade justice globally it can make a substantial difference to farmers' lives and provides an active expression of consumer desire for greater social justice. The movement to provide a better deal for producers has grown rapidly over the last few years so that schools, businesses and even towns are sourcing Fair Trade products (Fairtrade Foundation website). Consumer interest is now so great that supermarkets and transnational corporations such as Starbucks and Nestlé are producing their own Fair Trade brands. However, Fair Trade still only represents 2 per cent of world trade. But at £163 million a year and with a growing list of products, it has made an impact on securing rights for some of the world's most marginalised workers.

Good practice

Change the world in eight steps

The UN Millennium Development Goals are a set of achievable international targets set by member countries for reducing world poverty by 2015. By signing up to these goals, governments of both developing and developed countries have committed themselves to working together for a more just and sustainable future.

A useful resource which introduces the eight goals, and which provides a framework for learners aged 7–14, is 'Change the world in eight steps' (Oxfam 2006e). This is a set of A2 size posters, together with teachers' notes and classroom activities. Each of the posters acts as a stimulus for discussion of the goals by providing basic information, statistics, photographs, quotations and case studies. Each poster informs learners about issues in specific ways. The aim is also to help pupils communicate more confidently about major global issues and think about what their contributions and responsibilities in relation to these matters might be.

The international community has set the following eight goals for 2015:

Goal 1 Eradicate extreme poverty and hunger
Goal 2 Give every child a primary education
Goal 3 Promote gender equality and empower women
Goal 4 Reduce child mortality
Goal 5 Improve maternal health
Goal 6 Combat HIV/AIDS, malaria and other diseases
Goal 7 Ensure environmental sustainability
Goal 8 Build a global partnership for development.

Whilst the examples covered in the pack are concerned with poverty in poor countries, the range of activities helps pupils to make personal and local connections with each of the issues in their own lives and to understand the meaning of each of these goals in their own lives and community.

For example, the poster for Goal 7: Clean Up the Environment by 2015, shows a young Filipino boy who lives in a squatters' colony in Manila, the capital of the Philippines. Most of the people living there earn their living by scavenging through rubbish for things that can be sold, reused or recycled. The notes provide statistics about issues such as access to clean water and sanitation. They explain the crisis in rapidly growing cities of providing an appropriate infrastructure for their populations. At the same time activities are provided for primary pupils to introduce the issue of waste and recycling in their own classroom and for secondary pupils to explore the origins of slums and issues of climate change. All of these materials, including the classroom activities, can be downloaded from the Oxfam (2006e) website.

The Philosophy for Children Project

The Philosophy for Children Project, known as P4C for short, was developed more than 20 years ago by Dr Matthew Lipman, who devised an international education programme now being taught in more than 30 countries. In the UK the organisation which offers training, resources and co-ordination is the educational charity SAPERE. Organisations such as the Citizenship Foundation and Oxfam promote the work of this project because of the important contribution it makes to developing critical and reflective thinking skills, clear communication and a respect for the views of others. It is well suited to issues of social justice (and the global dimension more broadly) because it offers a clear approach to the ethical questions which children like to discuss: What's right? How should we treat our friends? What would a fairer society look like? Do cocoa growers get enough for the hard work they put in?

The project fosters a habit of thinking that can encompass uncertainty and disagreement and it also helps pupils simultaneously explore and understand their own difficulties and those of more distant others. As a result teachers have reported improved social interactions, particularly in young people with low self-esteem (North West Global Education Network 2006).

The ethos of the 'community of enquiry', the chief pedagogic tool of Philosophy for Children, helps to develop a range of values which are crucial in pluralistic societies. In a community of enquiry students generate and answer their *own* questions. A typical session is sparked off by a stimulus which may be a picture, a story (especially with young children), a website or a purpose-written text. Children sit in a circle and individually or in pairs formulate philosophical questions inspired by the stimulus. Their questions are voted on by the whole group and a dialogue on the question receiving the most votes then follows. At the end of the enquiry there is a debriefing to bring closure to each session. This may, for example, take the form of the children offering a final statement in relation to the question that they have been pursuing.

Here is an example from a primary school in Hampshire, following a two-day training course given by SAPERE.

I launched my Year 3 class into philosophical discussions starting with the thought-provoking story stimulus *The Tunnel* by Anthony Browne. They delighted me in their quick grasp of the idea of what a 'philosophical' question was (I simply showed them a few sample questions) and their excitement at asking and discussing questions which puzzled or intrigued them. Above all, they seemed to relax in the knowledge that they would not have to please me by giving a right answer. They did indeed want to argue their corner over such questions as: Is she imagining all this? Can people turn to stone and come back to life? ... In Years 4 and 5 each week I presented these children with a story or a picture, or sometimes just a question, which they themselves wanted to raise. I realised how quickly they grew as a community of enquiry, listening carefully, soon learning to respond to each other's comments and often changing their own thinking by the end of the session.

(SAPERE 2006)

The teacher commented that the enthusiasm for philosophical debate soon spread beyond classroom sessions to involve other staff and Learning Support Assistants. The response of children who often struggled with literacy was particularly impressive.

The North West Global Education Network has combined the Philosophy for Children Project with global citizenship particularly in order to reach children with educational difficulties and as a way to 'include the excluded'. The Network aimed to test the effectiveness of global citizenship activities and philosophy for children as tools to engage socially excluded young people in their own learning and to encourage them to become active, responsible citizens. The first step was a pilot project at a high school where members of the team worked with a group of pupils from Years 7–9 identified as having multiple social, cultural and emotional problems. This group not only grew in confidence and concentration but also began to understand the need to respect others. They generated the following questions, which addressed their own quandaries as well as global issues: why are there so many poor people in the world? Why do people fight in the world? Why do people get excluded?

This led the Network to take a further step and undertake a Philosophy for Children inclusion project with two pupil referral units (Key Stages 2 and 3) again taking a global social justice focus. This work also showed significant results, with positive changes in the confidence and behaviour of young people who had been seen as failing by their school. A full report of the project can be found on the North West Global Education Network website. The project focused on key themes as starting points with a different stimulus for each (see Table 7.1). Details of Philosophy for Children training courses can be found on the SAPERE website.

The Get Global Project

The Get Global Project (see website) was created by the education programmes of a number of development agencies and has the following aims: i) to provide an experience of being able to make a difference through action; ii) to develop skills of

Table 7.1 Using Philosophy for Children

Theme	Stimulus	Student-generated question
Diversity	Lancashire, Cumbria photo pack	Do negative images of this country generate racism?
Refugees	BBC Newsround website	How would you feel if you were an asylum seeker from another country?
Fair Trade	Comic Relief PaPa Paa Pack	Do the growers get enough for the hard work that they put in?

enquiry, participation and reflection; iii) to develop an understanding of the world as a global community, and to discuss the political, economic, environmental and social implications of this.

The Get Global Project provides a stand-alone process by which teachers can take KS3 and older KS2 pupils through a learning cycle from identifying a focus issue for study to taking different forms of action in relation to the chosen issue. The project uses a range of participatory learning styles and visual tools to develop the skills and confidence to discuss and resolve issues. The evidence from pupil evaluations during the extensive pilots suggested that the experience changed their views about being able to make a difference and that in particular they began to understand the role of awareness-raising as an important form of action. Get Global identified the following critical six steps in its work:

1   *Get asking questions*: students explore their understanding, values and attitudes towards global citizenship.
2   *Get an issue*: students generate important issues affecting their lives. They think about issues in a local and global context and choose one to take action on to improve the situation. They explore the root causes of issues.
3   *Get more information*: students find out more about their chosen issue through in-depth research and investigate how it affects people and environments locally and globally.
4   *Get planning*: students decide what action to take and how to implement it. They consider the feasibility of their idea and how to manage the practical implications.
5   *Get active*: students take action. They monitor and record their progress.
6   *Get thinking about it*: students reflect on what they have learned and achieved and what they would do differently next time.

The Get Global pack and video includes testimonies from pupils about the experience of working with this framework and examples of action they have taken, from introducing fair trade purchasing in their schools to setting up peer education projects and giving presentations to school governors to change recycling policy. The teaching pack offers a wealth of techniques, games and activities and exemplar planning, recording and evaluation frameworks. Whilst Get Global does not offer information about global issues as such it does provide a framework for a term's worth of sessions which can easily be implemented by the teacher. It addresses the interesting boundary between 'education' and 'campaigning' by offering a route within which the latter can be understood as one element in responsible citizenship action.

The Eye of the Storm

In 1968, immediately following the assassination of civil rights leader Martin Luther King, Jane Elliott, a young teacher in Iowa, devised a two-day exercise in experiencing racism which she hoped her class of 8-year-olds would never forget. The brutality of race hatred, she believed, had to be explained. In answer to the children's questions about why Dr King had been murdered she asked them whether they would like to find out what experiencing unfairness and discrimination felt like. With their agreement she explained what she was going to do over the two days. She divided the all-white class into blue and brown-eyed groups. On the first day she told the blue eyes that they were 'the better people in the room', gave them privileges and commented on their superiority all day. The brown eyes were told to wear collars. On the second day she reversed the roles. She told the class that she had been wrong the previous day and that actually brown-eyed people were better than blue-eyed people. On the second day the brown-eyed group scored better on the same test they had done the day before when they were told they were inferior.

A film called *The Eye of the Storm* was made at this time showing the process and its effects on the children over the two days. It has had a huge impact worldwide since that time and often proved highly controversial with teachers, parents and communities. Since then Jane has continued to conduct the exercise with adults worldwide and a number of later films have been made, including *A Class Divided*. This includes extracts from the original experiment set alongside the now grown-up children talking about how it had impacted on them and changed their lives. The film provides a powerful tool for changing attitudes with adults and young people. Without appropriate training it is unwise to undertake the exercise in one's own classroom. However, the film can produce a powerful effect in itself, in all-white and ethnically diverse classrooms. Often, for minorities, it gives an endorsement of their experience and an opportunity for others to see and listen to what their experience of discrimination feels like. The film also raises questions about a range of other discriminatory behaviours and their effects.

It is possible to find and play the whole film online in order to evaluate it or before using it with student groups. It is divided into five play sections and can be found at the Frontline website which also offers highly useful guidance for teachers on facilitating discussion of the film together with a number of clear and well-written lesson plans for pre- and post-viewing sessions with students. The value of using the film is that through the medium of a distant time and place students can feel, reflect on and discuss their own experiences of injustice as well as their own role in perpetuating discriminatory attitudes and behaviour. The film thus puts them in touch with how people behave when they are made to feel either 'superior' or 'inferior' and are treated as such. It then provides an opportunity for teachers to encourage students to reflect on their own behaviour and experiences. Participants sometimes get sidetracked into discussing the ethics of the original exercise carried out with young children. It is important to keep this discussion separate from reactions to what is happening on screen.

The Coffee Chain Game

Becoming involved in fair trade issues as part of understanding trade justice and taking positive local action is proving very popular and motivating to pupils in schools. The time lag between understanding the issue and being able to do something about it is short. Pupils very quickly feel that they can make a difference.

The Fairtrade scheme means that:

- Farmers are paid a significantly higher price for crops such as cocoa, coffee, bananas or cotton, than the market rate.
- Prices are fixed on a long-term basis, which allows farmers to predict their future income and plan ahead.
- Some payment is made in advance so farmers do not have to go into debt.
- A premium earmarked for community development is paid.

The Fairtrade logo on a product bought in a shop means that the company complies with the code of conduct of the Fairtrade Foundation. The Fairtrade school handbook (2004) together with the Fairtrade Foundation, Comic Relief and Oxfam provide a range of helpful guidance for schools.

The Coffee Chain Game (Oxfam 2006f), for use with pupils of 11 and above, includes introductory activities about coffee production and trade, a role-play and case studies from Uganda. It helps pupils to understand the whole of the supply chain from coffee bush to cup and the way in which those involved at every stage face complex decisions and expenses of different kinds. The process of the role-play challenges pupils to feel and reflect on the unfairness of the fact that of every £1 spent on coffee, growers currently get only 10 pence, when 50 years ago their share was at least 50p in every £1. It allows pupils to experience the tiny bargaining power of small-scale farmers compared with that of agribusiness corporations. It provides information and encourages pupils to consider the steps that might be taken by governments and companies internationally to create a fairer trading process. Figure 7.1 taken from the Coffee Chain resource summarises the current situation.

Starting points

Oxfam's annual catalogue for schools incorporates global education resources from a wide range of NGOs and commercial publishers which promote effective teaching and learning about the global dimension. See www.oxfam.org.uk/coolplanet.

Low coffee prices also have long-term and widespread effects on whole communities and countries where coffee is a major export

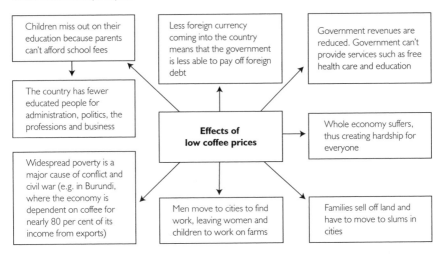

Figure 7.1 The effects of low coffee prices on coffee-exporting countries

Comic Relief provides useful materials for teaching about fair trade and cocoa at Key Stages 3 and 4. Available at www.papapaa.org.

Frontline (2006) at www.pbs.org/wgbh/pages/frontline/shows/divided provides a teacher's guide, transcripts, readings and interviews relating to the film *A Class Divided*.

Global Education Derby at www.globaleducationderby.org.uk. Summer 2005 Newsletter contains useful exercise for teachers to explore a range of perceptions and attitudes relating to questions of wealth and poverty.

Oxfam (2005c) 'Change the world in eight steps'. Posters and activities for 7–14-year-olds investigating UN Millennium Development Goals: www.un.org/millenniumgoals/.

Philosophy for Children Project resources, training, projects. Based at Oxford Brookes University. See www.sapere.org.uk.

Chapter 8

Values and perceptions

Robin Richardson

Developing a critical evaluation of representations of global issues and an appreciation of the effect these have on people's attitudes and values.

(DfES 2005a)

Understanding the issue

'The time will come,' wrote Anne Frank in her diary in 1944, 'when we'll be people again and not just Jews' (Frank 1997: 259). She longed to be recognised and treated as a full human being. It is because all human beings share the same basic humanity that all should be treated equally. It is essential in all education concerned with the global dimension to stress that human beings in all cultures and at all times in history have had certain basic things in common – physiological needs for food, shelter and good health, most obviously, but also social and psychological needs to belong to a community, to love and be loved, to have a sense of personal significance, and to feel safe and secure. It was to these latter kinds of need that Anne was referring. So was Shakespeare's Shylock when, in the most famous anti-racist line in English literature, he used metaphors from shared bodily experience to affirm that he and his community were paid-up members of the human race, with the same psychology and the same rights to justice as everyone else: 'If you prick us do we not bleed? If you tickle us do we not laugh? If you poison us do we not die?' (Act II, Scene 1).

All human beings have certain perceptions and values in common – yes. But shared humanity is not, so to speak, the whole story. Anne Frank shows in her diary that she was much more than 'just a Jew' – she was also a daughter, a teenager, a Dutch citizen, a budding writer, a sexual being, a friend. Yet Jewishness was a fundamental feature of her identity, not something incidental or peripheral. In the same way, every human being belongs to a mixture of homes, traditions, cultures, stories and relationships. In consequence, being different from most other people in terms of where one belongs is a fundamental and inescapable part of being human. To be human is to be different and is to be in constant interaction with strangers – people whose perceptions, experiences, narratives and agendas are different from one's own. The stand-up comedian Ken Dodd observes sadly sometimes in his act that what he likes about the British is that they are not foreigners. But differences of nationality and language, as also differences of age, gender, ethnicity and social class, are inescapable. They lead to, and are maintained by, differences in people's perceptions and values.

Human beings never exist outside cultural and social locations, and therefore outside situations and relationships of unequal power, and outside historical circumstances. No one is totally unaccommodated – or, it follows, unaccommodating. On the contrary, everyone is embedded in a cultural tradition and in a period of history, and in a system of unequal power relations. Everyone, therefore, is engaged in unending tasks and struggles to accommodate and adjust to others. How teachers help their learners to understand and to live with differences of perception and of value-system is the subject matter of this chapter. The Ken Dodd response to such differences is certainly beguiling. But removing differences of perception and values from the world is psychologically not beneficial, morally not desirable and politically not possible.

Action for change

The sub-title above is not really apt here, for the realities of difference and otherness are inescapable, part of the human condition. What *can* be changed, however, are the ways people form and hold their perceptions and values. The education system has a crucial role in this regard. The essential task, it can be said, is to develop 'open' views of the world, as distinct from 'closed' (Rokeach 1960). The distinction is outlined below. But first, it is relevant to recall a contemporary example of differing perceptions and values. 'In many influential circles in Europe,' the political philosopher Bhikhu Parekh observes, 'it is widely held that its over 15 million Muslims pose a serious and political threat.' He continues:

> Sometimes this view is explicitly stated; more often it is implied or simply assumed. On other occasions it takes the form of an attack on multiculturalism for which Muslims are held responsible and which is a coded word for them. It cuts across political and ideological divides, and is shared alike, albeit in different degrees, by conservatives, fascists, liberals, socialists and communists.
>
> (Parekh 2006: 179)

The historian and political commentator Timothy Garton Ash (2005) has suggested that there are six different ways of representing the anxiety to which Parekh refers. Briefly summarised, they are as follows: i) the problem is not Islam but religion in general, which is 'superstition, false consciousness and the abrogation of reason'; ii) the problem is that 'with its systematic discrimination against women, its barbaric punishments for homosexuality and its militant intolerance, Islam is stuck in the middle ages'; iii) the problem is Islamism, namely a particular interpretation of Islam; iv) the problem lies in the specific history of West Asia, including the Sykes-Picot agreement of 1916 for the dismemberment of the Ottoman Empire and the creation of the state of Israel; v) the problem is 'the West' – Western powers have for centuries oppressed Muslim countries and cultures; vi) the problem lies in the alienation of young people of Muslim heritage born and educated in European countries.

These six representations of self and other, 'us' and 'them', 'the West' and 'Islam', are not mutually exclusive. On the contrary, there are overlaps amongst them and in practice the representation someone holds is likely to be complemented and qualified by at least one of the others. It is logically impossible, however, for someone to hold all six with equal assurance.

Rokeach was interested not primarily in the content of people's minds but in how their minds worked. Open-minded people are ready to change their views, both of others and of themselves, in the light of new facts and evidence; do not deliberately distort, or recklessly over-simplify, incontestable facts; do not caricature or over-generalise; are not abusive when arguing; and do not claim greater certainty than is warranted. The open/closed distinction developed by Rokeach (1960) was used by the Commission on British Muslims and Islamophobia (1997) in its discussion of views on 'the West' and 'Islam', and subsequently revised by the Commission on the Future of Multi-ethnic Britain (2000) to evaluate all representations of self and other. The key issues include:

- whether the other is seen as monolithic, static and authoritarian, or as diverse and dynamic with substantial internal debates
- whether the other is divided into two broad categories, good and bad, moderate and extreme, or whether multi-faceted complexity, both in the present and the past, is recognised and attended to
- whether the other is seen as totally separate from the self, or as both similar and interdependent, sharing a common humanity and history, and a common space
- whether the other is seen as an aggressive and devious enemy to be feared, opposed and defeated, or as a cooperative partner with whom to work on shared problems, locally, nationally and internationally
- whether the other's criticisms of the self are rejected out of hand or whether they are considered and debated
- whether double standards are applied in descriptions and criticisms of the other and the self, or whether criticisms are even-handed.

This account of open and closed perceptions of self and other is admittedly abstract. It is illustrated in the rest of this chapter with three discussions of classroom activities, concerned respectively with teaching about the media, teaching about cultural identities and teaching about racism and prejudice. The discussions show practical ways and contexts in which pupils can learn to identify open and closed value-systems in the outer world, and can be supported in the development of openness themselves.

Good practice

Teaching about the media

In his ground-breaking study of the American press in the early twentieth century the commentator Walter Lippmann (1922, cited in Nesbitt 1971: 5) wrote:

> It is because they are compelled to act without a reliable picture of the world that governments, schools, newspapers and churches make such small headway against the more obvious failings of democracy, against violent prejudice, apathy, preference for the curious trivial as against the dull important, and the hunger for sideshows and three-legged calves.

A key educational task is evoked here – it is crucial not only to distinguish between closed and open, as outlined above, but also to devise strategies for teaching about 'the dull important' as distinct from 'the curious trivial'. This involves, researchers have shown, equipping people to understand underlying issues and historical contexts. Viewers who felt they were watching 'an incomprehensible and irresolvable litany of death and suffering', the Glasgow University Media Group found in a study of the effect of TV news, switched channels or simply walked away from their screens. They quoted a student who commented that the news 'never explains it so I don't see the point in watching it – I just turn it off and just go and make a cup of tea or something. I don't like watching it when I don't understand what's going on' (Philo and Berry 2004: 240).

The beginning of wisdom in studies of the media lies in appreciating the role played by selection, or more accurately selectiveness. There are processes of selective attention in the gathering, receipt, digesting and publishing of news, and then also in the reading and viewing of it. Selection necessarily involves prioritising and privileging, and also marginalising and sidelining. 'Imagine a typical American,' wrote a social studies specialist in one of the first books ever published on media studies in schools, 'who has just boarded the 8.02 a.m. bus on his way to work. His favourite newspaper is under his arm as he walks down the aisle, sits down, opens the paper and begins to read' (Nesbitt 1971: 5). He continued: 'There is far more to this commonplace encounter of a man and his newspaper than meets the eye', and proceeded to explain:

> On the one hand, the newspaper represents the end product of an elaborate chain of activities involving news gathering, transmission and processing by humans and machines. On the other hand, our man on the bus is the product of his experiences – recent and remote, transitory and permanent – which influence what the newspaper means to him ... [A]ny individual selects, distorts, remembers, understands, agrees with or disagrees with what he reads in the light of his individual experiences ... [T]he messages on the page ... are processed to make sense according to the pictures of the world already in the mind's eye.

Of course, the media themselves are a major source of 'pictures of the world already in the mind's eye'. The six pictures outlined above, for example, are formed and perpetuated by the media, and act as lenses or templates through which specific news items are both reported and responded to. To develop insight into selectiveness in the production and consumption of news, teachers can organise activities such as the following. Learners study differing accounts of the same event, for example the differences between a report on the website of BBC News and reports in various tabloids, and in their analysis they use the schedule of questions in Box 8.1 (adapted from Imran and Miskell 2003: 27).

Box 8.1 Understanding the news

What is fact and what is interpretation?
Distinguish the facts whose accuracy can be readily checked from statements of opinion and interpretation.

What language is used?
Are words neutral or are they emotive and loaded? For example, how are words such as *freedom-fighter*, *terrorist* and *vigilante* used? Or *invasion* and *liberation*? How does the report use the word *say*, implying that someone is telling the truth, and the word *claim*, implying that someone may not be? What choice is made between *Third World* and *Global South*?

Is the account balanced?
Is more than one point of view reported, and is each different point of view presented fairly and neutrally?

Complexity and uncertainty
When points of view are reported is it acknowledged that the people quoted are in certain respects uncertain, both in their perceptions of what actually happened and in their interpretations and opinions?

Quotations
Who is directly quoted and how are they referred to? For example, are they said to be 'experts', 'professionals' or 'representatives'? How much information is given about who they are? Does it sometimes happen that someone is quoted anonymously, and could the quotation therefore be fictitious?

Background
Reporters and newscasters frequently go for 'bang bang' items with immediate and attention-grabbing impact rather than provide 'explainers', giving information about the general context and historical background. What is the balance in the report you are looking at between explainers on the one hand and immediate facts on the other?

Cause and effect
Reports sometimes run two items together with words such as *following, later, subsequently, previously.* They do not actually say, when using such words, that there is a causal connection between the events. They do, however, imply such a connection. Do you see this happening in the report you are studying?

Motivations
Are words used which imply how someone is motivated and could it be that they are misleading? For example, the phrases *Muslim terrorist* and *Islamic terrorist* are frequently used, but the term *Christian terrorist* in reports from Northern Ireland has seldom if ever been used.

Freedom to make up one's mind
This is one of the most important questions of all. News channels claim to distinguish between providing facts and providing interpretations. But do they in fact do this? Are you confident that you can make up your own mind on the basis of what is reported, or can you see that you are being subtly (or perhaps unsubtly) led to adopt a particular point of view?

What are the assumptions about the audience?
Who does the reporter think they are talking to? That is, what knowledge and understanding do they assume the audience to have, and what predispositions and expectations?

Another valuable activity is for pupils to create their own newspaper-style or TV-style reports, based on real or imaginary events in their own school. Later in this chapter there is a list of episodes in school life that raise issues about prejudice and racism (see Box 8.2). Any one of these can be developed into a news story and pupils have then to grapple with the technical and ethical questions that are necessarily involved in how the story is to be presented.

Box 8.2 Responding to prejudice

- A local shopkeeper casually mentions in conversation with a teacher that he gets a lot of low-level racial abuse from certain pupils at the school. He's used to it, he says, and doesn't want to make a formal complaint.
- A Sikh boy at a primary school who wears his hair in a knot (*ghuta*) covered by a handkerchief (*patka*) is teased by other pupils because, they say, he looks like a girl. His distress is compounded when a teacher assumes he is a girl and tries to separate him from other boys when changing for PE.
- Geoffrey, who is of Traveller heritage, has annoyed Michael in the playground. Michael retaliates with anger, calling Geoffrey a Pikey, and appeals to other non-Traveller boys to support him.

- In an RE lesson a pupil produces a leaflet published in February 2006 by the British National Party. 'We owe it to our children to defend our Christian culture,' it says. And: 'Are you concerned about the growth of Islam in Britain?' The pupil says: 'My dad agrees with this. Do you, miss?'
- Pupils are queuing up in the canteen at lunchtime. There is some general pushing and shoving and a girl is pushed into another girl, knocking her tray out of her hands. The girl whose tray has been knocked turns aggressively to the other girls and calls them 'white trash' and 'white bitches'.
- A girl whose father is American comes home in tears, saying she has been verbally abused by a South Asian boy angry about the US invasion of Iraq.
- Simon, who is Jewish, is jostled in the corridor and told with anti-Semitic abuse that his life is going to be made a misery in retaliation for an action by the Israeli government earlier in the week.
- A girl from Turkey has recently joined the class. She is repeatedly referred to as 'Turkish Delight' by a group of other girls and doesn't appear to mind.
- Boys playing football in the playground are heard to call each other Nigger.
- In a school with a mainly South Asian heritage intake, a group of Year 7 Asian boys surround two older white pupils blocking their way, calling them names and saying 'This is our school'.
- A pupil reports that a piece of graffiti has appeared on a wall near the school saying, 'Death to all Pakis'.
- At the school gates, members of the BNP are handing out election leaflets.
- 'You only ever pick on Black or Asian kids,' says a pupil to a teacher. 'You're racist, that's why, same as most white people.'
- Graffiti appears at the bus stop saying 'Farmers are gay and suck ****'. This has been written about the children from farming families at a rural comprehensive.

A useful variation on this activity is to provide pupils with ten or so 'snippets' of news, or with about ten real or imaginary press releases. In groups, they imagine themselves to be an editorial team whose task is to put the items in a sequence and to allocate space and time for each. It is instructive if each group adopts the stance of a specific paper or TV channel.

It is increasingly the case that people nowadays receive a high proportion of their information from websites as distinct from the press or TV. To explore the implications further, pupils can be sent on 'webquests'. With regard to perceptions and values, for example, they can be asked to visit and write reviews of websites, looking not only at content but also layout, ease of navigation, and use of colour and graphics.

Teaching about identity

It is important that pupils should explore their own perceptions and value-systems, and identify the ways in which these have been affected by the times they live in and by nationality, class, gender, religious tradition and ethnicity. In this connection it is relevant to recall three overarching aims of education proposed by Martha Nussbaum (1997, cited in Walker 2005: 143): to develop the capacity to examine oneself and one's traditions critically; to see oneself as part not only of one's neighbourhood and nation but also of world society; and to cultivate a 'narrative imagination' – the ability to read intelligently the stories of people in locations different from one's own. The following lesson ideas, developed by teachers in Derbyshire (Richardson 2004), provide opportunities for such aims to be achieved.

We Are Britain

Learners study and perform the poems in *We Are Britain* by Benjamin Zephaniah (2003) and write similar poems about themselves, illustrated by photographs similar in style to the ones in Zephaniah's book. Instead or as well they commit to memory the poem *I too sing America* by Langston Hughes, readily downloadable from the website of the Academy of American Poets. They then write similar poems about themselves and their feelings about Britain. In addition, they write similar poems using other personas. They then create and illustrate time lines showing relationships over the centuries between England, Ireland, Scotland and Wales, noting different perspectives and stories in the four nations at different times, and in different social classes, and the impact of urbanisation and the Empire. They investigate current views of British identity and of how it is changing. Finally, they imagine identity as a mask that reflects aspects of heritage and community, and each designs and creates a mask to reflect their various loyalties, influences and affiliations.

Journeys

Using a resource such as *The Journey* (Callaghan 2003) about migrations to the UK from the Caribbean, or *Oldham Journey Teachers' Pack* (Burney 2005) about migrations from Bangladesh, learners conduct interviews with people who took part in a major journey (from another country to the UK, or from one part of the UK to another) in their youth, and construct pieces of prose which tell their stories. They include expectations before the journey began; things that happened on the way; initial feelings on arrival; the tasks of settling down and developing a sense of belonging; and how people's perceptions have i) persisted and ii) developed or changed over time. Historical perspective can be given by the booklet *Paul's Journey* (Oppenheimer 2006) about a survivor who came to the UK after captivity at Bergen Belsen.

Sibel's story

Learners use a Persona Doll to construct and tell the story of Sibel, a 5-year-old child from Iran whose family is seeking asylum in the UK. Information is provided by the teacher about reasons for leaving Iran and the dangerous journey to the UK. Imaginary family photographs are found on the internet and culturally relevant artefacts such as clothing are obtained from friends. Commonalities between Sibel and the learners are established, for example with regard to the likes, dislikes and worries of any 5-year-old girl in the world. As the story progresses there is consideration of cultural, linguistic and religious diversity and of how this influences values and perceptions.

To be a British Muslim

Learners attend to the testimony and experience of young British Muslims, as outlined and discussed on the websites of Muslim News, Q News and the Muslim Council of Britain, and in the report of the Commission on British Muslims and Islamophobia (2004). They identify commonalities, similarities and differences in the lives and identities of British Christians, British Jews and British Sikhs, and then also dual identities such as Black British, Scottish British, Mancunian British.

Problem or solution?

Learners debate three 'Big Myths', but also shared values, set out by the Inter-Faith Network (2004). The myths are: i) 'Well, they may say they're religious but no one believes any of that stuff'; ii) 'Religious people are just a bunch of fanatics'; and iii) 'Religion divides people – all the religions hate each other'. They then sort through some of the stories and case studies about practical inter-faith projects in various parts of Britain. For each project they ask and consider three questions: What do you see as the strengths of this project? What reservations or criticisms do you have? If you could meet someone from the project what would you ask?

Such activities are likely to lead to understanding that no one is just one thing. This was vividly expressed by a character in Ken Loach's film Ae Fond Kiss: 'I am a Glaswegian Pakistani teenage woman of Muslim descent, who supports Glasgow Rangers in a Catholic school, 'cause I'm a mixture and I'm proud of it' (quoted in Kettle 2004). A similar mixture is described by a leading theorist of modern multiculturalism (Sardar 2004: 12):

> I am a Muslim, a British citizen, of Pakistani origins, a man, a writer, a critic, a broadcaster, an information scientist, a historian of science, a university professor, a scholar of Islam, a rationalist, a sceptic, a traditionalist, and a partial vegetarian. All of these identities belong to me, and each one is important in a particular context.

Just as each individual is a mixture and continually evolving so is each group, community, culture, society or civilisation. No culture, no community, is just one thing. 'East' and 'West', or 'Islam' and 'West', are no more than metaphors and dangerous ones at that. So are the terms 'majority' and 'minority'. All communities are changing and all are complex, with internal diversity and disagreements. Neither 'minority' communities nor 'majority' communities are static. They change in response to their own internal dynamics and also as a result of the interactions and overlaps which they have with each other. This is a crucial point to bear in mind and to explore in all teaching about values and perceptions.

Prejudice and racism

It is frequently valuable to discuss real or imaginary events in schools. What should happen immediately, in the next few minutes? What should happen in the next few days? The next few weeks? What may have triggered off the event in the previous few minutes, or hours, or days? What should schools do to prevent such incidents occurring, and/or to prepare themselves for them when they do occur, so that they respond as effectively as possible? And, not least, what general principles should they draw out from such incidents? Scenarios such as those in Box 8.2 can be used initially with pupils in groups of three or four where they are asked to pick one in turn and suggest a response. Episodes such as these can be explored through role-play and other kinds of theatre, and through imaginative writing and art. Many of them require unpacking the differences and similarities between racist behaviour in schools and other forms of offensive behaviour. In this connection it is valuable to note guidance issued by the Department for Education and Skills (2006a). The principal similarity, the guidance observes, is that pupils who are targeted experience great distress. They may become fearful, depressed and lacking in self-confidence, and their progress at school may be severely damaged. The distress is connected with feelings of being excluded and rejected. Also, the distress is because a characteristic is picked out as a justification for the bullying that the person attacked can do nothing about – their size, whether they wear glasses, the colour of their hair, the colour of their skin, their religious or cultural background. Since all kinds of bullying cause distress, all are wrong.

Further, those who engage in bullying develop a false pride in their own superiority. Teachers and even parents are sometimes not aware of the miseries that are being inflicted, or of the cruelty that is being perpetrated. An additional similarity is that when dealing with incidents, staff must attend to i) the needs, feelings and wishes of pupils at the receiving end; ii) the needs, feelings and wishes of their parents and carers; iii) the children and young people principally responsible for the bullying; iv) any supporters they have; and v) any bystanders and witnesses.

The principal differences, the DfES (2006a) guidance continues, include the following:

- Racism has a long history affecting millions of people and is a common feature in wider society. People are seriously harmed and injured by it, and sometimes even viciously attacked and murdered. Words such Spotty, Fatty and Four Eyes are seldom used by adults and seldom or never used by adults to justify offensive behaviour. Racist words and prejudices, however, are associated with discrimination in employment and the provision of services, and with a range of criminal offences.

- The distinctive feature of a racist attack or insult is that a person is attacked or insulted not as an individual, as in most other offences, but as the representative of a family, community or group. Other members of the same group, family or community are in consequence made to feel threatened and intimidated as well. So it is not just the pupil who is attacked who feels unwelcome or marginalised. 'When they call me a Paki,' a nine-year-old child is quoted, 'it's not just me they're hurting. It's all my family and all other black people too.'

- Racist words and behaviour are experienced as attacks on the values, loyalties and commitments central to a person's sense of identity and self-worth. Often, therefore, they hurt not only more widely but also more deeply. 'They attack me for being an Arab,' remarks Ahmed. 'But I'm an Arab because my father is an Arab, and I love my father. Do they think I should stop loving my father? I couldn't do that, ever.'

- A message in all bullying is 'you don't belong'. In the case of racist bullying the message is not only 'you don't belong in this playground or this friendship group' but also 'you don't belong in this country'; it is therefore often even more devastating and traumatic for the pupil who is attacked than other forms of bullying.

- Racist attacks are committed not only against a community but also, in the eyes of offenders themselves, on behalf of a community – they see themselves as representative of, and supported in their behaviour by, their friends, family and peer group, and they may well feel it is right and proper to take the law into their own hands.

All these points are of fundamental importance as pupils learn about value-systems and perceptions in the wider world, and in their own immediate world close at hand. Anne Frank, quoted at the start of this chapter, would have expounded them vigorously and forcefully, and no doubt eloquently and beautifully, if she had been permitted to survive.

Starting points

A Faith Like Mine (Buller 2005) is a celebration of religious values and perceptions seen through the eyes of children.

Bullying Around Racism, Culture and Religion: How to Prevent it and What to do When it Happens (Department for Education and Skills 2006a) provides extensive guidance. Intended mainly for teachers but much of the material can be adapted for use in classrooms.

Citizenship and Muslim Perspectives: Teachers Sharing Ideas (Imran and Miskell 2003) contains background information about Islam and British Muslim communities and identities, and practical teaching ideas for citizenship education.

Coming Unstuck: Guidance and Activities for Teaching about Racism with 10 to 11– year-olds (Theodore 2004) is a substantial pack for teachers and pupils. It contains sections entitled 'direct racism', 'prejudice and multiple identities', and 'racism comes in many forms' and focuses throughout on values, perceptions and interpretive frameworks.

Here, There and Everywhere: Belonging, Identity and Equality in Schools (Richardson 2004) considers each national curriculum subject in turn in relation to teaching about similarities and differences, globalisation, conflict resolution and justice, and race and racisms.

Integrating Global and Anti-Racist Perspectives in the Primary Curriculum (Daffé *et al.* 2005) takes each separate national curriculum subject in turn and shows with a wealth of detail how each can contribute creatively to global education.

Chapter 9

Sustainable development

Ros Wade

Understanding the need to maintain and improve the quality of life now without damaging the planet for future generations.

(DfES 2005a)

Understanding the issue

The challenge of sustainable development first came onto the global political agenda at the UN Conference on Environment and Development in 1992. The significance of this 'Earth Summit' lay in the fact that issues to do with care of the environment and issues to do with development, previously largely treated as separate matters, were now seen as two sides of the same coin. The term 'sustainable development' was coined to embrace both the welfare of the planet and the welfare of people. This represented a considerable mind shift on the part of the world's leaders in recognising that human actions today can threaten both the present and the future of the planet (Quarrie 1992). Education was considered as absolutely essential to this process and commitments were made to integrate environment and development issues into education at all levels. Education for sustainable development (see below) grew out of this process and has since been further endorsed by the Earth Summit in Johannesburg in 2002.

Sustainable development thus starts from the premise that we are facing a major dilemma: how to reconcile the development needs of the poor and disadvantaged and at the same time address the environmental needs of the whole planet and the needs of future generations. This essentially is the challenge of sustainable development which directly confronts the dilemma that many human practices are unsustainable, whether in relation to people or the environment. For example:

> In 2006 one person in five will have less than a dollar a day to live on, ten million people, including 4.5 million children, will die from hunger or hunger-related diseases and at least 13 million people will be refugees. At the same time, the UK alone will produce 400m tonnes of waste, 30 billion tonnes of greenhouse gases will be produced worldwide and around 1 trillion dollars will be spent on arms.
>
> (Caesar 2005: 3)

The notion of ecological footprint, which compares the effects of human consumption of resources with the actual finite ecological resources of the planet, makes the dilemma even clearer. Ecological Footprint (2005) found that the ecological footprint of humanity 'on a global level ... is exceeding its ecological limits by 39 per cent'. This is clearly unsustainable since the authors point out that we would need 1.39 Earths to maintain our current levels of consumption.

The best known, if oversimplified, definition of sustainable development arose from the Brundtland Report (WCED 1987) which described it as 'a way of meeting the needs of the present without compromising the ability of future generations to meet theirs'. This, as with all definitions, begs many questions such as 'How do we define needs?' and 'Whose needs are we talking about?'. How such questions are interpreted will of course depend on people's values, ideology and political and cultural context.

The 1992 Earth Summit, for example, highlighted major North–South tensions as the rich and poor countries of the world often see the problem and its solution in quite different ways. Rich Northern governments want the poorer South to be responsible stewards of the Earth. Southern governments want the North to help eradicate poverty. The South sees imperialism, neocolonialsim and the strategies of the International Monetary Fund as largely responsible for unsustainable development. They resent Northern demands that they should not exploit their natural resources for their own benefit.

There are also major differences of opinion over the role of economic growth in relation to sustainability. The dominant global paradigm of capitalist neoliberalism stresses the importance of continued economic growth, with some safeguards to promote sustainability, but it does not question the basis for this economic growth and the likely effects of unchecked consumption. This view tends to predominate in government circles in the UK and USA along with the belief that it will be new technology which will build a more sustainable planet, rather than any deeper change in our lifestyles or consumption patterns. Others, such as Colin Hines (2000), challenge the whole economic model on which society is built and call for a paradigm shift towards more localised communities and a transformation of the present patterns of production and consumption. Jonathon Porritt (2005) argues for a new kind of capitalism which asserts the urgent need to value natural, human and social capital on an equal basis with manufactured and financial capital.

Issues of sustainability are now constantly in the news, not least in relation to climate change which has been identified as the greatest threat facing humankind at present (IPCC website). It is no coincidence that the most threatened and fragile environments, whether in Bangladesh or New Orleans, are homes to the poorest people and it is clear again that development and environmental issues are inextricably linked.

Action for change

Action towards creating a more sustainable future is occurring at all levels of society – personal, local, national and global. Rather than waiting for others to act, numerous individuals, families and organisations are taking responsibility for their own contribution to unsustainable/sustainable practices. Many people and local authorities are now aware of the need to use resources more wisely so they regularly refuse, reduce, reuse and recycle (Webster 2004). More people are aware of the need to use bus, train and bike, as well as car (Carfree Cities website) and there is a concern about more healthy ways of eating (Ethical Consumer website). A growing number of people see the connections between issues and espouse a deeper green lifestyle: using renewable energy, sharing a car, living more sustainably (Hickman 2005). Others belong to NGOs such as Oxfam, Christian Aid or Amnesty International and support particular campaigns, whether to do with debt, human rights or child labour. They are prepared to question unsustainable consumerism (Klein 2001) and the impact of globalisation on people's lives and communities (Roddick 2001).

It was noted previously that both the Earth Summits acknowledged the crucial role that education, formal and non-formal, has to play in changing unsustainable practices. This has led to the emergence of education for sustainable development (ESD) as an international field in its own right and 2005–15 has been identified as the UN Decade for ESD. Sterling (2006), working with the Education for Sustainability Programme at London South Bank University, developed a helpful framework which sees ESD as a series of nesting and dynamically related systems (see Figure 9.1). The model was originally designed for course development but it is also more widely applicable. At the centre of these nesting systems is education for sustainable development which is part of the wider world of education. This in turn is part of the social, economic and cultural environment which is set within the biophysical environment as evidenced in the view of the Earth from space.

Sterling (2001: 60–1) has also developed a useful model which outlines the main responses by educationalists to the challenge of sustainability. These are:

- Education about sustainability – this has a content/knowledge bias and is exemplified by the revised national curriculum which takes on board some sustainability concepts.

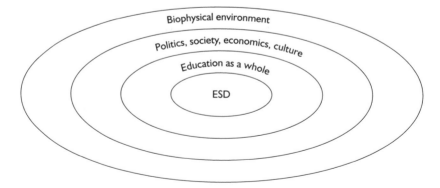

Figure 9.1 The nesting systems of ESD

- Education for sustainability – this goes further to include a values and capability bias. The emphasis is on 'learning for change' and includes critical and reflective thinking.
- Education as sustainability – this subsumes the first two responses but emphasises the process and quality of learning which is seen as creative, reflexive and participative.

Sterling accepts that within formal education the first response is the most common but that the other two are necessary if there is to be a real transition towards sustainability. The third response is the most difficult to achieve as it requires a paradigm change within education itself so that teaching and learning model the deeper processes of sustainability – what could be called sustainable education.

Good practice

Whilst there are differences in the national contexts of Wales, Northern Ireland, Scotland and England, there is nonetheless a strong commitment to ESD in all their educational policy documents. Of all of them, probably Wales has the strongest commitment (ACCAC 2002) although only certain elements of the policy are statutory, since the policy provides justification and support for schools and teachers who understand the importance of ESD. In addition, the DfES (2006e) produced an action plan for ESD, and Ofsted (see website) has completed a pilot inspection of ESD which is likely to be developed further. Whether ESD can be assessed by a system which depends on quantifiable rather than qualitative data is questionable but this initiative does demonstrate an increased awareness of its importance by government.

Good practice in ESD has to draw on a wide range of disciplines and it needs to question and look for new answers to present unsustainable ways of living. This section suggests some possible ways forward.

Promoting ESD in schools

Within the education sector, NGOs like the Development Education Association, the Council for Environmental Education, the World Wide Fund for Nature and Oxfam have led the way in promoting ESD. They contributed to the UK government's Sustainable Development Education Panel (see website) which defined ESD as education which 'enables people to develop the knowledge, values and skills to participate in decisions about the way we do things individually and collectively, both locally and globally, that will improve the quality of life now without damaging the planet for the future' (DETR 1999: 31). After consultation the panel went on to endorse the following key concepts which provide a useful starting point for teachers in planning for ESD:

- Interdependence
- Citizenship and stewardship

- Needs and rights of future generations
- Diversity
- Quality of life, equity and justice
- Sustainable change
- Uncertainty and precaution in action.

These concepts are supported by a list of skills and aptitudes, and values and dispositions. Full descriptions and support materials can be found on the QCA (2006c) website.

For the concept of 'interdependence', for example, the panel identified the following values and dispositions:

- Compassion for all humanity and concern for social justice now and for the future
- Concern for and appreciation of all living things, their needs and inter-relationships
- Appreciation of the earth and universe as a source of inspiration and challenge to human creativity.

Education for sustainable development permeates all areas of school life as it is, at heart, about a way of living and being. Above all, it is about the ethos and value base of the institution and the relationships that sustain this (Morris and Schagen 1995). Thus, knowledge, skills and values are part of a whole and cannot be treated as if they were separate. Research with tutors and students in Initial Teacher Education and Training (CCCI 2002) indicates that it is values and dispositions that are the most crucial in effective learning.

In consultation with pupils, parents and governors, teachers at Argyle Primary School developed a whole school curriculum underpinned by the principles of global citizenship and sustainable development (Argyle Primary School 2005). Their aim was to design a curriculum for the twenty-first century. In order to do this, they examined the ways in which the world is changing to help identify the challenges and opportunities which their pupils will face. The school adopted a holistic approach and their forward-thinking policy brings together the taught curriculum, informal curriculum and management of the school's resources. Box 9.1 shows some examples of how the school is trying to integrate ESD values into a whole school framework.

Box 9.1 Extracts from Argyle Primary School documentation

Through the core curriculum, including:
- Promoting recycling in What a Waste! (Y3)
- Campaigning on global development issues in *If The World were a Village* (Y6)

- Pupils contacting and writing to decision makers (e.g. mayor or MP) through persuasive writing units linked to humanities and citizenship in Y4, 5 and 6.

Through the informal curriculum, including:
- As peer mediators (Y5 and 6)
- Through promoting and helping to run environmental initiatives such as recycling, energy saving
- Through inbuilt flexibility to respond to current events, e.g. raising money for disaster relief (tsunami and Pakistani earthquake appeals)
- Through feedback from the school council to classes, head teacher and governors.

Staff, governors and parents have worked to develop sustainable practices, including:
- A commitment to energy conservation following the guidance of an energy audit commissioned from the Carbon Trust. This includes replacement of electrical and lighting products with energy efficient alternatives on a rolling programme
- A commitment to waste minimisation including re-use of paper in class, double-sided photocopying where possible, re-printing on used paper for internal documents, increased use of email to replace paper memos and newsletters
- A commitment to water conservation including installation of water-saving taps and rainwater harvesting for watering the garden
- Recycling of waste including paper, cans and plastic bottles; composting fruit and garden waste
- Purchasing of fair trade teas and coffee for staff
- Implementation of a School Travel Plan to reduce the school's carbon dioxide emissions from transport.

Pupils are fully involved in implementing sustainable development initiatives, including:
- organic fruit and vegetable gardening.

Developing communities for sustainability

Whilst it is possible to find many examples of good practice by individual teachers in individual classes, these still tend to focus on the knowledge dimension of education about development. In order to bring in the other two dimensions identified by Sterling, good practice needs to incorporate interdisciplinary and whole-school activities, the hidden or informal curriculum and the management and procurement of school resources.

Whilst teachers may decide to start by their own personal action, if there is to be real change, 'whole school communities need to come together, to share their own visions of sustainability and to place learning for sustainability at the heart of school life and the formal education system' (WWF 2006a). Activities from futures education (see Chapter 1) can provide some excellent materials for reflecting on shared visions and for considering future threats and challenges. For example, a futures timeline (Hicks 2001) can be used with staff or pupils to provide a framework to consider possible and probable futures. When MA Education students in Chichester were asked to identify three events or experiences which influenced their personal journeys to ESD, some felt that this had been a very gradual process and cited their upbringing and backgrounds, others mentioned books or films and some could even trace their development to a particular critical moment when their awareness changed. To truly live sustainably requires nothing less than a complete change in one's relationship with others and the world – what one might call an 'ontological epiphany' (Wade 2006).

Global Footprints Project

This project was co-ordinated by the Humanities Education Centre in Tower Hamlets and involved teachers all around the UK. The aim of the project was to encourage schools to estimate their 'global footprint' and to take action to reduce it. It was inspired by the idea of the ecological footprint but sought to add in the social and economic components of sustainable development. Schools responded with a wide range of approaches and activities, some of which can be found on the Global Footprints website. One particular activity provides a very useful starting point for all schools, namely the Global School Challenge. This is an interactive quiz which enables pupils to find out whether they are treading lightly or heavily on the earth. It starts with questions for staff and pupils to answer as individuals and then looks at the school as a whole.

For example, under the heading 'Energy Efficiency', one is asked to select one of the following options:

- The school has an action plan for reducing energy consumption and costs and uses energy indicators with targets. These are fully acknowledged by and involve the whole school community. Measures include insulation, heating and water temperature controls, sealed/double glazing and low energy lighting
- The school has a clearly stated aim of reducing energy costs but no specific action plan: measures such as fitting low energy light bulbs and better controls on the heating are being adopted
- The school has 'turn it off'/'save it' stickers around the school to remind pupils and staff to save electricity
- The school has made no efforts to save electricity.

After the quiz has been filled in, participants are given a score which can be used as a baseline from which to assess progress. This is both fun and an effective way to introduce ESD as a whole-school issue.

World Wide Fund for Nature's Development Framework

WWF UK has worked with teachers and whole-school groups to support them in reflecting on and developing their ethos and practice towards ESD. This work is essentially about relationships and processes within the school and acknowledges that there is no 'one size fits all'. Since each school is different so each will have different starting points, different routes and a different journey to make. WWF's Development Framework, which was drawn up in conjunction with teachers and which utilises research carried out by London South Bank's Education for Sustainability (EFS) programme, has proved to be a very useful tool for schools. Whole staff participation (including support staff) and the involvement of pupils was considered essential in the creation of supportive learning communities and effective long-term change. The Development Framework has now been adopted by the DfES and can be found on both the TeacherNet Sustainable Schools and WWF's websites together with information about online courses for teachers and a range of other useful resources.

Climate change

Climate change is probably the most urgent issue on the planet at this moment and educators may feel they are in a difficult position, coming to their own understanding of a complex and controversial problem at the same time as trying to help children and young people engage with the issues. No single subject can address the challenge of climate change as it highlights the interconnectedness of environmental, social and economic issues at local, national and global levels. Climate change demonstrates the need for positive action on all levels and, as such, it is an ideal theme to bring a school community together in looking at issues of sustainable development.

Some things we know:

- The world will heat up by between 1.4°C and 5.8°C this century. Anything over 2.0°C will lead to extremely dangerous consequences for the planet (Porritt 2005: 15).
- Carbon dioxide, due to our burning of fossil fuels, is the main problem pollutant and is the largest single contributor to greenhouse warming (Myers and Kent 2005).
- The world's economy is totally dependent on oil and yet the most optimistic forecasts predict that the world will run out of oil in 2050 (Orr 2005).
- People living in the poorest and most fragile areas are already feeling the effects of climate change (Lynas 2004).
- We live in a very unequal world. Africa, for example, contributes only about 3 per cent of global greenhouse gas emissions (TIDE 2005: 20).

In a letter to Tony Blair, Laura Nunnerly (11), from the first carbon neutral village in England, said 'hopefully other villages, towns, cities or even countries will follow us and reduce the energy consumption so reducing global warming and protecting and conserving the environment for future generations. If we don't we might find our planet uninhabitable' (*The Guardian* 2006b). Laura's concerns raise the important issue of what one might call 'personal sustainability' (Maiteny 2004) which is essential for our own well-being and ability to contribute to change. Sustainability is often presented as a negative, as meaning that one has to give things up or deprive oneself of things which enhance well-being. However, surveys in the UK show that people are no happier today than they used to be, despite the material benefits that they enjoy (Layard 2005) and a recent OECD report shows life satisfaction in the UK to be well below that of Mexico, a much poorer country (McRae 2006: 65). Beyond a certain minimum threshold of material welfare, it appears that it is not more money that makes people happier, but good relationships with family, friends, community and the environment (Layard 2005). Sustainability can therefore be presented as very positive, something that will make people's lives better as well as enhancing the life of the planet and the lives of others.

Teachers in Development Education (TIDE) in Birmingham has been working on issues of climate change after a visit to West Africa where teachers learnt about the Gambia's increasing vulnerability to rising sea levels, desertification and flooding. Their subsequent work is based on an enquiry approach and 'offers opportunities for primary, middle and secondary school children to learn to distinguish fact from opinion and to think about the future' (TIDE 2005: 3). The development process was crucial to the teachers' work and drew on the expertise of group facilitators, climate change scientists, campaigners and local government officers. Local teacher groups worked collaboratively to produce ideas and activities for use in their schools. Curriculum areas covered included Literacy, Science, Geography, DT and ICT, Citizenship and PSHE as well as some elements of Art and Design, History and RE.

The schools involved all used 4 key questions as a common framework:

- What is climate change?
- Why does it matter?
- What can we do about it?
- What have we learned and how?

The following examples from this TIDE (2005) publication indicate some possible approaches.

Positive action

In one activity the children are asked to draw around their hands and on each finger list one activity that they will undertake. For children involved in the TIDE project these included, 'I will walk to school, I will switch off lights, I will not leave the TV on standby'. Then on their other hand ask them to list actions for others to undertake, such as school council, family and government.

Diary of an energy waster

Working individually, ask children to write an imaginary diary entry about a person who wastes energy in every aspect of their day. They then pass this on to another child, who highlights an area of waste. This is then passed on to a third child, who suggests ideas for improvement and then a class discussion is held.

Future scenarios

Ask students to imagine two possible future scenarios: i) a Mediterranean scenario where warming continues unabated; ii) a Big Chill – a mini ice age resulting from interruption of the Gulf Stream by Arctic melt-water. Then ask the students to investigate the evidence for each scenario and choose which they would prefer to experience in 50 years' time. Then ask them to imagine that they are 50 years in the future and to consider how the climate and their lifestyles might have changed. What would be the impact on other low-lying countries, such as Bangladesh? Finally, ask them to write a letter back to someone in the present day telling them about the changes. Ask them to compare their lifestyles and suggest the things that could be done to slow down, minimise or mitigate the effects.

These activities and others on climate change scenarios are to be found in an excellent resource produced by TIDE (2005) *Climate Change – Local and Global: An Enquiry Approach*.

Starting points

Hicks, D. (2001) *Citizenship for the Future: A Practical Classroom Guide*, Godalming: World Wide Fund for Nature UK.

London South Bank University (2005) *Education for Sustainability: Education in Change*, Unit 7, Education for Sustainability Programme, South Bank University.

Peace Child International (2002) *Rescue Mission Planet Earth*, London: Peace Child International.

Smith, J. and Armstrong, S. (2002) *If the World Were a Village*, London: A.C. Black.

Sterling, S. (2001) *Sustainable Education: Re-visioning Learning and Change*, Dartington: Green Books.

TIDE (2005) *Climate change – Local and Global: An Enquiry Approach*, Birmingham: Teachers in Development Education.

Chapter 10

Interdependence

Teresa Garlake

Understanding how people, places, economies and environments are all inextricably interrelated, and that choices and events have repercussions on a global scale.

(DfES 2005a)

Understanding the issue

The issues facing young people today are more complex than ever. Television, information technologies, international sport and increased travel opportunities mean that the wider world has an immediate and central place in their lives. But if they are to be able to be fully aware of the part that they play in the world and become active participants in it, then they need to understand how it works. In order to do this they will need to understand the concept of interdependence.

We live today in a world where everything is literally connected to everything else. The clothes that young people choose to buy or the food that they eat will affect a producer in another country. The impact of a choice that is as simple as whether to walk to school or not will be felt across the globe. With more than 25 million carbon dioxide-producing cars on the road, the UK is a major contributor to climate change (CAFOD website). Environmental damage does not respect national borders.

The process through which individuals, groups, companies and countries become increasingly interdependent is called globalisation. It is not a new phenomenon. Connections across the globe have always existed – the valuable trade route known as the Silk Road linked Rome and China from the second century BC. More than five centuries ago, when the Spanish, Portuguese and English arrived in the New World, the countries of the world became more integrated into one global economy. The colonial links that followed were rarely mutually beneficial and became a way of transferring wealth and power from the poorer to the richer countries, leading to many of today's inequalities. By the end of the nineteenth century, countries were even more closely connected through the opportunities for trade that were opened up by steamships and railways. Cultures were linked as migrant labour helped the development of the world's richest countries such as the USA.

Over the last twenty-five years globalisation has taken on a faster pace. It is important to remember that this increasing integration has brought enriching cultural influences to countries: today we are able to enjoy music, literature and languages originating in many different parts of the world. But the increasing availability of consumer goods, such as soft drinks, hamburgers and music, mean that the world is becoming more homogeneous. Global producers such as Nike and Sony promote a lifestyle as well as a product (Klein 2001).

A key feature of globalisation has been the dramatic growth in international trade. Yet trade rules, regulated by the World Trade Organisation (WTO), make it harder for poor countries to get a good deal when they trade with richer ones. Whilst poorer countries attempt to increase their income by exporting more raw materials, they have no control over world prices. About 10 million people in West Africa alone depend on cotton for their livelihood. In the US, cotton subsidies mean that industrial-sized farms receive payments in excess of $1 million. The cotton that they produce is then sold very cheaply in West Africa. This dumping has caused losses of $400 million for African cotton producing countries and, although ruled illegal by the WTO, it will be some years before change is implemented (Oxfam 2005b). Poor countries lose £1.3 billion export income every day through unfair trade rules. This is 14 times what they receive in aid. (CAFOD website)

In our increasingly globalised world there are winners and losers. For some, globalisation offers new opportunities and improved standards of living. For others, it works against the interests of the poor. Some see it as inevitable, others as a force that must be resisted. Whatever their opinion, young people need to be given opportunities to grapple with one of the most controversial issues of our time.

Action for change

If education is to be meaningful it must give young people the tools to take action on issues which affect them and to influence decision makers. Article 12 of the United Nations Convention on the Rights of the Child (UNICEF 2006b) encourages children and young people to participate in discussion of such issues, developing the skills that will allow them to become active citizens. The wide range of individuals and movements across the world which have come together to raise their voices against globalisation are a source of inspiration (Roddick 2001).

At the end of November 1999 an estimated 100,000 people converged on a meeting of the WTO in Seattle, USA. In this first large-scale anti-globalisation protest, they called for fairer trade with less exploitation. Almost six years later, in July 2005, more than 250,000 people marched in Edinburgh, Scotland demanding that world leaders 'make poverty history' (Wikipedia website).

Whilst these protests have received widespread coverage, far away from the eyes of the world media much smaller community groups are taking on the world's giants and seeking change. In 2003 the villagers of Plachimada in Kerala, South India, pitted themselves against perhaps the world's biggest brand name. Coca Cola sells nearly 400 brands of soft drinks in over 200 countries (India Resource Centre website).

After Coca Cola had opened its largest bottling facility in India, villagers found that they had much lower levels of water in their wells and that the water had been contaminated and was impossible to drink, cook with or bathe in. Whilst they could never afford the fizzy drinks that were transported across the country to be bought by urban elites, women found that they had to walk 4 km to fetch clean water. Villagers decided to take on the global giant and, after three years of protest, production at the plant was stopped in 2005. Thousands of communities across India continue to protest against the company's operations (India Resource Centre website).

One of the most striking features of globalisation has been the development of new technologies. In many parts of the South communities are taking steps to ensure that they are not left out. In Uganda rural women decided to use the internet and e-mail to get information that would improve their productivity as farmers. When they found that the wealth of material in English, Chinese and Spanish was of little use, they set out to develop their own. Today at Nakaseke Telecentre women farmers can access a CD-ROM which gives practical advice on how to boost crop yields and manage livestock. The material gets them thinking about what else they can produce and how to collaborate with friends. Advice is given in the women's first language and, because the text on the computer screen is read out, the programme is also helping the women to learn to read. The knowledge that the women have gained has made them role models and improved the respect that their ideas are given in their community (The Communication Initiative website).

Throughout the world people are seeking ways to manage the process of globalisation. Whether this is by protesting against the inequalities and marginalisation that globalisation can bring or by seizing the opportunity to take advantage of some of its benefits, these actions are a reminder that it is always possible to take action for change.

Good practice

The activities in this section provide starting points for exploring the concept of interdependence and then the complex nature of globalisation. Pupils are encouraged to explore their own values and attitudes and, through this process, to develop their awareness of the relevance of globalisation to their own lives.

In keeping with sound educational principles the first three activities begin by exploring children's personal connections to other communities and parts of the world.

The next two activities look at information and communication technologies which play a key role in the process of globalisation. This is best represented by the internet. This had more than 140 million users in mid-1998. By 2006 this had risen to 1,022,863,307 (Internet Usage Statistics website). ICT may open up many ways to improve people's quality of life yet it is still out of reach for most of the world's poorest communities. While in the UK we send an average of 3 million texts every hour, more than a billion people have never used a telephone (Global Eye website).

The final part of this chapter contains two activities that look at trade. Since fashion is close to the hearts of many young people, activities focus on the garment industry. The clothing and textile industries are the largest industrial employer in the world. More than 23.6 million workers are employed in the garment industry worldwide and almost 75 per cent of these are women (Maquila Solidarity Network website).

People who help us

This activity is most suitable for younger children. It helps them to recognise the interdependencies that exist between members of a community by focusing on their own school. Pupils can then move on to consider local and global connections.

You will need

Blank postcard size cards.

Instructions

Talk with children about the different roles that exist in their school: head teacher, teachers, teaching assistants, cleaners, lunch-time supervisors, dinner staff, pupils, caretaker, visitors to the school, parent helpers etc. Write out a card with each role on it.

Give each small group of children a card and ask them to discuss the ways that this person helps them and others in the school community. They should also think about how they help that person (for example, children help the cleaner by tidying the classroom at the end of the day).

Children mime or devise a role play, depending on age, of the person on their card. They perform this to the rest of the class who try to guess who the helper is.

Discuss with children how each person plays a very important role in the community. What would happen if that person was not there? Point out that we all depend on others and go on to consider those who help us in the wider community.

Further work

Children could go on to draw the person on their card to make a classroom display. They could also write a thank you letter to the person, giving some details of how that person helps them.

Food matters

Purpose

By looking at a range of food packets children realise that they are dependent on many different countries for their food.

Preparation

Ask children to bring in a range of packets of food and other food items from home. You will need to supplement this with items from as wide a variety of countries of origin as you can. For younger children you will need to highlight the country of origin on the packet or attach your own labelling.

You will need

A large world map and enlarged photocopies of a world map.

Instructions

Give each child a selection of food items and a world map. Ask them to locate the countries of origin of the foods on a world map.

Bring the class together and discuss the range of countries from which their food comes. Talk about what children have discovered. Were they surprised to find out where their foods come from? Is most food produced in the UK or in other countries? Why are many of our foodstuffs grown or produced in the South (make the links to climate zones)? Are there parts of the world from which there are no foods in the class? Why might this be? Think about one particular country and ask children if they can imagine anything that might happen there that would make it difficult to keep buying that food – changes in weather conditions, import restrictions, lower prices, war etc. How would these changes affect the growers of the foodstuffs (loss of livelihoods, not being able to transport crops to markets etc.)?

Further work

Ask pupils to carry out a survey and look at the origin of as many different items in the classroom as they can. Where are their books printed? Where might the wood in their desks or rulers come from? What are their clothes made of (cotton, rubber) and where are these materials grown?

Older pupils could go on to consider how many of these countries are in the North and how many in the South. Manufactured goods are worth more than raw materials. Which countries make most money in trade and why? Make links to the activities in Chapter 7.

Reflect on this Martin Luther King quotation: 'Before you have finished your breakfast this morning, you will have depended on half the world'. Children could draw a poster to illustrate this, putting down some items and their countries of origin.

Global connections

Through asking each other a range of questions pupils discover their connections with other parts of the world.

You will need

A copy of the activity sheet (Figure 10.1) for each person.

Instructions

Give a copy of the activity sheet to each person. Children go round the room asking questions and filling in their sheets. They should note down the name of the person on their sheet and, where appropriate, the name of the country. They can only ask each person one question.

As a whole class, discuss the connections that children have with other places. Are they surprised by the range of connections that they have? Talk about the different types of connections: cultural, environmental, technological, commercial. Remember that some links are less obvious than others, for example through medicines, or raw materials such as cocoa. What do these observations tell us about the nature of interdependence? You will find a copy of Figure 10.2 useful to photocopy and to feed in to the class discussion.

Further work

Point out to the class that all the points on the activity sheet are examples of globalisation. In small groups, ask them to come up with their own definition.

Global connections activity sheet

Find someone who…

1	Has travelled to another country
2	Is wearing something made in another country
3	Likes music from another country
4	Can name two foreign companies that work in the UK
5	Has read about another country in the papers recently
6	Has been to McDonalds recently
7	Has electrical equipment that has been made in another country
8	Uses the internet at home
9	Likes food from another country
10	Can name a sports star from another country
11	Has a family car from another country
12	Has eaten chocolate today
13	Has taken medicine in the last month
14	Walks to school rather than drives

Figure 10.1 Global connections activity sheet

Global connections information sheet

1   Tourism is the world's biggest global industry. The number of tourists has risen from a mere 25 million in 1950 to 700 million today (World Tourism Organisation 2006). People also travel to work. At any one time there are approximately 120 million international migrant workers who send valuable earnings back to their families (International Labour Migration website).

2   The garment industry is one of the world's largest employers. In the UK the cost of clothes and footwear has fallen by a third in the last 15 years. This is partly because more clothes are made in developing countries where labour costs are cheaper (Garlake 2003).

3   Music constantly changes in response to historical and cultural connections. Arabs brought the guitar into Spain and Portugal from the thirteenth century onwards. Reggae, calypso and ska from the Caribbean are now popular forms of UK culture.

4   The UK attracts more foreign investment than any other country in Europe and is second in the world behind the US. In 2003/2004 this investment created more than 25,000 new jobs (Directgov 2004).

5   The media has a powerful influence on our lives and what we know about other countries. However, news about other countries is often confined to a few inside pages.

6   McDonalds is the largest and best-known global foodservice retailer with more than 30,000 local restaurants serving nearly 50 million people in more than 119 countries each day (McDonalds website).

7   The German electrical equipment company Siemens is one of the world's largest companies, working in more than 190 countries. It employs more than 461,000 people directly around the world, and many more indirectly through other contractors (Siemens AG website).

8   Today over a billion people have access to the Internet. However, half the world's population has never made a phone call (Internet Usage Statistics website).

9   Indian food is now the most popular food in the UK. Britain has around 8,000 restaurants which employ 70,000 people – more than the steel, coal and shipbuilding industry put together. Spending on Indian food is over £2.5 million each year (Grove and Grove 2006).

10   Brazil is the only nation to have qualified for every World Cup final. More than half the Brazil side that won the 2002 World Cup played for European clubs; Ronaldo, the best of them, had not played in Brazil since he was 17 (*The Observer* 2004).

11   In the first three months of 2002 people in the UK bought a record number of imported cars. Imported cars account for over 75 per cent of new car sales (Garlake 2003).

12   Chocolate is made from cocoa. Many farmers in the South are at the mercy of price fluctuations of cash crops on the world markets. In recent years prices have plummeted. Farmers have seen their livelihoods dissolve and countries have lost valuable export earning. Ghana is the world's third largest producer of cocoa. The crop accounts for 35–40 per cent of the country's foreign exchange. The US is the world's biggest importer of cocoa, and wants a free market (Divine Chocolate website).

13   Developing countries are home to around two thirds of plant species. Half of our medicines are derived from plants and a quarter of all prescription drugs have their origins in the tropical rainforests.

14   Transport produces 28 per cent of current carbon dioxide emissions and this proportion is growing rapidly. Greenhouse gases, mainly carbon dioxide, methane and nitrous oxide, have been blamed for heating up the world's temperature which, in turn, contributes to more unstable and extreme weather patterns. The richer countries of the world, with a quarter of the world's population, produce an estimated 60 per cent of greenhouse gas emissions (DEFRA website).

Figure 10.2 Global connections information sheet

Connect!

Pupils keep a log of their ICT usage in order to build their awareness of the impact of ICT on their lives. They then go on to look at how the use of technology is unevenly spread across the globe.

You will need

A copy of the activity sheet (Figure 10.3) for each pupil.

Preparation

Ask pupils to keep a log of their use of ICT over two days using the activity sheet.

Instructions

Discuss as a class how pupils use ICT in their lives. Encourage them to analyse the purposes of their usage. Do they visit websites as part of their homework, for entertainment or to buy something?

In groups, ask pupils to develop a list of the ways in which ICT is used. These may include communications, education, entertainment, shopping/business,

---

Using ICT

Over the next two days keep a record of all the times that you use ICT.

	Day 1	Day 2
Mobile phone (number of calls made)		
The internet (number of websites visited)		
E-mail (number of messages received/sent)		
Text messaging (number of messages received/sent)		
Computer games (number of minutes/hours)		

Can you think of any other ways in which you have used ICT?

_____

_____

Figure 10.3 Using ICT activity sheet

information gathering and campaigning. They should then list five advantages and five disadvantages of ICT.

After some discussion and feedback time, give pupils information on the digital divide (see Box 10.1). What has surprised pupils about this information? Since most of the world's population does not have access to ICT, how might people's lives in the South be affected? Pupils may wish to refer back to their lists of advantages and disadvantages. Suggestions might include: lack of knowledge, exclusion, isolation etc. Do pupils feel that the benefits of ICT outweigh the disadvantages?

Box 10.1 The digital divide

More and more people in the world today are benefiting from new technologies which are often seen as a powerful weapon in the fight against poverty. Technology can give people the tools to become more productive and prosperous. Helping farmers to share their knowledge can mean higher crop yields. The internet allows traditional craftspeople in the South to reach markets all over the world.

However, new technologies are still out of reach of most of the world's poorest people. Only 16 per cent of the world's population is connected to the internet (Internet Usage Statistics website). A garment worker in Bangladesh would have to save eight years' wages to buy a computer (CAFOD website). Even with the necessary equipment, connections can often be unreliable and expensive. For many illiteracy is also a big obstacle and since most websites are in English they are inaccessible to most of the world's people.

Many people now argue that mobile phones rather than computers are the way to provide people with access to technology that they need. Although more than a billion people have never used a telephone this looks set to change. Seventy-seven per cent of the world's population is within range of a phone network and mobile phones can be shared within communities. Since 1999 new subscriptions to mobile phone networks in Africa have grown from 72,000 to 25.5 million in 2005 (Global Eye 2005).

ICT in action

Through researching case studies pupils consider some of the differences that ICT can make to people's lives.

Preparation

There are a wide range of case studies available on the internet. One such site is Hands On: Ideas to Go (2006) which has a section called 'Making the Connection'.

There follow some useful starting points.

SOLAR-POWERED RADIOS – SIERRA LEONE

In a country emerging from the strife of civil war, information and communication technologies are few and far between. This case study shows how solar-powered radio and a new radio station are encouraging social engagement and education. See Hands On: www.tve.org/ho/doc.cfm?aid=1607&lang=English.

NETWORKING ON HEALTH – AFRICA

Costs and distances mean that health workers in remote areas of the South are often unable to keep in touch with other professionals. The HealthNet project uses hand-held computers to allow health workers to access information and seek specialist opinions. See: www.healthnet.org/healthnet.php.

VILLAGE PHONES – BANGLADESH

The Village Phone programme allows some of the poorest people in Bangladesh to improve their living standards. Women are given loans to buy cell phones. They then sell mobile phone services to other members of the community, making a living while they pay off their loans. See: www.grameenphone.com/modules.php?name=Content&pa=showpage&pid=3 (search under 'village phone').

COMPUTER CENTRE REVITALISES COMMUNITIES – UGANDA

At the Nakaseke Telecentre, villagers from the age of four are taught computer applications, how to use the internet and send e-mails, and can learn from the CD-ROMs held in the telecentre's library. Farmers can now get advice on how to make the most out of their land and there is an electronic link with Uganda's main hospital to get the best medical advice. See: www.comminit.com/strategicthinking/pdsmakingwaves/sld-1905.html.

Instructions

Ask pupils, in small groups, to research one of the projects listed above and prepare a short report for the rest of the class. They should consider how the project uses ICT, who benefits from the project and what changes the use of ICT has brought to people's lives.

Once the groups have reported back, discuss pupils' findings. If they had money to spend on technology as a way of reducing poverty, which project would they support? Which use of technology do they feel is most worthwhile and why? Has their research made them think differently about their own use of ICT?

Focus on fashion

Pupils explore their attitudes to the clothing industry and discover the web of connections that are made through trade.

Preparation

A few days in advance ask pupils to bring in a range of fashion adverts taken from magazines.

You will need

An outline copy of a world map for each pair of pupils.

Instructions

In groups of four ask pupils to discuss and note down what factors influence their choices over the clothes that they buy. These may include cost, style or colour, advertising, what their friends are wearing, a good fit etc. Groups should report back to the rest of the class.

Look at the adverts and ask pupils to consider what image or lifestyle the clothing is trying to promote. Who are the adverts aimed at? Are they for well-known brands? How influenced do pupils feel they are by advertising?

Now point out to pupils that the clothing industry is one that connects people around the world. Ask pupils to look at the labels in their clothes. As a class they should record where these have been made and find the countries on a world map. Do they notice any patterns? How often is clothing bought in a different country from that in which it was made? Do manufacturing countries tend to be located in the North or South? Are they considered to be less or more economically developed?

Further work

Note down pupils' opinions and findings from this lesson and go back over these after carrying out further work, including the next activity. What has most surprised pupils? How have their attitudes changed?

Jean journey

In this activity, pupils consider the nature of interdependence by looking at the countries that are involved in the making of a pair of jeans.

You will need

A transparency or slide of the activity sheet (Box 10.2) or a photocopy for each pair of pupils. An outline copy of a world map for each pupil.

Box 10.2 Jean journey activity sheet

A PAIR OF JEANS

This pair of jeans is normally sold for £29.95 at Cromwell's Madhouse in Ipswich, Suffolk

Brass rivets and buttons made from Namibian copper and Australian zinc

Jeans sewn by Ejallah Dousab, aged 21, in Tunisia. She is paid 58p per hour

Cotton grown in Benin. The farmer makes about £15 profit on his year's harvest

Jeans stone-washed using pumice from an inactive volcano in Turkey

Jeans made and dyed in Italy

Synthetic indigo used for dyeing from Germany

Zip teeth made in Japan

Polyester tape for zips produced in France

Thread for seams from Northern Ireland

Thread for seams dyed in Spain

Jeans sold in Ipswich, Suffolk

(Source: Garlake 2003)

Instructions

Begin by asking the class how many of them own a pair of jeans. Discuss the sort of prices that are paid for jeans. Where do they buy them? Do they prefer brand names? Why?

Point out that if you measured the distances travelled by all the components that go into a pair of jeans it would come to about 40,000 miles. Project the activity sheet onto the interactive whiteboard or distribute photocopies. Ask pupils to find each country on a world map.

As a class discuss the range of countries that are involved in producing a pair of jeans. Which countries do pupils feel benefit most in terms of money earned from the production processes? What might be some of the effects of this global production process (transportation costs and the effects of this on the environment, people from all over the world being tied into a global economy, the increasing interdependence of countries etc.)?

Starting points

Choc-a-lot: A Chocolate Flavoured Resource to Explore Global Trade in Cocoa (2004) (Reading International Solidarity Centre). An activity booklet which allows secondary pupils to explore all aspects of the global market through the chocolate industry and cocoa trade.

Donnellan, C. (2005) *The Globalisation Issue*, Independence Educational Publishers. A collection of previously published articles from magazines, government reports, lobby groups etc. presented in a lively A4 magazine format which makes this ideal material for secondary pupils.

Ellwood, W. (2001) *The No-Nonsense Guide to Globalization*, New Internationalist. Ideal for background reading, this accessible book gives a clear overview of the global corporate system.

Garlake, T. (2003) *The Challenge of Globalisation*, Oxfam. This secondary teachers' handbook concentrates on subjects relevant to pupils' own lives (sport, new technology, the fashion industry) and encourages pupils to discuss the moral and ethical issues surrounding globalisation.

Positively Global (2005) Leeds Development Education Centre. A set of five booklets which explores globalisation and looks at how young people can respond. Themes include education, debt relief, health, the media and migration.

TIDE (2001) *Globalisation: What's it All About?* Teachers in Development Education. A resource book for secondary teachers which features case studies, activities, games and background information.

NB For examples of work on interdependence at primary level see: Young, M. and Commins, E. (2002) *Global Citizenship: the handbook for primary teaching*, Chris Kington Publishing and Oxfam.

Chapter 11

Human rights

Margot Brown

Knowing about human rights including the UN Convention on the Rights of the Child.

(DfES 2005a)

Understanding the issue

In a recent document directed at journalists there is a picture of a street scene in an unspecified location in Africa. On the street is a huge billboard with the legend 'Unbalanced news is also a human rights abuse'.

The juxtaposition of the words 'human rights abuse' and 'unbalanced news' may challenge some preconceptions about what are human rights and their abuse. Media coverage would lead us to believe that human rights abuses refer almost exclusively to torture, terrorism and conflict and that it happens mostly 'out there'. Of course at one end of the spectrum, human rights abuses are categorised by such events but human rights are also universal and apply to all people everywhere. Their abuse can be glaring, physically damaging and horrifying but also can be pervasive, subtle and ongoing. As Eleanor Roosevelt said in 1958:

> Where, after all, do universal rights begin? In small places, close to home – so close and so small that they cannot be seen on any maps of the world. Yet they are the world of the individual person; the neighbourhood he [sic] lives in; the school or college he attends; the factory, farm or office where he works. Such are the places where every man, woman and child seeks equal justice, equal opportunity, equal dignity without discrimination. Unless these rights have meaning there, they have little meaning anywhere. Without concerned citizen action to uphold them close to home, we shall look in vain for progress in the larger world.
>
> (Office of the UN High Commissioner for Human Rights website)

Human rights span gender, ethnicity, ability, language, religion, age and culture. This gives them their strength but also brings responsibilities. Tom Paine, the eighteenth century English radical, said:

A declaration of Rights is, by reciprocity, a Declaration of Duties also. Whatever is my right as a man, is also the right of another, and becomes my duty to guarantee, as well as possess.

(cited in CEWC 2001: 1)

The concept of reciprocity is one which is now accepted as an important element of human rights education. The fact that the quotation above comes from the eighteenth century prompts the question 'Where did human rights begin?'. Many would agree that the concept of universality in the field of human rights began with the founding of the United Nations in 1945 and the Universal Declaration of Human Rights in 1948 but the underpinning values and desire for justice and equality go back much further. Amnesty International has a chronological wall frieze for schools which begins with the Laws of Hammurabi in 2500 BC in what is modern day Iraq and ends with Rigoberta Menchu of Guatemala in the 1990s. The title of the frieze, 'A Long March to Freedom', highlights a key value underpinning human rights and reminds us that human rights are still what one might call 'work in progress'. Amnesty succinctly describes human rights as follows:

Human rights can be defined as those basic standards without which people cannot live in dignity as human beings. Human rights are the foundation of freedom, justice and peace. Their respect allows the individual and the community to develop fully.
    Rights can be put into three categories:

1. *Civil and political rights.* These are 'liberty-orientated' and include the rights to: liberty and security of the individual; freedom from torture and slavery; political participation; freedom of opinion, expression, thought, conscience and religion; freedom of association and assembly.
2. *Economic and social rights.* These are 'security-orientated' rights, for example the rights to: work, education, a reasonable standard of living, food, shelter and health care.
3. *Environmental, cultural and developmental rights.* These include the right to live in an environment that is clean and protected from destruction, and rights to cultural, political and economic development.

These classifications are not always clear cut however as some rights may fall into more than one category.

(Amnesty International 2001: 2–3)

Action for change

This chapter opened with reference to a billboard in an African street. On the billboard, in addition to the declaration about unbalanced news, were the words 'Don't sit doing nothing. Help fight the wrongs of society'. The belief that action springs from meaningful, transformative education links well with the balance of 'rights and responsibilities' in education. The very term 'responsibilities' implies a more active approach to change. Young people come to school with many misconceptions about rights, from 'I have a right to … stay up late/watch TV/go out with my friends/ come home late', to the view that 'human rights are "huge" – they involve atrocities, repressive governments, torture – and I can do nothing about these'.

Human rights education has a responsibility to challenge such misconceptions. Saying you have a right does not necessarily mean that you have. Rights can be legal or moral and human rights are enshrined in international law. Nevertheless, in explaining about human rights and human rights infringements and denials, young people should not be left feeling disempowered and that nothing can be done. It is therefore important that, whenever possible, action can be offered as an antidote to powerlessness.

Action can encompass the change of behaviour in the playground where pupils no longer exclude one of their classmates from a game because she is 'different', to being a member of the school's Amnesty International Junior Urgent Action Club. Junior urgent actions are monthly appeals designed specifically for young people aged 8–12 working with the help of an adult. The actions are part of Amnesty's worldwide letter writing campaign on behalf of victims of human rights violations.

A recent case (Amnesty International 2005) suggested that 'a short polite letter' be written to the authorities in Myanmar (Burma) on behalf of a 4-year-old girl, Ei Po Po, who was being held on her own by police. She and her parents normally live in India as refugees. The briefing paper for the adult leaders of the Club gives details of the case, including a map, practical guidelines on the postal costs of letters of concern, points for the letter and an address to which to send it. There is also additional information about the country.

In itself, the letters written by school pupils will not change the stance of the Burmese police but Amnesty has proof of the success of letter writing campaigns in both boosting the morale of the prisoner and putting a brake on the behaviour of the oppressor. Providing an opportunity for practical action which shows solidarity with other young people in difficult situations can energise pupils in schools here and give them a sense of purpose.

In the case of Ei Po Po, a letter from Amnesty to the Club one month later said: 'Do you remember sending a letter last month to Myanmar asking the government to free Ei Po Po? Good news! She has now been released and is in the care of relatives – thank you to everyone who wrote to Myanmar on her behalf!' News of the impact of the letters does not always come so quickly or with a happy ending, but Amnesty does give regular updates so that pupils, in both primary and secondary schools, are kept informed and involved.

In the UK, school councils are often seen as a contribution to Article 12 of the UN Convention on the Rights of the Child (UNICEF 2006b) – giving young people a voice in decisions which affect them. Both primary and secondary schools are frequently very good at planning elections to councils, a process which can contribute to an understanding of democracy and citizenship. However, when the school council has been elected the impact varies from school to school. There is still work to be done to ensure that, after the process of election and meeting, all councils are given the ability to make meaningful decisions and see them carried through.

In 2006, Vernor Muñoz, UN Special Rapporteur on the right to education, issued a statement to promote the implementation of the plan of action for the first phase of the World Programme for Human Rights Education (2005–7). He stated his strong belief that human rights education is an integral part of the right to education. 'Integrating human rights into education systems contributes to ensuring the construction of quality education and to improving standards of living for all' (Muñoz 2006). He concludes,

> human rights education promotes a rights-based approach which enables the education system to fulfil its fundamental mission to ensure the full development of the human personality and the sense of its dignity, and strengthens the respect for human rights and fundamental freedoms.

Many schools in England are focused on the requirement of *Every Child Matters* (DfES 2005b) and its impact. UNICEF (2006c) has recently published a very useful mapping of the principles of *Every Child Matters* and the Convention on the Rights of the Child.

Good practice

Media coverage and human rights

Surveys over the years have consistently shown how influential television is in forming young people's views of the world. Many countries are only in the news when disaster, corruption or human rights abuses are reported and it is rare to be given the full context for these stories. Uncritical acceptance of such unbalanced news creates negative stereotypes and inaccurate perceptions. A MORI poll for DfID (2004) found that 89 per cent of 11–16-year-olds cited TV news as their most frequent source of information about developing countries.

In 'Making sense of the media', Catling (2000) reports on research evidence that shows children as young as four to six years old have both accurate and misconceived knowledge of other places and issues such as global warming. He goes on to comment on pupils' sources of information, which include video, films and computer programmes, and the need for adult mediation in relation to these sources.

The importance of adult intervention and explanation is also highlighted in the Department for International Development report, *Viewing the World* (DfID 2000b). An exchange between a group of 15-year-olds on third world debt led the report's writer to remark,

> The problem is that without factual knowledge or explanation children put together ways of understanding from other resources. These could include overheard commentaries from adults or peer groups or imagery drawn from

films, television or computer games. Some of this is likely to be false or even racist.

(DFID 2000b: 138–9)

The report also found that 'young people were apparently put off development issues by forced participation in charitable events at schools' and that '15 year olds showed very low levels of interest' (p. 13). It is clear therefore that, in relation to developing responsible young global citizens capable of making informed choices about issues of concern, considerable work has yet to be done. It is also clear from such research that young people have a great interest in human rights which can itself provide a useful starting point for exploring these issues.

At a time when a 'soundbite' is often seen to be essential, the need for context and analysis of media coverage of human rights issues has never been more urgent. This is especially true of the human rights stories from the South which often focus on the horrific, rarely give context or follow-up and even more rarely link with issues of refugees and asylum seekers in the UK by considering their reasons for leaving in order to come here. This compartmentalisation of issues in the news is damaging to our understanding of the universality of human rights.

With this in mind, the Centre for Global Education is involved in a three-year project with pilot schools in the north-east of England to explore media coverage through a human rights framework. This has required Year 9 school students to: i) learn about their rights; ii) explore the three topics of child exploitation, poverty and conflict; and iii) develop a radio programme which encourages them to make their own analysis of these issues and present their findings. The project team includes expertise from the BBC World Service, with contributions from BBC York and BBC Cleveland. The project has been developed in as democratic a way as possible, with teachers taking a lead in the direction of the content and with pupils involved in the evaluation of the drafts and contributing views which influence the revisions.

One unit of work aims to help: a) students critically review media coverage from a human rights perspective and b) reflect on how this influences their response to reporting, whether print, radio or television. It also helps them consider the situation behind the headlines. This involves a short video produced by UNICEF (2006d) to launch their campaign against child exploitation. This 3-minute film is introduced by Robbie Williams who reads a poem by Simon Armitage. The poem speaks of countries being rich in natural resources, such as hardwood trees, diamonds and another resource 'more precious than gold' (the name of the film). This 'fruit … grows wild and free in towns and villages … and is ripe for picking after twelve or thirteen summers'. The visual images which accompany these and following lines make it clear that the 'fruit' is the young women of the village who are being trafficked to the UK and Europe. At the end Robbie Williams says that we all have a responsibility to these young women and a duty to act. For the teachers in the project, this film provided an opportunity for tackling difficult issues, stressing the interdependence of people and the human rights that bind us together. Questions such as the following were then asked: If there was no 'market' for young women in

Europe, would the trafficking take place? Where is the source of the problem? What are the links?

The activity below (Figures 11.1 and 11.2) is part of this unit of work and is used to begin the process of unpicking the viewer's expectations and how we 'read' images and language.

Morocco and England linking

A project linking primary teachers, student teachers and teacher educators in Morocco and England, through a focus on human rights, was intended to sow seeds of change in both communities. Human rights education and citizenship education are separate statutory subjects in Morocco at both primary and secondary levels where both the Ministry of Human Rights and the Ministry of Education are involved in curriculum development.

A 10-year-old commented, 'Democracy is about us in school as well as out in the world'. This child was taking part in a lesson on human rights where a cartoon was used to stimulate lively discussion. The cartoon shows a teacher facing a group of children seated in a classroom; the teacher says, 'I said today we would learn about democracy – I did not ask for your opinion!'.

Lesson I	**Audiences and great expectations**
Objectives	**What to do?**
To raise awareness of links between stereotypes and expectations	Each student in the class receives one of the five different *Expectation* cards.
Learning outcomes	Without looking at each other's cards, students answer only
Students will have: • identified how stereo-typing can influence perceptions	the questions they read on their *own* card about their different expectations of the video. (NB. This works best if the class is working in silence.)
You will need ...	Teacher plays video once and then (without any discussion)
• A copy of the 'More Precious than Gold' video • Sets of *Expectations* cards for each group	gives out the post-viewing response questions. Students (again in silence) write their individual answers to the questions about whether their expectations were met and if
Time: 30 minutes	not why not.
	Students form small groups, made up of (approximately) one student from each of the five *Expectation* groups.
	These groups share their reactions to the video, using their written answers to help structure the discussion.

Figure 11.1 Audiences and great expectations

You are about to watch a three-minute video with the title 'More Precious than Gold'. What do you expect: • it will be like? • will be in it? • you will see? • you will hear?	You are about to watch a three-minute video with Robbie Williams in it. What do you expect: • it will be like? • will be in it? • you will see? • you will hear?
You are about to watch a three-minute video about child trafficking. What do you expect: • it will be like? • will be in it? • you will see? • you will hear?	You are about to watch a three-minute video about prostitution. What do you expect: • it will be like? • will be in it? • you will see? • you will hear?

You are about to watch a three-minute video about Africa.

What do you expect:

• it will be like?
• will be in it?
• you will see?
• you will hear?

Figure 11.2 Audience *Expectation* cards

This scene took place in the small town of Khemisset, Morocco. It was observed by a party of visiting teachers and tutors from York schools and York St John University College as part of work linking primary and special schools, together with teacher-training institutions, in the UK and Morocco. It was largely funded by the British Council initiative 'Connecting Futures' and focused on four strands: human rights, citizenship, intercultural learning and inter-faith understanding. The initiative aimed to build understanding, learning and respect between young people and educators from different cultural backgrounds.

The objective was for each school to teach about its partner community, through French, focusing on the four strands mentioned above. To that end, when each group visited the other country, they collected a box of artefacts, books, posters and realia which were used to teach about the daily life of the pupils in Khemisset and York. The classes then corresponded with each other and sent class-made books to help the process of learning. This was not intended as a 'pen-pal' exchange but rather that the children would be learning about life in their partner country through a curriculum which focused on the four strands. This was sometimes a problem for the UK teachers who, unlike their Moroccan partners, did not always have an obvious curriculum focus within which to place this work. However, music, maths, geography, art and literacy were all found to have potential and a wealth of classroom work was prepared in addition to the primary languages work.

Through reciprocal exchange visits everyone's cultural perceptions were challenged. The Moroccan teachers and tutors were as surprised about what they found in York as the educators from York were when they visited Khemisset:

> Being in this country we were able to follow, through the media, lots of signs which prove the freedom of expression, such as the anti-war march which took place in London, and seeing the posters 'Not in Our Name'.
>
> (Moroccan tutor)

> We learned about religious time – exact and prompt, and secular time – not so exact, as we experienced over the week.
>
> (English teacher)

> I was interested to see women's dress and their public demeanour and realised how many preconceived ideas I had brought with me (now firmly quashed!).
>
> (English student teacher)

The literacy hour in the York schools gave the teachers the opportunity to develop work on language awareness. The Word House Activity (Brown and Durie 2000), which is used to show how many languages have contributed to English over the centuries, was extended to include an Arabic family. In the original there is already a 'family' of French words. The use of French as the language of communication was important for different reasons. First, it gave children the opportunity to develop their language for a real purpose. Second, it gave them the opportunity to begin to develop a language of rights and responsibilities. Finally, it put the children on a more equal footing with their partners. All the children in Khemisset with whom we worked speak Arabic or Tarifit as a first language. For them, too, French is learned in school. It has to be said that the French of the children in Khemisset was much more developed than that of the York children.

Rights in daily life were also part of the learning. An English teacher commented that 'We learned some of the reasons why the women often wear the veil, some of which were unexpected'. The issue of the hijab (the term used for the traditional veil for Muslim women) is often described only in the terms of male dominance, denying the rights of women and girls to choose their clothes. One of the Moroccan teacher education tutors was upset that his wife had chosen to wear the hijab after the birth of their daughter. He would have preferred she did not. The group were fortunate to meet with the editor of a Moroccan investigative magazine published in French. A special edition (*Telquel* 2002) asked the question, 'Why is the hijab gaining ground? We see it everywhere more and more. But the reason is not necessarily because of Islamism'.

The magazine explored different views on wearing the hijab through a series of interviews with women who did, or did not, choose to wear it. Comments from wearers included: 'Wearing the veil is a gift from God' and 'Today I do not pray and I do not fast, but I continue to wear the veil in order not to shock my parents and friends'. Non-wearers said, 'The veil is a new form of feminism' and 'The veil is a negation of the female body'.

This range of views exemplifies the complexity of Moroccan society, and how important it is not to see cultural or religious groups as homogeneous or unchanging, particularly when passing on cultural and religious understanding in the classroom. It is also not always easy to identify denial of rights where there are different cultural expectations.

From the beginning, there was an emphasis on getting to know as much as possible about others' culture, faith and ways of teaching human rights and citizenship. Although the pupils in Khemisset were more familiar with the Convention on the Rights of the Child than the York children, the Moroccan teachers were impressed with the autonomy of the latter. This included the way in which children worked together, helping each other and the way in which they interacted with the teacher, all of which can be identified as the skills of human rights in action. These observations made it clear that knowledge on its own is not sufficient. The Moroccan teachers knew their pupils' knowledge of rights was greater yet without the skills, it had not been translated into action. The overwhelming impression left with the York teachers was that of commitment to learning and the desire for the right to education. The pupils in all the Khemisset schools were intent on gaining as much as possible from their school experience. The absence of high technology, glossy books and a range of teaching strategies did not seem to matter.

After one year of fairly intensive coverage of culture and faith in the York schools and human rights and democracy in the Khemisset schools, it was decided that the classroom-based work would be more effective if there was a common theme and 'food' was agreed on. This topic and its component parts may not seem extraordinary in themselves yet the whole process was about rights and responsibilities, about discussion, negotiation and consensus-building in action. In arriving at a plan, there were deep philosophical discussions between the partners about belief, culture and the right to be different. The exploration of these issues led to one of those wonderful moments when one knows there has been a genuine connection of minds and hearts.

After two years of working together, what will be the output? The groups in each country have already done many things. A board game, 'On the Right Track' (Waters 2003), developed by a York teacher, was used as part of the shared work with teachers and students from Khemisset. This has now been translated into Arabic by one of the Khemisset tutors. It will also be translated into French and it is planned to distribute sets of the game to all primary schools in Morocco. There will be a special page on the Moroccan British Council website and the UK teachers are working on a 'Big Book' based on life in Khemiset with text in Arabic, French and English. A photo pack is also being planned which will collate some of the innovative classroom work developed during the project. There is also a plan to bring the children together through video conferencing. The Centre for Global Education has produced a Human Rights Trail of York (see Box 11.1). The Khemisset visitors followed this and when the York student teachers visited them, they devised together a trail for Khemisset. In short, this initiative has generated an enormous amount of work which will carry the themes into schools and teacher education institutions in both countries for a considerable time to come.

Box 11.1 Extract from York Human Rights Trail

See if you can follow this route around York. You have a map and a simple version of the Universal Declaration of Human Rights (UDHR). There will be places to stop and link an Article from the UDHR with what you can see. Try and find something which shows you human rights 'in action' (e.g. Article 26: a right to education, a school, a library).

As you come out of St Martin's Church there is a Starbucks Coffee Shop.

What was it before it was a café?

Continue along Coney Street to Mansion House, the official residence of the Lord Mayor.

When was it built?
Is there a right associated with this?

From St Helen's Square turn right into Stonegate. On the RH side you will see the Teddy Bear Shop. There is a reused ship's figurehead propping up the corner.

Who is commemorated at number 32?
What right is linked with this?

Continue walking towards the Minster. At the crossroads of High/Low Petergate you can see the goddess Minerva, the goddess of wisdom and drama.

Minerva has the symbols of wisdom and drama with her. What are they?
If wisdom is a quality needed for implementing peace, can you think of others?

Continue into King's Square. Often street entertainment is taking place here.

Is there any today? What is it?
Can you attach a right to street entertainment?

Walk down the Shambles until you reach No. 36 on the RH side.

What is not allowed in this building?

Inside is the Chapel to St Margaret Clitherow, the wife of a butcher who openly practised Catholicism at a time when the law of the land forbade it. Go into the chapel (be respectful) to find out what happened.

When was she canonised?
Why and when was she put on trial and how was she put to death?
Which rights were abused?

(Source: Brown *et al*. 2004)

Rights and responsibilities

Human rights can be explored by young children as well as older pupils, developing a sense of justice and responsibility for themselves and others. Since human rights are universal, the global dimension is both implicit and explicit. The same rights apply to children in Botswana, Bolivia and Bhutan, and in the curriculum in primary schools it is possible to introduce rights and responsibilities through a range of curriculum areas, including history, geography, maths and Personal, Social and Health Education (PSHE) as seen in *Our World, Our Rights* (Brown and Jones 2006). It includes practical classroom activities for different subjects and for younger as well as older primary pupils. UNICEF and Save the Children have produced excellent resources for the primary classroom. For children aged from 3–7, *First Steps to Rights* (Hand 2003) has some very useful activities, including a human rights 'feely bag'. Children love the sensation of trying to guess what is in the bag and then linking it to a right. These interactive activities help teachers respond to the requirement in the Convention on the Rights of the Child that children's rights should be made 'widely known, by appropriate and active means, to adults and children alike' (Article 42).

Being active not only keeps young people healthy but can also help them learn. The Human Rights Trail mentioned above (Brown *et al*. 2004) leads participants through the streets of York, linking events, buildings and key people in the past and the present to the Universal Declaration of Human Rights. They follow a walk round the city and mark on their trail booklet what they have identified. Box 11.1 gives extracts from this walk. This has been very popular and there are versions for primary schools and English and French speaking adults. It is, of course, possible to develop a similar trail in almost any location and classroom-friendly versions of the Universal Declaration and the UN Convention on the Rights of the Child are available from the websites of the major human rights agencies such as UNICEF UK (2006c).

Starting points

Brown, M. and Jones, D. (eds) (2006) *Our World, Our Rights*, Amnesty International. This is a revised edition of the successful handbook for primary school teachers. It contains lesson plans, activities, games and case studies.

Hand, Pam (2003) *First Steps to Rights – Activities for Children Aged 3–7 Years*, UNICEFn. An important resource for introducing human rights at Foundation stage and Key Stage 1.

Human Rights in the Curriculum: a series of handbooks for secondary teachers from Amnesty International which integrates citizenship and human rights into subject areas: French (2002); Spanish (2002); History (2002); Mathematics (2004). Each handbook contains photocopiable resource sheets and comprehensive teachers' notes.

Jarvis, H. and Midwinter, C. (1999) *Talking Rights; Taking Responsibility. A Speaking and Listening Resource for Secondary English and Citizenship*, UNICEF. An excellent resource for secondary schools with a particular focus on participation.

Save the Children Fund (2000) *Partners in Rights: Creative Activities Exploring Rights and Citizenship for 7–11 Year Olds*, SCF. A very useful pack for the primary classroom.

When Rights are Left: Anti-slavery International (undated): a series of books for secondary teachers of English, geography, history and citizenship. These books introduce issues of bonded labour, trafficking and other forms of modern slavery.

Chapter 12

Diversity

Hilary Claire

Understanding and respecting differences and relating these to our common humanity.

(DfES 2005a)

Understanding the issue

Diversity is not just about differences between groups and individuals, but about 'identity'. Identity answers the questions: 'Who am I? Who is like me? Where do I belong? What do I believe in? What can I do?' Identity thus belongs to the future as much as the past since it is always in process. Different groups are not united in a single identity since we all have 'multiple identities'. Sometimes our ethnic, gendered, age related or cultural identity is paramount, at other times it may be our national identity, global identity or even democratic identity. As globalisation dissolves geographical and national boundaries it has intensified the multiple nature of identity in society. Associated with substantial movements of people, rapid communications and economic interdependence, globalisation often blurs the boundaries between ethnic and national groups.

For some people 'British identity' excludes non-Christians and minority ethnic groups (Commission on British Muslims and Islamophobia 1997). Such notions of identity feed 'the new racism' – by concentrating on religion and culture, but without mentioning the word race. Globalisation also means that identities reflect international political and environmental concerns. The political problems in the Middle East may be reflected in hostility between communities in our schools. Shortly after 9/11 I was in a nursery school where some 4-year-olds were chasing two Muslim boys. 'Osama Bin Laden,' they were yelling, 'your Dad's Osama Bin Laden.'

All human beings belong to 'the human race' and despite external markers such as skin colour there are more genetic similarities between peoples than differences. Racism is a product of history in which people who oppressed and exploited others justified their actions on the grounds of their own cultural superiority. Feelings of superiority and fear of 'otherness' have been carried forward through unexamined beliefs about people designated as of a different 'racial' group, separating out those who are believed to 'belong' in Britain, and those assumed to belong somewhere else. In addition to people of colour, people of Irish and Jewish heritage and Travellers also experience racism. In contrast to such outmoded essentialist views about 'race', everyone has ethnicity – shared cultural, religious, regional and linguistic markers of our identity in a specific community.

Even though 'race' *per se* does not exist, 'racism' is a useful term which encapsulates three different ideas. These are: i) *Institutional racism* – in which certain groups are marginalised or discriminated against (e.g. higher numbers of Caribbean boys being excluded; people of colour being underrepresented in positions of authority in school and society); ii) *Street racism* – direct abusive behaviour to individuals and groups – graffiti, name calling, personal attacks; iii) *Cultural racism* – patronising, stereotypical or hostile attitudes towards minority cultures which, although they may be officially 'celebrated', are still actually seen as 'not as good as' the majority culture. Cultural racism often results in the majority wanting minority groups to adjust and assimilate.

Islamophobia means fear and hatred of Islam. It is a particular form of racism which has arisen in the context of international terrorism and the anti-Western stance of some fundamentalist groups. To fear and hate Islam and by extension all Muslims because of political extremists, is a bit like fearing and hating Christianity and all Christians because the racist apartheid regime used the Bible to justify its stance. As the Commission on British Muslims and Islamophobia (1997) points out, it is vital to distinguish between the religion Islam, which the majority of Muslims in the world follow, and the ideas of politically motivated extremists. Islam, like other faiths, is concerned with a just and tolerant society. It is not racist to condemn violence, extremism and suicide bombing, but this should not imply condemnation of Islam *per se*.

Research by Jones (1999) and Gaine (2005) reveals the extent of racism in mainly white schools, challenging any belief that diversity and racism are only issues for 'multicultural' classrooms. It should be noted that the concept of a *trans*cultural society (rather than multicultural) more appropriately suggests a two-way traffic, a mingling of attitudes and customs. Transculturalism recognises that globalisation has brought people together – we all engage now with issues and people whose lives and experience may be very different, but are now part of our consciousness. Whatever our differences we share aspects of our common society – whether music, food, shopping, politics or literature.

Whilst multicultural practice aims to 'celebrate diversity' it can end up by stereotyping people which feeds racism rather than challenging it. We do need to understand about each other's cultural practices for mutual understanding, and all pupils need to feel that they are included in the school curriculum. However, children can feel exoticised or ignored in the normal curriculum, if 'their' festivals are only seen as one-off occasions (Claire 2001: 60).

Action for change

Throughout society, nationally and globally, individuals and groups are working to challenge stereotypes and xenophobia. As Iqbal Sacranie, Secretary General of the Muslim Council of Britain (website) wrote in his 2005 report, 'There is no need for a label "moderate". Islam means peace. It rejects all kinds of excessiveness'. Jews for Justice for Palestinians is a British organisation of Jews who oppose Israeli policies that undermine the human rights of the Palestinian people.

In Britain the Race Relations Amendment Act (Office of Public Sector Information website), which followed from the Stephen Lawrence Inquiry in 1999, put schools under a legal obligation to promote good race relations and provide full equality of opportunity for all pupils. Schools have a specific duty to draw up a race equality policy which shows how they will challenge and prevent racism and discrimination, tackle racial bias and stereotyping and promote equal opportunities for all pupils, regardless of their ethnic group. They must also take specific action to tackle any differences between racial groups in terms of their attainment levels and progress, the use of disciplinary measures, and admissions and assessment.

Moreover, there is a specific duty to establish strategies to help raise the attainment levels of those ethnic minority pupils who are underachieving. The DfES Ethnic Minority Achievement website (2006b) has a wide range of clear and relevant guidance and many links to other government sites. Look for 'Aiming High' materials on refugees, minority groups (including in mainly white schools) and travellers. Another useful website is Ethnic Minority Attainment, a resource base for teachers developed by Birmingham, Leeds and Manchester LEAs with funding from the DfES, which contains many practical ideas and links.

In addition, there are many initiatives to promote greater acceptance of cultural diversity. The Kick It Out project (see website), for example, is a national project to confront racism in sport, sponsored by the major football clubs. There are also many initiatives at national and local authority level which acknowledge the contribution of Black Britons in UK society. For example, see the websites of the Science Museum, Berkshire Family History, Black History Month, Origination and 100 Great Black Britons. Where such work is simply relegated to Black History Month, criticisms of tokenism are justified, although this may be a good starting point for teachers new to the area.

Good practice

Self-esteem

Siraj-Blatchford and Clarke (2000) emphasise the necessity for children in the Early Years to learn tolerance and respect from the adults around them. However, they point out that to 'treat everyone the same', when there are real differences in gender, religion, ethnicity and language, is in fact discriminatory. Young children need to learn to pay attention to other people's points of view, communicate positively and effectively, and cooperate. It is essential to involve parents in policy development on equality and diversity and teachers may need to speak to parents of children who make offensive discriminatory remarks to ensure that they understand the school policy for equality.

Teachers are at the forefront of dealing with the diversity of identities through strategies which build tolerance and mutual respect in young people. The other side of the coin is that when personal and collective identity feels threatened, people may retreat defensively or become aggressive. Adolescents are particularly prone to such responses (INSTED website). As a child or adult, it's painful and damaging to feel that who you are is disrespected by others – whether it's what you look like, what you believe in or who your family and community are. One way to counter this is by developing positive self-esteem in pupils. To feel good about yourself and have a positive sense of identity – a feeling of belonging and being valued – can make the difference between openness and tolerance of others and belligerence and hostility.

A primary school in London decided to survey all of Key Stage 1 to find out about their attitudes to themselves and to school. Noting the number of children who reported that they sometimes experienced 'unkind words' (some of which it would be safe to assume would be racist, given hostilities in the community), the senior staff organised a 'Friendship Week' for the whole school which addressed some of the issues that had arisen. This was a proactive week with a Theatre in Education group running workshops for the pupils, with children learning songs and games.

In another class a Year 4 teacher helped turn round hostile attitudes which included elements of racism and sexism with a simple game. Every day a pupil's name would be pulled out of a hat. The teacher made sure that the first few names were popular children so that they could model the kinds of things that could be included in a very positive climate. The child would leave the room while the others brainstormed all the good things they could say about her. These were scribed by the teacher who facilitated the brainstorm by asking them to think in categories such as work, art or music, concentration, sport, helpfulness, tries hard, etc. The child came back in and the children read out all their positive statements. The child then made a shield which represented what had been said. This continued till every child had been included and the display board filled with positive shields.

Curriculum opportunities

There are many opportunities for teachers to address multiple identities and trans-culturalism, to build positive identities and mutual understanding, and to encourage young people to engage actively with anti-racist work. Here are examples from Citizenship, History and Religious Education (RE).

Citizenship

The KS1 and 2 guidelines on Citizenship and the KS3 and 4 statutory curricula, all recognise the importance of valuing different identities and communities and challenging racism. Two examples of teaching about diversity within the Citizenship curriculum follow.

A classroom activity to illuminate multiple identities involves the teacher giving pupils 5 or 6 post-its each. Individually, they write a couple of words about themselves on each one, using the following categories (alter or add as appropriate). They can use several post-its for any category.

- Relationships
- Things I'm good at
- Things I enjoy out of school
- What I believe
- Places I have connections with
- My personality
- My goals or ambitions.

Then in groups of four they play a game similar to rummy. One person starts with a post-it in the middle of the table, and the others put down a post-it, either to match it or to which they think it has links. After all the post-its have been laid out the teacher helps the groups to create larger sets, joining up smaller sets and discussing overarching categories. This game works with people of all ages, including adults, though characteristics and discussion of categories will be significantly more sophisticated. The outcome is the same – you learn about other people, you consider your own characteristics and individuality, and you realise the many ways in which we share interests or background. The example shown in Figure 12.1 is from a Year 2 group.

A second example shows how teachers can help children understand stereotypes. These may represent a necessary shorthand for making sense of the world, but people who think stereotypically do not make good learners. Mathematically, the logic of stereotyping can be expressed as: all Xs are Y. This is an X therefore it is a Y. It's the 'all' in the first statement that creates the problem. This breaks down as soon as you acknowledge that only *some* Xs are Ys. If being an X is very distinctive, and you don't know much about X other than something equally distinctive (called Y) then you may believe, for example, that all girls are interested in dolls, all boys love football and all Jewish people refuse pork.

Now change 'all' to 'some' – instantly there are people who don't fit your stereotype. You will need to ask, not assume. This X may be a Catholic, but he may accept birth control. This woman wears a hijab, but doesn't necessarily support fundamentalists. This Iranian may be a refugee, not a supporter of the current regime in Iran. In the interests of clear thinking and to counter stereotypes we need to find every opportunity we can to keep pressing this logic in the classroom. Numbers matter too. With children, to consolidate the concept, there will be opportunities to quantify and provide visual support using Venn diagrams. For example, how many girls really do love playing with dolls, or might prefer to join the football game? How many children from all cultural and faith backgrounds love fish and chips? Of

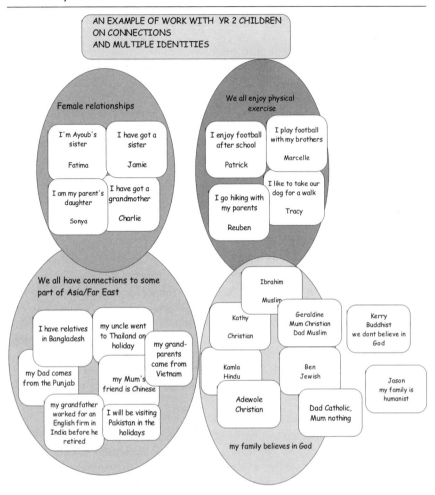

Figure 12.1 Connections and identities

roughly 1,000 million Muslims in the world, by far the majority have no sympathy with fundamentalist Islamic sects.

History

History is a particularly powerful vehicle for developing attitudes about diversity and social justice. As the QCA (2006b) points out, history helps pupils:

- gain experiences that help them to make connections between themselves, their communities and the wider world
- develop awareness and understanding of a range of peoples and cultures and a respect for many different attitudes, views and beliefs

- recognise the need for a just and equitable society and their own role in making this possible
- explore current issues within an historical context to make sense of the world around them and develop the skills and attitudes necessary for active involvement as citizens.

A Year 5 class in a London school researched black footballers in the past as part of Black History Month. This was a community project organised by the Head and their own teachers, in which they liaised with the local football club which was affiliated to the campaign to kick racism out of football. The class went to the club where they learned more about black footballers in earlier decades and, in the process, developed their own ICT and literacy skills through the preparation of material to take back to their school.

Year 3 commemorated Black History Month with detailed work on Harriet Tubman, the black activist who led slaves from the southern states of America to freedom in the north on the so-called 'Underground Railway'. They presented their work to teachers and parents in the school assembly and made a book which was 'published' in multiple copies and given to each class for their book box. In another school, children in Year 4 each chose a person they wanted to research for Black History Month and scripted a short drama about this person's life, which they presented to the whole school. Memorably, one girl researched and then dressed up as Sojourner Truth and proclaimed the famous 'Ain't I a woman?' speech at assembly.

Even very young children can begin to learn about significant people from history. The nursery and reception classes in a different borough found out about Rosa Parks in the USA. Their teacher told the children the story of how Rosa was thrown off a bus when she refused to move from the 'whites only' seats. Then they made a bus in their role play area, using chairs. One child took the role of the bus driver who ejected Rosa, another was Rosa herself and others were passengers, white and black. In this multicultural school, white children were as avid as black children to protest against Rosa's treatment and support her.

In work with a Year 2 class on significant people (not part of Black History Month), two parallel classes learned about three different individuals – Ruby Bridges, who at 6 years old was part of integrating schools in the 1960s in the southern states, Bessie Coleman, the first black female aviator, and Frederick Douglass. This work included role play and hot seating with the teacher taking the roles of Ruby, Bessie and Frederick. Through this work, the children discussed historical situations of racism and how it had been challenged – by white and black people – and voiced their own experiences and commitment to anti-racist action (Claire 2002).

In Year 6, as part of their work on Britain since the 1930s, two parallel classes chose to find out about the role of Commonwealth soldiers in WWII and the experience of Commonwealth immigrants to Britain in the post war years. Again, children researched historical instances of racism, and through this, explored their own attitudes and commitment. Like the work on significant people, this was not for Black History Month, but a decision by senior staff and teachers about the interpretation of the History curriculum to take an inclusive approach. The BBC resource (Claire 2006b) has several suggestions about how to permeate the primary History curriculum rather than do 'add-on' work for one small part of the year.

Religious education

Rather than celebrations of difference, teachers who move beyond specific rituals and look for overarching principles in religious and ethical belief systems help their pupils consider our common humanity. Issues for both monocultural and multicultural schools may span a wide spectrum. The following quotation from a headteacher is thought-provoking:

> Unfortunately, the anti-semitism amongst a significant minority of our parents, as well as the racism demonstrated by some new arrivals to this country have made the need to tackle such issues very important – again – but in some ways more difficult because we are now dealing with asylum seekers and refugees who voice opinions which we find unacceptable. There is also quite a lot of 'you're not a good Muslim' from some parents and children directed at non-Hijab wearing girls etc. We have also recently discovered children being told that they will go to hell if they are not Muslims.
>
> (Personal communication 2006)

Promoting respect and tolerance requires attending to prior experience, stereotypes and oversimplifications, not avoiding them, and appreciating that some children may hold narrow views about religious and cultural affiliation. History tells us that newly arrived communities may have identities and allegiances which will be modified through their children and grandchildren. In contrast to the simplifications and stereotypes that some resources embody, Eleanor Nesbitt's research (2004) indicates how families within minority cultures respond to their new environments. People start to celebrate Christmas and birthdays and alter their dietary regimes. Life is more fluid than the orthodox textbook versions suggest. Typically, resources and celebrations deny the diversity of belief and practices *within* any particular community. There is seldom space for children – or their parents – to say, 'Yes we are Jews, or Muslims, or Sikhs, but we don't do things like that in our family!' Even while celebrating the culture, multiculturalism often exoticises communities as 'not like us', concentrating on differences in music, food, clothes and celebrations, especially in Early Years work.

The RE curriculum, which emphasises learning 'from' and not just 'about' religions, aims to counter this problem, but may not get to the much deeper roots of hostility and racism if these attitudes are not recognised and are allowed to fester away under the surface. For example, a Year 2 teacher realised with dismay that her carefully planned lesson on the Jewish Sabbath was being undermined by a small group of Muslim boys whispering 'people of the devil' to each other. A student teacher, asked to find out and tell his class about Judaism, summed up his views in the following stereotype: 'Jews believe they are the chosen people. They worship one God. Women are separated from men in the synagogue.' Both oversimplified and misleading about reform or liberal Jews, such a statement could potentially feed or provoke hostile responses.

In contrast, Linda Whitworth (2004) describes strategies to counter ignorance, misunderstandings and prejudice against any religious group. This involves inviting someone from the faith group itself to talk honestly and openly to children, and encouraging the pupils to ask about things they don't understand or want information about. Whitworth describes how a practising adult Muslim in the classroom talking directly to the children provided personal stories and explanations, and dealt with questions. A young student, Fatima, was able to explain at first-hand, why she wore the hijab in public, to a mainly non-Muslim Year 5 group. A Muslim neighbour was invited to talk to Year 4 about the meaning and importance of the Five Pillars of Islam.

Increasingly, rather than concentrating on just one 'festival', schools are looking for overarching symbolic ways to be inclusive about culture and religious practices, in whole school projects. All members of the child and adult community contribute recipes and there are opportunities to cook and eat the foods, learn and perform dances and songs, and explore the variety of ways in which people celebrate light, or peace, or sunshine, or harvest, or the end of winter, *across* faiths and cultures. It may mean you can't 'do Divali' (the Hindu festival of lights) in two sessions but that Divali would become part of a larger exploration of the importance of light for our lives, whatever our faith or secular heritage.

Cultural racism

Cultural racists (see above) may know quite a lot about 'another culture' but that doesn't mean they think it has any merit compared to their own. In fact, the superiority of their own ways of doing things may just be confirmed. If, instead of multicultural celebration, we looked at a curriculum which acknowledged interwoven cultures and histories, we might be better placed to develop positive attitudes and mutual understandings. It is not just that a very large number of people actually have connections to the wider world – but that looking for opportunities to acknowledge multiple identities builds bridges rather than barriers.

This requires that we explore the shared human qualities that exist across the varied communities found in Britain. This means moving away from idealised versions of 'their culture' in publications which oversimplify and stereotype, and permeating the curriculum with an inclusive agenda (Claire 2006a). Maths, art, and design and technology can all draw inspiration from batiks, kente cloth, beadwork, sculpture and modern political art from Africa. Going back in time, the Egyptian and the Mayan pyramids, the extraordinary interior of the Alhambra built by Muslims before they were excluded from Spain in 1492, the Taj Mahal built by Shah Jehan, the floating cities and irrigation systems of the Aztecs, the Great Wall of China and the monumental stone structures of Great Zimbabwe represent significant cultural and scientific achievements from outside Europe.

Recently, because of the threats of war, we have been alerted to the heritage of sculptors from Mesopotamia (now Iraq) who made the magnificent friezes commemorating their rulers' victories (Artlex website). The Greek sculptures and Egyptian treasures in the British Museum are well known, but the bronzes and sculptures of Benin craftsworkers in the sixteenth century are also there, not just as evidence of historical conquest, but of the genius of people whose culture and talents are largely ignored in the West. All this is accessible through the British Museum website for those who cannot take their students there in person.

I have mentioned the possibilities of permeating the History curriculum but there are other curriculum opportunities to challenge cultural racism. The mathematical knowledge of Middle Eastern people who established our number system, scientific inventions of African Americans like Garrett Morgan who invented traffic lights or Lewis Latimer who invented the filaments for light bulbs, and the survival and tracking skills of Australian Aborigines or South African San people all challenge cultural racism, and help children appreciate the diversity of cultural achievements.

With younger children, there are opportunities to move from exoticising minority cultures, to acknowledging how far our lives have become intermingled, through quite conventional work on the food which is now available in any supermarket and in most market stores – the spices that are used for curry, and the fruits and vegetables which come from abroad.

Fiction, poetry, drama and music all help children recognise commonalities, as well as acknowledge differences. Theatre in Education projects exist in many parts of the UK and will bring drama into schools which allows children to empathise with the pain of racism, as well as reconsider their own attitudes. Through a source such as Letterbox Library (see website) it is easy to obtain material which features Black children in ordinary domestic settings, not celebrating any special religious ceremony, but just going to school, dealing with a new baby in the family, or facing up to changing friendships or the challenges of adolescence. Such books are not just for minority children, they are for everyone, even more so in monocultural communities, where minimal personal contact with children from minorities only serves to succour stereotypes and misunderstandings.

Linking with a school in a nearby town or with a very different community within the same LEA can be a powerful educational experience, for both schools, as a case study from Oldham facilitated by Manchester Development Education Project (2006b) describes. Westwood Primary, an inner city school in Oldham with 99.9 per cent of pupils of Bangladeshi heritage, linked with Holy Trinity Primary, a rural school with pupils almost entirely of White British heritage. Lancashire Global Education Centre sponsored a similar link between urban, multicultural St Mathew's School in Preston, and White rural, Tarleton Holy Trinity. Children sent each other Christmas and Eid cards, studied maps of each other's location, considered issues of racism and finally visited one another. All this contributed to children understanding more about a different community whose members actually lived quite nearby.

Global school linking is actively encouraged by the DfES (2006c). Teachers need to be aware of the pitfalls of such partnerships, however. Children can assume that one school in India is representative of all India and there is a danger of reinforcing stereotypes about developing countries. The UK One World Linking Association (website) also warns against the 'feel-good' and essentially patronising attitudes that linking can sustain when it is regarded as an opportunity for charity – 'How can an equal partnership evolve when one partner is the recipient of charitable giving from the other? True partnership means that both partners are changed by the relationship'. Not only should pupils be asked to examine taken-for-granted attitudes about Western values but linking should be within an economic and political context which focuses on the causes of inequality and recognises that, unlike short-term charity, raising awareness and taking action against it can contribute much more in the long term.

Starting points

Claire, H. (ed.) (2004) *Teaching Citizenship in Primary Schools*, Exeter: Learning Matters. Most chapters refer to issues of diversity and inclusion but see, in particular, the chapters on RE and History with Citizenship.

Claire, H. (2006b) *Black Britons: from Romans to the Second World War*, London: BBC Active/Pearson. Teacher's activities book with DVD. Contains a variety of suggestions about integrating Black history into the KS2 curriculum with classroom activities.

Richardson, R. (2004) *Here, There and Everywhere: belonging, identity and equality in schools*, Derbyshire Advisory and Inspection Service, Stoke-on-Trent: Trentham Books. Useful and practical material which can be used for staff meetings, e.g. how to deal with playground racism, grids for each curriculum area to audit and monitor inclusive practice. Has an excellent resource section.

Richardson, R. and Wood, A. (2000) *Inclusive Schools, Inclusive Society: race and iidentity on the agenda*, Stoke-on-Trent: Trentham Books. Mainly addresses issues to do with inclusion of young African Caribbean pupils, but contains extremely helpful chapters about the concepts of race and identity. It summarises curriculum work and positive management of relationships in schools endeavouring to be inclusive.

Siraj-Blatchford, I. and Clarke, P. (2000) *Supporting Identity, Diversity and Language in the Early Years*, Buckingham: Open University Press. Important and helpful guide to good practice, including stages in which this can be developed and a chart of good practice for multicultural settings and diversity.

Training and Development Agency for Schools, http://www.multiverse.ac.uk. Excellent site sponsored by TDA for raising achievement in multi-ethnic schools, with links to official reports on e.g. race equality practice, schemes of work, reviews, articles.

Chapter 13

Global citizenship

Julia Tanner

Gaining the knowledge, skills and understanding of concepts and institutions necessary to become informed, active, responsible citizens.

(DfES 2005a)

Understanding the issue

Citizenship is a highly complex and contested concept. In its narrowest sense, citizenship refers to a legal status in relation to a particular sovereign nation state, conferring particular rights and responsibilities on the individuals with that status. In many countries in the industrialised West, definitions of citizenship are underpinned by Marshall's (1950) conception of citizenship as consisting of legal, political and social rights. However, contemporary political and social theorists have suggested that true citizenship involves not just formal rights, but also real participation in the life of local communities and the nation state, and have explored how some groups and individuals are excluded from social and economic activity, and from the political processes that might challenge the status quo which perpetuates their exclusion (e.g. Lister 1997; Commission on the Future of Multi-ethnic Britain 2000). Janoski (1998) argues that the right to participation in civic society is as important as legal, political and social rights. Other commentators have argued that narrow concepts of national citizenship have become outdated in the twenty-first century, where local communities and nation states have become more diverse through global population movements, and where many citizens now have multiple loyalties and identities. Held (1996) therefore proposes a model of 'cosmopolitan democracy', which acknowledges the interlinking local, national and global aspects of contemporary citizenship.

The argument that in an increasingly globalised world, where humankind faces globalised problems, we need to start thinking of ourselves as global citizens (e.g. Boulding 1990; Kelly 1995; Osler and Vincent 2002; Oxfam 2006a; Shallcross and Robinson 2006) is particularly strong. Thus Kelly argues:

> Positive views of citizenship ... have sought to transcend nationalism, to seek for unity in the notion of shared humanity and to define citizenship as international citizenship. ... The current emphasis on individualism that is divorced from any

collective, democratic responsibility, on competitivism rather than co-operation, on market forces rather than social policy as a solution to social problems ... is leading society away from democracy as well as away from the concept of citizenship.

(Kelly 1995: 183)

In an excellent introduction to the idea of global citizenship, Nigel Dower examines the ethical, social and political arguments for and against the view that we are global citizens, emphasising, in particular, the moral dimension. He suggests that the global citizen is someone who adopts the value perspective that 'all human beings have certain fundamental rights and all human beings have duties to respect and promote these rights' (Dower 2003: 7).

In an important contribution to the debate about the nature of contemporary citizenship, Osler and Starkey (2003) point out that these new broader understandings of citizenship have implications for citizenship education. They propose a reconceptualised education for 'cosmopolitan citizenship' which acknowledges the reality that:

Processes of globalisation and increased interdependence mean that no one, wherever they live in the world, can remain completely isolated within a single nation. All human lives are increasingly influenced by events in other parts of the world. One of the most visible manifestations of this is that local communities have become more diverse. If democracy is now re-conceptualised as cosmopolitan, then the actors within the democracy are, by extension, cosmopolitan citizens.

(Osler and Starkey 2003: 245–6)

As implied by Osler and Starkey, if citizenship is a complex and contested concept, then citizenship education is also an area of controversy and sometimes heated debate (Heater 2001, Osler and Starkey 2005, Halsted and Pike 2006). Historically, narrow conceptions of citizenship education have focused on education *about* citizenship (e.g. constitutional history, political institutions, the rights and responsibilities of citizens etc.) and were largely concerned with producing politically literate citizens. Broader conceptions of citizenship education relate to education *for* citizenship, emphasising the need to nurture active citizens with a commitment to certain value positions and the ability to act as autonomous, critically reflective individuals who participate in political debate and campaign actively for change where they deem it appropriate (Halsted and Pike 2006: 40). This is reflected in the anticipated attainment level for a majority of pupils in England at the end of compulsory schooling (i.e. age 16):

Pupils have a comprehensive knowledge and understanding of: the topical events they study; the rights, responsibilities and duties of citizens; the role of the voluntary sector; forms of government; provision of public services; and the criminal and legal systems. They obtain and use different kinds of information, including the media, to form and express an opinion. They evaluate the effectiveness of different ways of bringing about change at different levels of society. Pupils take part effectively in school and community-based activities, showing a willingness and commitment to evaluate such activities critically. They demonstrate personal and group responsibility in attitudes to themselves and others.

(QCA/DfEE 1999: 31)

Global citizenship initiatives are firmly in this broader tradition, reflecting the reality that pupils must be prepared not only with knowledge, but also with the skills and values necessary to face and respond to the challenges of the twenty-first century. Contemporary economic, social and political trends mean that individuals, communities, nation states and supranational institutions are increasingly bound together in an interdependent globalised web of complex connections and interactions, and that many local communities and nation states are more diverse. At the same time, we face unprecedented issues of environmental sustainability, such as climate change and resource depletion, and social and economic injustice, which could, ultimately, threaten the survival of humankind on planet Earth.

Action for change

Millions of people around the world are already thinking and behaving as active global citizens, campaigning and taking practical action to fight injustice and inequality, and improve the lives of others. In the past too there were important international movements, such as those to abolish slavery, to limit the nuclear arms race, and to end apartheid in South Africa. Today, the need for people to act together across national boundaries is ever more urgent. The major issues facing humankind, such as global warming, environmental degradation, resource depletion, extreme poverty, acute health inequalities, religious sectarianism, human rights abuse, global economic instability and political oppression, all require concerted international action if they are to be adequately addressed.

Throughout the world, concerned individuals are involved in initiatives to promote international and intercultural understanding, active in international solidarity campaigns, and engaged in practical projects to improve the life chances, choices and opportunities of other people in far-flung places. In addition, there are many organisations working internationally to protect the environment, challenge economic, social and political injustice, and support positive change in deprived communities.

The interdependence between the local and global is encapsulated in the phrase 'act locally, think globally'. We all have the opportunity to make small life changes, such as buying fairly traded goods, reducing our car use, recycling materials, or taking energy conservation measures, which make a contribution to tackling major world issues. The next section provides some examples of how the 'act locally, think globally' principle is embedded in effective education for global citizenship.

Issues of international development are finally becoming mainstream in the first years of the twenty-first century. The United Nation's Millennium Development Goals, the Commission for Africa and the Make Poverty History campaign all reflect the growing understanding amongst politicians and people alike that global inequalities and injustices must be addressed. In the United Kingdom, the Department for International Development has been active in promoting development education in schools and in civic society through the 'Building Support for Development' strategy and the Development Awareness Fund. A major element of this strategy is to provide opportunities for the citizens of all ages to gain real understanding of global and development issues, enabling them to make connections between their own lives and those of people elsewhere in the world, and to have the knowledge, skills and confidence to make informed choices for positive change.

As described in Chapter 1, many educators, including academics, classroom teachers and development education agencies, have championed a global dimension in the curriculum. In recent years in the United Kingdom, much of this effort has coalesced around the concept of education for global citizenship.

This concept has been most fully elaborated by the Oxfam education team in *Education for Global Citizenship: a guide for schools* (Oxfam 2006a). In this a global citizen is defined as someone who:

- is aware of the wider world and has a sense of their own role as a world citizen
- respects and values diversity
- has an understanding of how the world works
- is outraged by social injustice
- participates in the community at a range of levels, from the local to the global
- is willing to act to make the world a more equitable and sustainable place
- takes responsibility for their actions.

(Oxfam 2006a: 3)

Oxfam proposes a curriculum for global citizenship which includes three elements – knowledge and understanding, skills, and values and attitudes.

The *knowledge and understanding* element comprises five critical concepts: social justice and equity, diversity, globalisation and interdependence, sustainable development, and peace and conflict. Taken together these are key organising concepts for understanding how the world works, for exploring how the global is part of our everyday lives, and for understanding how our local actions have global implications.

The vital *skills* sets identified are: critical thinking, the ability to argue effectively, the ability to challenge injustice and inequalities, respect for people and things, and skills in co-operation and conflict resolution. These skills are all essential for informed and truly participatory citizenship at local, national and global levels.

The *values and attitudes* include: developing a sense of identity and self-esteem, empathy and a sense of common humanity, a commitment to social justice and equity, valuing and respecting diversity, concern for the environment and commitment to sustainable development, and, critically, the belief that people can make a difference. These are all aspects of pupils' personal, social and moral development, and are vital elements in an education that fully prepares children and young people for the opportunities and challenges of adult life in the twenty-first century.

The examples provided in the next section illustrate the development of these key elements of effective global citizenship work in schools.

Good practice

The Crick Report, *Education for Citizenship and the Teaching of Democracy in Schools* (1998), became the blueprint for the compulsory citizenship curriculum in Key Stages 3 and 4 and the framework underpinning the Key Stages 1 and 2 non-statutory guidelines in England. It identifies three main strands in citizenship education – political literacy, social and moral responsibility, and community involvement. The report and the consequent curriculum guidelines have been criticised as marginalising the international dimension, but as Brownlie (2001) demonstrates, these three strands are significant in developing global as well as national citizenship.

Crick defines *political literacy* as knowledge and understanding for becoming an informed citizen. This includes understanding how the political system works in Britain and also developing the skills of enquiry and communication which will make citizens effective in the life of the nation. Politically literate global citizens need to know about international political institutions, such as the United Nations and the World Bank, and to understand their role and function. They also need to understand how social, economic, religious, cultural and political processes are intertwined and how they operate in an increasingly globalised world. They need to understand the critical challenges facing humankind, and accept their responsibility for working towards finding sustainable solutions to these challenges. The skills of enquiry and communication are important for effective citizenship at local, national and global levels.

Crick suggests that *social and moral responsibility* is concerned with developing self-confidence, and socially and morally responsible behaviour towards people in authority and each other, considering problems in society originating in political, spiritual, moral, social and cultural differences, understanding and empathising with points of view or experience other than one's own, and expressing personal opinions.

In the global context, this means pupils accepting that they have responsibilities towards other people and to the planet which is humankind's home. They also need to understand that their actions may have consequences for other people in far-flung places, and for the environment. They need to be aware of and sensitive to diversity, and open-minded in their response to differences of view arising from diverse life experiences. They need to be able to empathise with people whose lives may be very different to their own, due to their social, political, cultural and economic circumstances. They need to be able to formulate and express informed personal opinions in a way that respects difference and democratic debate.

The third strand in the Crick Report relates to *community involvement*, including developing the skills of participation and responsible action in school and community, and learning about the role of community and voluntary groups, the media, and European and global issues.

Education for global citizenship offers many opportunities for community involvement at local, national and international levels. Children and young people in school can participate in practical projects such as tree-planting or energy conservation; in intercultural exchange through school twinning or international visits; or through campaigning on global issues.

Participation, engagement and action

In education for global citizenship, *how* pupils learn is seen as being as significant as *what* they learn. Typical classroom approaches include active teaching and learning strategies such as simulations, games, brainstorming, discussion and debate, role play, communities of enquiry, ranking exercises, fieldwork, guest speakers, problem-solving, drama, research, small group presentations, and the use of many different types of resources – photographs, information texts, statistics, reports, the internet, music, personal testimony, DVDs and videos, etc. These approaches are used because active, experiential and participatory approaches motivate pupils, engage their interest, and provide memorable experiences which encourage deeper learning.

As the Oxfam Development Education team point out in a recent publication (Oxfam 2006g), participatory methodologies are now established best practice in education, and are not unique to global citizenship work. They also emphasise the importance of the process of learning for developing pupil autonomy and critical thinking skills, stating that:

Education for global citizenship offers a process by which young people can

- absorb new information
- judge its bias and reliability
- analyse it
- synthesise it through a process of reflection on their own current views
- draw their conclusions
- make informed choices
- take considered action.

(Oxfam 2006g: 2)

Active, participatory and experiential approaches are also important for authentic learning. Authentic learning activities are those which have real purposes, audiences and outcomes, and as the Crick Report makes clear, authenticity is a critical characteristic of effective citizenship education. If we want pupils to participate, and develop a sense of agency and responsibility, then they need opportunities to work in real-life contexts, to engage with genuine issues, to take action and to have an impact (Claire 2004: 12). An interesting example of primary children taking local action in response to a real local and global problem was reported in *The Times Educational Supplement*:

> Kings Norton Primary School in Birmingham has not only managed to fit Safe Routes to Schools into its curriculum – its pupils are influencing the decisions of local politicians.
>
> Transport is a huge issue for the school, which is situated on the busy Pershore Road, a main arterial route through south Birmingham, with traffic jams, heavy lorries thundering past, and frequent accidents. Children were asked to complete on-line surveys on how they came to school and the information was used as part of the school's travel plan. The survey highlighted real issues for those walking to school. A main pathway was blocked with overgrown ivy, and drivers were parking on double yellow lines opposite the school, causing a hazard to the children crossing the road.
>
> Kings Norton School Council was invited to put its case to Birmingham City councillors. The pathway has now been cleared, and some of the children's suggestions have been incorporated into a transport consultation for the area. 'I think it's brilliant', said the senior teacher responsible for citizenship. 'They've developed confidence in talking in an adult environment and in expressing their opinions in a way that understands that people have to make priorities.'
>
> (*The TES* 2004: 28)

The need for genuine pupil participation in decision-making represents a challenge to the traditional patterns of authority and power in schools, but as Osler and Starkey point out, effective citizenship education must recognise children as citizens now rather than merely 'citizens in waiting' (2005: 43) and so must draw upon pupils' own interests and perspectives. They stress the need for 'listening schools', where the principles of democracy and participation are institutionalised within school structures, not simply taught as abstract concepts.

Fair Trade Schools

Many schools find that the issue of fair trade provides a practical starting point for education for global citizenship. There are a number of reasons for this. First, learning about fair trade enables pupils to see the connection between their everyday activities, e.g. buying chocolate, and the lives of other people in distant parts of the world. Second, most children and young people have a strong sense of fairness and can readily understand the principle that the people who grow our food and make our clothes and other things we need should be paid a fair price for their products and labour. Third, fair trade is an issue where everyone can make a difference. Individuals and organisations can use their power as consumers to support fair trade products, thereby promoting decent pay and working conditions for workers in poorer countries, and can campaign for change in international trading practices. Fourth, there are many excellent resources available to support teachers who want to incorporate fair trade issues in their teaching. These include resources for all age groups and most subject areas, and exemplify the principles of active and participative learning. A very useful list of websites and classroom resources can be found in the *Fair Trade School Handbook* (Dalrymple n.d.) published by Leeds Development Education Centre.

The Fair Trade Schools Project provides some examples of good practice. The Project worked with eleven primary, secondary and special schools in the Leeds area and had three aims – to incorporate fair trade in a curriculum, take practical action to support fair trade, and to ensure that the fair trade message was communicated to the wider school community. The project culminated in the publication of a handbook which offers guidance to teachers and school leaders who want their school to become a 'fair trade school'. The Head of Geography in one secondary school describes how she addressed the three project aims:

> The basis of the fair trade work that I have carried out at school has been a group of enthusiastic pupils. They are currently in Y10 but began the work in Y9 ... These pupils have taken the lead in organising events and assemblies.
>
> I tried to identify different areas in which we could include fair trade in the geography curriculum. I used a great resource called 'The Chocolate Game' which pupils found very entertaining and it really helped them to see the inequalities involved in trade. I was also keen to have a school-wide event and took advantage of a poetry competition organised by Divine Chocolate. The fair trade group designed a powerpoint presentation to show at an assembly and I distributed a fair trade video and teaching materials to the geography department. This meant that all the pupils learnt about fair trade during assembly and a lesson. They were encouraged to enter the competition by the English department and I received some outstanding entries ... The pupils also ran a stall at parents' evening when they gave out chocolate and informally chatted to them about fair trade.
>
> (Dalrymple n.d.: 10)

Monahan (2006) reports that a significant number of schools now run co-operatives which offer fair-trade goods, with a turnover in excess of £100,000 annually. Such pupil-led enterprises enable pupils to develop many business and interpersonal skills, and also to learn that there is more to business than profit. As Harriet Lamb from the Fairtrade Foundation comments,

> What they are going to do with any dividends is one of the trickiest discussions young co-operative members will have to undertake. The aim of any business is to make a profit, but the wonderful citizenship lesson here is being part of something with a strong social worth, not only because of what they do with their surplus cash, but also understanding the difference buying fairtrade can mean for farmers in developing countries.
>
> (quoted in Monahan 2006: 27)

School linking

In the United Kingdom there is a long tradition of town twinning. Many towns are twinned with one or more towns, often in Europe. The focus of these twinning arrangements is usually intercultural understanding fostered through exchange visits of groups of citizens, including teachers. In many secondary schools there are long-standing arrangements through which modern foreign language departments organise mutually beneficial pupil exchange visits with partnered European schools. During these visits pupils typically live with the family of their exchange partner and attend school with them, thus experiencing daily life in the country of the language that they are learning. Although the main aim of such visits is to provide pupils with an intensive experience of immersion in the target language, opportunities for developing knowledge and understanding of a different culture are also seen as important.

The last decade has seen the rise of a new movement promoting school linking between schools in the UK and in the less economically developed countries of the South. North–South school linking is strongly promoted by the government as a means of promoting the global dimension in the curriculum (DfEE 2005a), and there is an aspiration for every school to develop such a link. At its best North-South school linking can make learning more powerful and meaningful, by enabling pupils in both schools to communicate and find out about each other's lives. This authentic contact can provide relevance and reality, enriching many areas of the curriculum, offering real-life case study material and making otherwise abstract concepts such as interdependence more concrete. It undoubtedly has potential to foster active global citizens of the future through engaging pupils in their learning. As Temple (2006) argues, school linking can:

- Bring a global dimension to teaching
- Foster genuine understanding of the lives of people in other countries
- Challenge stereotypes and narrow perceptions in a real and lasting way
- Help pupils to celebrate and value the diversity of ways of life in the world today
- Help pupils and teachers to realise that we have as much to learn from others, as we have to learn about others
- Lead to friendships between pupils and teachers, across the world, and genuine solidarity in working together for a better world.

There are, however, many potential pitfalls and challenges associated with North–South school linking, as pointed out by Clare Short, then Secretary of State for International Development, in a speech to the Secondary Heads Association in April 1999.

> I want every school in the country to have the opportunity to develop a link with a school in South. Some of the most exciting development education work in schools results from links with schools in developing countries. Linking is an

area which needs great care. I am not interested in links which are one-sided, or which are based simply on charity because they do not create mutual respect and learning. But where links are based on equality and mutual learning, and on a genuine commitment to both sides, the results can be remarkable.

(Short 1999)

Indeed, as Temple warns, school linking is not something to be approached lightly. It is, she says:

A demanding, complicated and time-consuming process that doesn't automatically lead to good global citizenship education. A bad school link, one undertaken without enough thought or preparation, is worse than none at all.

(Temple 2006)

A damaging school link is one which fuels negative stereotypes. In exchanging information about their lives, UK pupils may focus on their possessions and consumer lifestyle, and develop a sense of material/economic superiority, which can easily transmute into feelings of intellectual or moral superiority (Graves 2002). This, of course, is counterproductive to the aims of education for global citizenship, which seeks to build mutual respect for diversity. To counteract this possibility, teachers need to ensure that the chosen activities suit and enrich the curriculum in both schools, emphasising the value of sharing perspectives and learning from one another (see also Chapter 14).

Experience suggests that school linking arrangements falter if the partners do not spend enough time considering or sharing their motives with one another, or fail to work through practical issues such as how to secure the resources (human, financial and other) to set-up and sustain the link long term. However, there is now an emerging body of best practice in relation to school linking, and *A Quick Guide to North–South School Links* (Leeds DEC n.d.) provides invaluable advice on establishing an effective and mutually beneficial link, and avoiding the common pitfalls. It recommends a detailed process of thinking about, planning, negotiating, agreeing and evaluating a link, through a framework of five questions, offering practical guidance in relation to each stage.

Starting points

Action Aid (2003) *Get Global! A skills-based approach to active global citizenship.* Funded jointly by Action Aid, CAFOD, Christian Aid, Oxfam, Save the Children and DfID, this major publication provides a unique six step method for developing active global citizenship in any subject area.

DEED (2005) *To Begin at the Beginning: Bringing A Global Dimension to the Early Years.* This substantial handbook for early years practitioners from Development Education East Dorset provides practical ideas for developing young children's knowledge and understanding of global issues across the Foundation Stage curriculum and includes an extensive resource list.

Leeds Development Education Centre (2005) *Global School Guide.* A practical booklet offering realistic advice to teachers and school leaders who want to embed the global dimension in both the curriculum and ethos of their school.

Oxfam (2006a) *Education for Global Citizenship: A Guide for Schools.* An indispensable guide to education for global citizenship, providing a rationale and definition of global citizenship, and detailing progression in knowledge and understanding, skills, and values and attitudes.

Young, M. and Commins, E. (2002) *Global Citizenship: The Handbook for Primary Teaching.* An award-winning, comprehensive manual for teachers which includes ideas for INSET, assemblies and classroom activities, and photociopable worksheets for geography and literacy.

Part III
The global classroom

Chapter 14

The wider world in the primary school

Fran Martin

This chapter looks at a number of key issues that arise when teaching about the wider world in primary school. It also includes examples of good classroom practice and references to useful educational resources.

Key issues

Both a study into the needs of teachers and learners (Davies *et al.* 2005) and primary school teachers on a recent course in Worcester identified a number of important issues in relation to teaching about global citizenship. These included:

- The relevance of a global dimension to primary school pupils
- Teacher knowledge, or lack of, and associated levels of confidence in tackling global issues
- How to teach about global issues in such a way that children will not feel overburdened
- The challenges of another initiative in an already overcrowded curriculum

This chapter will address some of these concerns as they relate to primary classroom practice.

The relevance of a global dimension

One of the first concerns that primary teachers often have about developing the global dimension in the curriculum is that the wider world is seen as being conceptually beyond children's grasp. Davies *et al.* (2005) cite a primary teacher who comments:

> Some of our children are ... only just beginning to be aware of themselves, so if you're at the level of a young child beginning to be aware of yourself and your environment and the difference between yourself and the environment, it's difficult to think of things further afield.
>
> (Ibid.: 95–6)

These views are understandable – they reflect the powerful and long-lasting influence of the way in which Piaget's work has been interpreted and applied in an educational context. Piaget identified discrete stages of development which young children move through as they mature and as a result of increasingly wide and varied experiences of the world. This model of development suggests that children are only able to begin to 'decentre' (view things from different perspectives) and cope with more abstract ideas towards the end of primary school as they reach the age of eleven (Wood 1988). However, these views are in direct contrast to those expressed by children themselves both in this book (see Chapter 3) and in Davies *et al.* (2005).

Piaget's theory of development has also led to a 'concentric circle' approach to the curriculum which assumes a progression from the concrete and local in the early years to the abstract and global towards the end of primary and beginning of secondary school. However, Donaldson (1978) has long since provided evidence of young children's ability to think abstractly and about complex issues. Catling (2003) and Martin (1995, 2006a) cite research into young children's understanding of the world which indicates that it is not only appropriate but essential to focus on a global dimension from an early age.

There is a growing tradition in the field of primary geography and developmental psychology of researching children's private geographies, i.e. the understandings of the world they carry around in their heads as a result of personal experiences. Briefly, children's personal geographies are made up of direct *and* indirect experiences of the world (Catling 2003). We cannot ignore the fact that children come into contact with the wider world on a daily basis from a very young age – through what they watch on television, the food they eat, the internet, the clothes they wear, the commercials and music they enjoy. The idea that the personal has to be the local is therefore mistaken.

In addition, Martin (1995, 2006a) has shown how, in terms of people and place, there are two conceptual elements to children's understanding of the wider world. One of these might be called 'a sense of distance and location' (where is it, how far away is it?), the other 'a sense of place' (what sort of place is it, how do people live there?).

> The former is a complex concept for young children to grasp and is often best developed within a local study framework where locations and distances of known features can be considered. The latter is about developing a sense of place and therefore involves drawing comparisons between one place and another. It is well within the grasp of young children and can be very successfully taught using a variety of approaches.
>
> (Martin 1995: 3)

Young children do not need to understand where people and places are in order to develop ideas and concerns about them. Indeed, it could be considered irresponsible of us to ignore these developing ideas and the attitudes and values associated with them, some of which might be stereotypes that lead to prejudice and bias. Research shows (Wiegand 1992) that, if left to secondary school, these ideas and attitudes can become deeply entrenched and then far harder to change. Yet the ideas and attitudes pupils hold about 'otherness' or diversity will have a profound impact on how they respond to global issues and change in the future.

A sense of agency

'How can I look at issues in such a way that children don't get depressed or give up because the problem is too big for them to do anything about?' said a teacher on a recent course. If children feel that there is nothing they can do about the issues that they study then it is likely that they will shut off from such matters and relegate them to being 'out there' or 'not my problem'. Concern about the development of such attitudes was one reason for the current emphasis on action and participation in the new curriculum for citizenship education. Identification of injustice and examination of its causes is not enough, pupils need to feel empowered and to understand that there are a number of things that they can do, as individuals and with others, to make a difference.

Stephen Pickering, Education for Sustainable Development Officer in Worcestershire, said at a conference:

> Did you know that light travels at 186,000 miles per second? At the moment we can push a space rocket up over 1,000 miles an hour … to reach the nearest star that might possibly have an environment that we could inhabit we would need to travel at the speed of light for thirty generations. Thirty generations of people living, sleeping, breeding on a space ship because we've messed up our own earth. Just imagine if you happened to be born into the twenty-ninth generation? What a shame! But then imagine what it would be like to be the thirtieth and to arrive. Wouldn't you want to look after the place?
>
> (Pickering 2006)

The emphasis here has the concept of care at its heart – care for self, care for others and care for the environment that sustains us now and for the future. This provides a positive stance from which to view global issues but is not, in itself, sufficient. It also requires developing an understanding of how, when there is evidence of people and environments not being cared for, we can do something to make a difference. Each of the writers in Part II has made practical suggestions about positive action for change in relation to the focus for their chapter.

Embedding the global dimension

Primary schools, arguably more than any other phase of education, have been subjected to countless government initiatives over the last 15+ years – three versions of the National Curriculum, the introduction of the National Literacy and Numeracy Strategies, Citizenship and PSHE, Excellence and Enjoyment, the National Primary

Strategy and Every Child Matters to name but a few. In the face of all this change it may seem as though embedding a global dimension in the curriculum is yet another thing to fit in.

Oxfam's guide for schools (2006a) makes a strong case for the relevance of global citizenship to all areas of the curriculum. They show how it is a *perspective* on the world and a *way* of teaching, rather than an additional extra and, as Young and Commins point out (2002: 8), 'if you look you will probably see that you are already covering many of its principles'. The content may therefore remain the same, but the perspectives brought to it, and thus the resources and pedagogical approaches used, may change. Indeed, there is some evidence to suggest that where teachers do bring a global dimension to the curriculum, pupils are more motivated and achieve higher standards (Hirst 2006).

The task of the primary teacher is both easier and harder than that of the secondary teacher. Easier because primary teachers have an overview of the whole curriculum for their class and can plan for a global perspective in a more holistic way; harder because there is the challenge of having sufficient subject knowledge to be able to identify appropriate global perspectives in all areas of the curriculum, not just one or two. This implies the need to work as a team, drawing on the strengths of the group of staff or cluster of schools to which you belong. An example of how this has been achieved in one school is given below.

Classroom practice

Football and the wider world

How could a photograph of David Beckham (or any other internationally famous footballer) be used to develop a sequence of activities that have learning relevant to both specific subject areas and the global dimension? Table 14.1 provides an overview of a medium-term plan. The key questions and ideas in column one suggest that the activities should be enquiry-led and give a clear indication of the main purpose of each section or week in terms of children's learning. The remaining columns show links, where appropriate, to subjects, the key concepts explored in this book and Oxfam's skills, attitudes and values for global citizenship (Oxfam 2006a).

If the example of the merchandising industry that surrounds football is explored it is possible to identify a 'ladder of participation' which exemplifies progression in global citizenship (DfID/Action Aid 2000a). Here are four main steps on that ladder:

- *Gain knowledge* – What do big football clubs sell and how much do things cost?
- *Develop skills and understanding* – Why do clubs sell these things? Why do fans want to buy them? Where do they come from? See trade game on sports shoes (Figures 14.1a and 14.1b).

Table 14.1 David Beckham and football

Key questions/ideas	National Curriculum subjects	The eight concepts	Oxfam's objectives for global citizenship
Is football played all over the world? Where is it most popular?	Geography: locations, lifestyles	Diversity Interdependence	Sense of common humanity
Manchester United as a global industry – merchandising, who makes the money? Sports Shoe Trade Game and Fair Trade Where are sports shoes made? How much do they cost? How is the cost of a shoe divided among people in the process? Is the distribution of wealth fair?	Geography: identification of locations where sports shoes are made. Sequencing stages in process – manufacturing to retail. North–South divisions in wealth distribution Mathematics: cost of goods, how much goes to each group of people who contribute to the process Environmental education: pollution caused by transport of goods from one side of the world to another	Global citizenship Human rights Social justice Interdependence Sustainable development Values and perceptions	Critical thinking Ability to argue effectively Ability to challenge injustice and inequalities Co-operation and conflict resolution Empathy and sense of common humanity Commitment to social justice and equity Concern for the environment Belief that people can make a difference
Is there anything we can do to make a difference? E.g. Buy local goods wherever possible/buy Fair Trade goods/donate to charities who help reduce poverty	Citizenship: basic knowledge of trade rules; taking positive action by supporting Fair Trade		
Football and Conflict What teams/sports do we support in our class (doesn't have to be football)? How do we show that we support our team? What examples of football hooliganism do we know about? Why do people fight over football? How can differences of opinion be resolved peacefully?	English: discuss (and define using a dictionary where necessary) relevant vocabulary linked to football and football hooliganism. Play Odd One Out using vocabulary PSHE/Citizenship: provide scenarios in which something happens at a football match and ask pupils to consider, and then role-play what might happen next. Give three versions and ask rest of class to decide on most appropriate action	Conflict resolution Diversity Human rights Values and perceptions	Critical thinking Ability to argue effectively Co-operation and conflict resolution Sense of identity and self-esteem Empathy Value and respect for diversity Belief that people can make a difference

---

Procedure

Divide class into 5 groups. Each group receives an instruction card and a role card.

After about 10 minutes discussion arrive at a figure that you think is reasonable for the time, costs and expertise that are involved in your work. Be able to justify the amount you suggest.

Teacher asks each group for their figure and compares the total with the 'actual' figure the shoes sell for in the shops.

Small groups then reconsider the amount they think they are worth. At this point groups can be re-formed into ones that have at least one representative for each of the key roles in the process of sports shoe production. These groups then discuss and attempt to arrive at a solution that everyone is happy with.

Teacher then asks for examples of agreements reached.

Compare with 'actual' (simulated) figures below and discuss the issues that this raises.

If a sports shoe retails in the UK for £60.20 ...

£7.20 goes to the factory (usually in the 'South') where it was manufactured, broken down as:

* £4.80 raw material costs
* £1.20 other production costs (of which wages are £0.24)
* £1.20 profit for the factory owners

£20 goes to the owner of the brand name, broken down as:

* £6.60 research and design costs
* £5.20 promotion and advertising costs (including sponsoring people like Tiger Woods and David Beckham)
* £8.20 is profit for the brand name owners

£30 goes to the retailer

£3 is paid in transport and taxes

Figure 14.1a Sports Shoe Trade Game

* *Form opinions* – What do we think about how the wealth from sports shoes is shared between different people? Is it fair? Why do some people get more money for their 'bit' than others? Is this how it should be?
* *Take action* – What can I/we do to make a difference? Making choices about what sorts of things we buy, where we buy them, Fair Trade etc.

Two sources that will provide useful information on the 'taking action' aspect are the Fair Trade website and their publication *Fair Trade School Handbook (2004)* which is available through that site.

The same sequence can be applied when focusing on football and conflict as the following activity suggests:

Each group gets this instruction card A sports shoe costs £60 How much of the selling price do you think your group should have to cover your costs/needs?	**Raw materials suppliers** You have to supply: • Leather • Plastics • Glue • Any other raw materials as required
Factory workers You need wages to: • Feed your families • Pay for housing • Pay for your children's schooling • Pay for healthcare	**Brand name owners** You have to: • Promote the brand through advertising and sponsorship • Pay designers for new product ideas • Pay researchers to 'assess' the market and what people want
Retailers You have to: • Maintain high street shops • Employ staff to deal with customers • Keep a large stock of shoes	**Manufacturers** You have to: • Buy the raw materials • Run the factory • Pay the factory workers

Figure 14.1b Sports Shoe Trade Game (continued)

- *Gain knowledge* – What vocabulary do we use to describe football and football hooliganism (e.g. fan, hooligan, thug, violence, support, loyalty, pride, intolerance, racism, supporter, criminal)?
- *Develop skills and understanding* – What do each of these terms mean and how do they relate to each other? (see Leat (1998) and Higgins and Baumfield (2001)). Each word is written on a separate card, the cards are then placed face down on a table, and in pairs or small groups children turn over three cards at random. They decide which is the Odd One Out and why. They can then either decide on a different Odd One Out, choose a fourth card that would keep the Odd One Out the same, or select a new set of three cards. This deeper understanding of the vocabulary then supports the following activity using the cards.
- *Form opinions* – On the basis of the cards, why do we think people are sometimes violent at football matches? What do we think are suitable courses of action in each case? Why? In what ways can conflict be resolved without violence?

Is violence ever justified? Are all football hooligans fans and supporters of the game? Are all fans hooligans?

- *Take action* – What can I/we do to make a difference? How should I/we behave in challenging situations? How can we show we are proud of the team we support in peaceful ways? How do we feel when our team wins/loses?

Eco-warriors

Shelley Primary School in West Sussex (2006) has been planning and teaching in an integrated, cross-curricular way since 2004 because staff believe this makes for enjoyable teaching and learning, it enables subject links to be supportive of other themes and dimensions, and it meets the aims of more recent government initiatives such as *Excellence and Enjoyment* (DfES 2003) and *Every Child Matters* (DfES 2005b). An example of one of the school's cross-curricular themes is given in Figure 14.2. This demonstrates how the school plans through key questions (regular font) to ensure enquiry-led learning, it links these questions to NC programmes of study (*italics*) and identifies links to the eight key concepts of the global dimension where appropriate (**bold**).

The topic has been planned with geography and science as the lead subjects, using literacy, ICT, art and PSHE skills to support them. Examples of the pupils' learning journey questions and statements are shown in Box 14.1. As the topic drew to a conclusion, staff ensured that the children were given sufficient time to plan their Shelley Sustainable School, encouraging them to discuss and apply the geographical and scientific insights they had gained through the term. The children researched newly built eco-schools around the country on the internet and then included some of these ideas in their own plans.

The children's involvement through enquiry, and their designs and learning journeys are ample evidence of how this school is using children's interests as a starting point and empowering them in meaningful ways that are not tokenistic. Encouraging the children to engage in an online forum discussion on national environmental issues gives them access to a wide range of views and perspectives, which enables the staff to address the issue of 'balance'. The staff plan topics collaboratively, with each teacher offering support from their own area of expertise. In this way global dimension concepts are embedded within the subject framework from the start.

School linking

Many schools are interested in, and being actively encouraged (DfES 2004) to develop a link with schools in other countries. This is seen as an excellent way of embedding a global dimension in the activities of the school. However, as research is beginning to show (Disney 2004, Martin 2005), school linking is not without its own challenges, not least whether the link is perceived as being mainly about fundraising or a true partnership (see Chapter 13).

Geography

Programmes of Study: Geography: KS2 5. *Knowledge and understanding of environmental change and sustainable development. a) recognise how people can improve the environment or damage it and how decisions about places and environments affect the future quality of people's lives. b) recognise how and why people may seek to manage environments sustainably and to identify opportunities for their own environment.*

How can we improve the quality of our environment?

In groups, design an Eco-School using the knowledge from QCA units. How can we make Shelley School a more environmentally friendly place to work?

What's in the news? Find out about environmental schemes in the area and how these can be used in our Eco-School.

Geog. 6e) attempts to manage the environment sustainably.

Interdependence, Sustainable Development, Global Citizenship, Values and Perceptions

---

Eco-warriors scheme of work:

How can we improve the quality of our environment?

Literacy

Link design of new Eco-School to writing in Literacy-newspaper report; leaflet; proposal.

ICT

Take part in the online forum to discuss the issues surrounding environmental change (www.wwf.org.uk)
3a) email, online discussion
Using information and online games to investigate sustainable development and Eco-Schools.
1a) find and use relevant information.
Use digital images – manipulate images for fact sheet.

Art

Observational Sketching in school grounds/map work of proposed changes including digital photos.
Art 1a) to select and record from first-hand observations.
5c) to use a range of materials and processes including ICT.
Plan a fact sheet on Recycle/Reuse/Reduce using ICT text boxes.
Develop drawing techniques in readiness for publication of their individual project.
2b) developing their control of tools and techniques.

Science: QCA Unit 6A *Interdependence and Adaptation.*

INDEPENDENT PROJECT: Environments: rainforest; jungle, savannah, tundra etc. How have animals adapted to these environments? How have humans impacted upon them? As an Eco-Warrior how could you improve it? Children to include a food chain in their project.
Sc2: 5a) ways in which living things and the environment need protection.
CLASS ACTIVITIES
What plants would you plant in an Eco-School? (e.g. Buddleia for butterflies to start a food chain; to be introduced into our school to bring in new animals e.g. hedgehogs)
Sc2: 5d) to use food chains to show feeding relationships. 5e) How nearly all food chains start with a green plant.
Why do plants need light? *Sc2: 3a) effect of light.*
How do plants make their food? *Sc2: 3b) leaf=new growth; 3c) root=water and minerals; stem=transport.*
How do soil conditions affect plant growth?
How can animals and plants be identified and assigned to groups? *Sc2: 4a) keys; b) same as key question; c) the variety of animals and plants makes it important to identify and group them.*
How are animals and plants suited to their local habitat/environment? *Sc2: 5b) different plants and animals are found in different habitats; c) how animals and plants in two different habitats are suited to their environment (link to INDEPENDENT project).*

QCA 6B *Micro-organisms.* How are micro-organisms helpful and harmful? How can the use of micro-organisms sustain our environment? (compost, sewage etc.)
Sc2: 5f) micro-organisms are living, they can be beneficial and harmful.
Attainment Target (AT1): 1a) 1b) 2j) 2k) 2l) Do conclusions agree with predictions? l)

QCA 5B *Life Cycles.*
How do flowering plants reproduce? *Sc1: 1a) What are the best conditions for germination; b) Testing ideas (cress seed investigation); 2b) first-hand experience will be used to answer questions (investigation skills); 2d) fair test; f) observation and measurement; g) check observations; h) communicate data; j) draw conclusions; l) explain observations; Sc2: b) Life processes common to plants including growth, nutrition and reproduction; 1c) make links between life processes; 3a)b)c)d) reproduction.*

Biodiversity, Interdependence, Sustainable Development

PSHCE

Your worth as an individual – link to being an eco-warrior, having your own opinion.
6. 1b) recognise their worth as an individual.
Emotional intelligence. Coping with your emotions and those of others.
1: 1a)
Diversity, Human Rights

Figure 14.2 Eco-warriors scheme of work

Box 14.1 The Eco-warrior's learning journey

We will investigate the meaning of sustainable development and how this will impact on our futures.

How can we make our own school more environmentally friendly?

We will find out the places around the school that we like and do not like and say why, and what we could do to change them.

We will find out how we can improve our environment through growing plants and improving the food chains around the school.

What are the ideal conditions for plants and animals to thrive?

We will investigate how we can order and organise information about plants and animals.

We will investigate the life cycles of plants and animals and the part their environment plays in this.

How can micro-organisms help us in creating our Eco-School?

We will discover more about sustainable energy supplies and recycling and develop strategies for our own school.

We will use all of our knowledge about plants, animals and the environment to design an Eco-School for the future.

We will take part in an online forum to support and question our ideas.

[Children were faced with an issue about placing a new school in a particular area and having to discuss the issues of sustainability for the community and environment, building methods, position and design. The World Wide Fund for Nature forum (www.wwf.org.uk) enabled links to be made across areas of the curriculum and questions were posed to focus the learning further. This was to be a final outcome for the classes: to debate with children from all over the country about environmental issues.]

We will sketch key areas for improvement around the school.

We will use digital images to support the changes we propose for the school.

We will also produce a plan for making the environment of Shelley School into a better place for all of our futures.

During a day conference (TIDE 2006b), teachers explored a number of key questions which challenged their thinking:

- To what extent do we fully explore why we want to establish a partnership before we consider who, where, what, when and how?
- What do we hope our pupils will learn from partnership activities? What do they actually learn? How do we know?
- How is a school partnership affected by the world views and values of all those involved? Are we aware of what each other's (teachers and learners) world views are and the impact these might have?

Our exploration of the third question was underpinned by the understanding that we all learn from any contact with a partner school, that this contact cannot be separated from other experiences in school, that children learn from *all* these experiences and that these will be affected by the school's overall ethos and educational vision. In other words it is crucial to see partnership activities within the broader context of school life as a whole and to question whether the curriculum, formal and informal, is compatible with the aims of the partnership. We agreed that the formal, planned curriculum presented less of a challenge because at least it was something that was explicit and recorded for all to see. However, the informal and sometimes unplanned curriculum presented more of a challenge.

There is a growing concern in education (Disney 2004; Martin 2005; Temple 2006) that one partnership activity – that of fundraising for the partner school – is counterproductive to the type of learning originally intended. Fundraising most commonly takes place where the link is with a school in the 'South' and as a direct response to the economic disparity that is evident between the two schools. The danger of responding to poverty in this way is that children often associate economic poverty with intellectual and emotional poverty (Graves 2002) and this can lead to feelings of superiority on the part of UK children which undermines other work that might have taken place to develop pupils' understanding of diversity, interdependence and social justice. Not only this, it undermines any attempt to develop a partnership that is based on *mutual* goals. With regard to the latter, Temple offers the following advice:

> The aim of school linking shouldn't be purely to help the partner school, through fundraising or otherwise. School links based on charitable aims, however well meaning these may be, are very unlikely to become real partnerships and can be a very negative experience for pupils and teachers in both schools. Links based around fundraising can reinforce power differences between partner schools and compound pupils' negative perceptions and stereotypes. Fundraising can take place within a good school link, but be very aware of the distinction between fundraising to facilitate linking activities and fundraising to help the partner school. Successful linking is about partnership: a working relationship based on respect, in which both partners make equal contribution, even if they are very

different in terms of the wealth of their resources. It is about understanding that both partners can learn things from, as well as about, each other.

(Temple 2006: 14)

Useful resources

Connecting to the wider world

Starting with children's own ideas and concerns is a pedagogically sound approach to the global dimension. However, we may sometimes wish to introduce global issues that children have not identified for themselves. How can we do so in such a way that they still feel connected to the issue and that it should matter to them?

Research has shown that stories are a powerful way of enabling young children to engage with abstract and complex issues (Egan 1989). Stories, particularly if they focus on family life and children who are of a similar age to those in your class, can present complex issues in a straightforward (but not simplistic) way. One book that lists a number of stories and provides examples of how to use them to develop an understanding of wider issues is *Start with a Story: supporting young children's exploration of issues* (TIDE 2002).

Supporting teacher confidence

If, as a staff, you wish to conduct some in-house staff development, a good place to start is *Global Citizenship: the handbook for primary teaching* (Young and Commins 2002). Chapter 2 of this excellent book provides a number of whole-school in-service activities designed to support teachers' understanding of how to implement global citizenship.

If you prefer to seek external advice and support, Development Education Centres are a very good place to begin. The website of the Development Education Association provides information about the work of DECs and an A–Z of these is listed under regions. Most DECs have resources for loan and/or sale and a member of staff who can offer advice and support. Some of the larger DECs will also have a programme of in-service training on offer.

Keeping up to date with current global issues is quite a challenge. The following websites may be helpful: Global Eye is a site devoted to providing resources to support teaching and learning about current issues aimed at primary and secondary; Oxfam's website is for teachers and pupils; the World Wide Fund for Nature's site is for teachers, with a strong emphasis on sustainable development. WWF's main site (2006b) is useful for subject knowledge on wildlife, habitats and threats.

School partnerships

The *Times Educational Supplement* (2006) magazine, *Teacher*, provided a double-page spread on global partnerships. There is a thought-provoking article on the issues and reviews of a number of resources for supporting both school linking and how to make global citizenship central to a school's ethos.

There are a number of websites that provide advice on setting up a school partnership. The British Council (2006b) and DfES (2006d) focus on how to find a partner school, how to get funding and how to support the link. A more recent and welcome addition to internet resources is the 'Toolkit of good practice', which is being developed by the UK One World Linking Association (see website).

Chapter 15

Global citizenship in the secondary school

Harriet Marshall

This chapter explores the various ways in which global citizenship can be introduced into the secondary curriculum. In particular it discusses a range of whole-school issues, from professional development to schools linking, and gives examples of good classroom practice.

Introducing the key issues

Global education can be delivered in a variety of ways in secondary schools. Figure 15.1 (Marshall 2005b) illustrates some of the ways in which schools can develop a global dimension. Most of these methods focus upon the important affective and participative dimensions of global education, whilst also being clear about the cognitive requirements of global citizenship. Throughout this chapter case studies of good practice will be offered which draw upon at least one of these criteria.

Schools wanting to adopt an international or global dimension may choose one or a combination of these curricular and extra-curricular elements. There is little agreement about which is more effective and of course such a question would be dependent upon the aims of global education for that particular school. However, the DfES strategy document *Putting the World into World-Class Education* (2004) and the Global Gateway website (2006), run by the British Council on behalf of the DfES, clearly emphasise school linking and the Teachers' International Professional Development Programme (British Council 2005) as important ways of adding a global dimension to schooling. Meanwhile there is a range of textbooks and resources available related to global citizenship, and supportive networks of NGOs (non-governmental organisations) exist throughout the UK. Alternatively some schools have chosen more radical methods of internationalising, such as through the incorporation of the International Baccalaureate Diploma (see IBO website) in addition to, or as an alternative to, A-Levels.

Teachers and schools are faced with many choices and issues when developing a global dimension in the secondary school. For example:

- Which approach to global education should a school take?
- How can a school train and engage staff in this area?

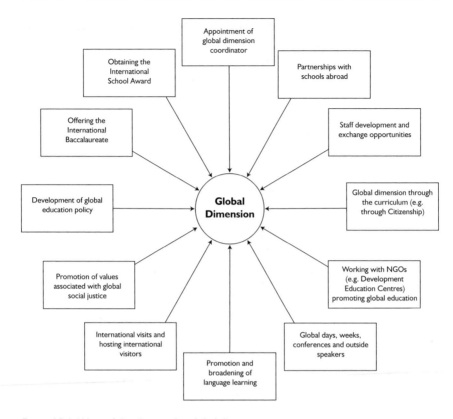

Figure 15.1 Ways of developing the global dimension

- How should schools organise student and staff conferences, global weeks, international visits and so forth?
- How can a school develop the global dimension inside mainstream curricula?

Some of these issues relate more to classroom practice whilst others relate more to whole-school issues.

Whole-school issues

Chapter 1 gave examples of the several issue-based educations which can contribute to a global dimension. It is possible to identify a number of such traditions, each suggesting different foci, such as human rights, anti-racist, global interdependence or internationalist. Ultimately, a school needs to adopt the approach best suited to staff and student dynamics and corresponding interests within the school. Whatever the school chooses, it is useful to adhere to the four dimensions of global education highlighted in Chapter 2 when planning whole-school activities. Thus a school will need to consider which issues to focus upon (such as poverty, human rights or conflict) and how issues are spatially interconnected at local–global levels. An understanding should also be gained of the need to place issues in their temporal context, acknowledging the past and present but emphasising the future, and that the holistic and participatory process of global education involves substantial forward-planning.

Teachers' Professional Development

These four key dimensions of global education can be incorporated into any staff development and training session. A specified space and time for such development is highly recommended if a school wishes to incorporate the global dimension at a whole-school level. Local Development Education Centres (DECs) and NGOs promoting global education such as Oxfam, Save the Children and ActionAid, offer advice, assistance and training sessions for staff wishing to develop global awareness programmes in their school. Advice about INSET and professional development can also be found at the Global Gateway website. Additionally, the British Council (2006a) and organisations such as Education Action International offer or facilitate staff exchange opportunities designed to foster a more international outlook in their teaching (discussed later).

Teachers' professional development programmes need to address the following issues which are often perceived to be of concern to staff delivering global education:

- *Pedagogy*: How to engage with the participatory pedagogy of global education.
- *Permeating the curriculum*: How global education can best work within and across mainstream curricula.
- *Practising global education outside the classroom*: How to go about organising outside visitors, global days/weeks/events, assemblies and exchanges.

These three 'Ps' may also be accompanied by a concern that teachers have more generally about dealing with controversial issues in the classroom (see Chapter 5).

Whilst it might seem difficult to permeate subjects due to the compartmentalised and assessment-orientated nature of the National Curriculum, supporting resources are at hand. *Developing the Global Dimension in the School Curriculum* (DfES 2005) gives examples of how different curriculum areas can incorporate the eight key concepts of global education. The Development Education Association has published specific advice for secondary school subjects on how they can incorporate a global dimension, e.g. for Citizenship (DEA 2001), Science (DEA 2003b) and Geography (DEA 2004). A school may wish to allocate a specific period of time for teachers to research and reflect on how their subject can contribute to the global dimension. A clear and detailed whole-school strategy on delivery of this dimension is vital. Such a document should be negotiated by staff, perhaps with student consultation, in a teacher training session.

Activities

A wide range of whole-school global activities can be used by schools, including global days, theme weeks, assemblies, conferences, workshops and exchange visits (see Box 15.1). Schools can select which activity best suits the topics, students, learning space and context.

Box 15.1 A global conference

Case 1: A global conference for Year 10 students

A two-day global conference was organised by a small group of staff in conjunction with a local Development Education Centre for about 120 14–15-year-old students. Prior to the conference students were able to sign up for a choice of workshops on a variety of global topics such as:

– Human rights and Amnesty International   – Fair trade and chocolate
– Deforestation and the environment   – The Trading Game
– World music   – Racism

The conference began and ended with whole-group sessions involving a quiz, an activity and student feedback. *If the world was a village of 100 people* is a world-shrinking interactive activity which includes statistics such as 20 people are undernourished but 15 are overweight. The day took place during the school week immediately following an examination week and offered students choice and participation. Student feedback from the event was, on the whole, extremely positive. Whilst the conference was time-consuming to organise, as teachers needed to co-ordinate the workshop leaders (generally from outside the school) and negotiate timetabling, most staff felt the conference had been rewarding and a great success.

Oxfam's Cool Planet website (2006b) provides a calendar of 'global' days, such as International Women's Day (8 March) or One World Week (October), for organising assemblies or theme weeks. Those wanting to organise model United Nations days or Earth Summits should contact organisations such as United Nations Association (see website) which can provide schools with resources and guidance. A globally focused theme week for the whole school can also be effective as Case 2 shows (see Box 15.2).

Further help with planning a focus week can be obtained from local Development Education Centres or other NGOs – for example GLADE, the Centre for Global and Development Education in Somerset, has designed a global focus week booklet for planning and resourcing such events.

Box 15.2 Landmines

Case 2: Landmines week

A group of sixth-form students launched a whole-school awareness campaign about landmines in their local secondary school. They invited a speaker to take an assembly, erected fake landmine sites around the school, distributed leaflets about landmines and gave a presentation to Year 7 and 8 students about the issue. Because of the way every student in the school came across the issue (they had to physically walk around imaginary landmines in corridors), the topic was brought up in classrooms across all departments, as well as in the staff room. Two years after the event students still had vivid memories of it and conveyed to me just how significant the week had been as a globally orientated activity.

Working with non-governmental organisations (NGOs)

Global education NGOs can give advice about (or provide) resources, staff training and arranging outside speakers. In the UK there are a large number of local, national and international NGOs and projects interested in helping schools incorporate a global dimension. Many of these, such as the Council for Education in World Citizenship (2006) and Teachers in Development Education, Birmingham, can be found in the Development Education Association's A–Z of members. Some Local Education Authorities (LEAs) also have international education advisors or personnel able to inform teachers about such groups. Many groups have extensive experience of working with schools and teachers and can offer support in creating resources, organising workshops and engaging in small research projects (see Box 15.3).

The school in Case 3 also piloted a new Year 7 project which incorporated African issues into their curriculum. As the school was developing a range of approaches to its global dimension it hoped to gain an International School Award in the near future.

Obtaining the International School Award

The British Council International School Award (ISA) has been given to over 670 schools since 1999. The scheme consists of three different tiers or categories – the foundation level (introducing internationalism), the intermediate level (developing internationalism) and the full ISA. There is a long list of aims for the ISA, including supporting the development of 'an international ethos embedded throughout the school', 'a majority of pupils within the school impacted by and involved in international work' and 'year round international activity' (Humanities Education Centre 2006). The assumptions behind this award are that the ISA will raise awareness, encourage whole-school activities and collaborative working across disciplines, and enhance students' understanding of global citizenship.

Box 15.3 Going global

Case 3: One school goes global: launching and publicising the global dimension with the help of NGOs

Having identified some of the ways the school was already engaged in global education activity, e.g. through active Comenius projects and international school links, one comprehensive in the west of England publicly launched itself as a 'global school'. There was much activity throughout the week which culminated in an afternoon and evening of events, interactive exhibitions and talks. Having rarely worked with local global education organisations before, the school's international education co-ordinator was pleased to discover the resources of Save the Children, Christian Aid, Amnesty International, the Refugee Awareness Project (Refugee Action) and their local Development Education Centre, all of which were represented at the event. Save the Children ran a well-received teacher training session on developing a global dimension in the classroom and the Asian Arts Agency funded a successful Indian dance workshop for students. The event involved staff, students, parents and members of the local community and the co-ordinators were appreciative of the resources, expertise and support provided by the NGOs. Attendees described the positive impact they felt the event had had in the feedback books provided, where recognition was also given to the efforts made by the co-ordinator.

Important in obtaining the award is the presence of an international school policy and an international co-ordinator. An example of key aims and objectives is given from a school in Oxfordshire on the Global Gateway website:

> To enable our students to know more about global issues and to: celebrate the rich and diverse heritage represented in our school and local and national communities; understand complex international interdependencies in the global economy; respect and value different cultures and beliefs; enjoy regular contact with students and adults living in different countries.

The international co-ordinator is often someone especially interested in the global dimension who may have been involved in school linking or global education events in the past. However, any individual taking on this role will require the full support of the head and other staff members as the global dimension needs to be both embedded and sustainable. There should then be no danger of the global dimension being lost should the co-ordinator leave the school.

Whether or not a school chooses to apply for the International School Award, those interested in developing their global citizenship programmes need to begin by conducting a self-audit in order to identify what the school is already doing. Examples of international or global citizenship audits are available at the Global Gateway and Oxfam (website) whilst an alternative 'global footprints' audit is available from the Humanities Education Centre (website).

Schools linking and teacher partnerships abroad

The Global Gateway website also provides advice and help to schools wishing to foster schools linking. Organisations such as the Link Schools Programme, the UNESCO Associated Schools Project, the UK One World Linking Association and the British Council (2006b), all provide support. Some grants are available from the British and Foreign School Society and the Teachers' International Professional Development Programme which provides opportunities and funding for staff exchanges and study visits. Other programmes exist such as that designed by the British Council for international placements for head teachers. Whilst much evidence for the effectiveness of international exchanges is anecdotal, the belief that such exchanges can have a significant impact on the school community prompted a competition inviting bids from schools to send teachers on international visits (run by Teachers TV). Underlying many of these initiatives is the belief that anything that helps teachers see themselves as global citizens will enhance their teaching.

Language learning

It is not surprising that many language-focused secondary schools (such as specialist language colleges) are involved in global citizenship programmes and many have gained the International School Award. Indeed, the relationship between global citizenship and language learning has received much attention and Audrey Osler argues that:

> Good language teachers must necessarily be cosmopolitan citizens. The languages classroom is a key place in which the knowledge, skills and attitudes necessary for cosmopolitan citizenship can be developed and practised ... The participative learning styles which characterise good practice in language teaching and learning are also those which support education for democratic citizenship.
>
> (Osler 2005: 21)

Comenius and British Council language learning, teaching and exchange programmes are clearly an important part of global citizenship in schools. Other language learning projects are being run online, such as E-pals, which facilitates cross-cultural exchanges. However, it is important to remember that not all language teaching is 'global' unless other key elements of global citizenship are also present.

Alternative approaches

In my own study (Marshall 2006) of the relationship between global education traditions in the UK, I found that international education is very much associated with international schools and the International Baccalaureate. The International Baccalaureate Organisation provides primary, middle years and diploma programmes (the latter being the most widely adopted) which offer alternative curricula with a specific international focus. Working with over 1,700 schools in 122 countries the IBO aims to 'develop inquiring, knowledgeable and caring young people who help to create a better and more peaceful world through intercultural understanding and respect' (see website).

Whilst most international schools are privately funded, there has been an increase in the number of state schools in the UK choosing to adopt the IB Diploma as an addition or alternative to A-Levels. A study of one such school revealed how much this impacted upon teachers' and students' understanding of global education (Marshall 2005a). In particular, teachers who taught on the programme described how it had affected their teaching in Key Stages 3 and 4 because the pedagogy and international outlook of the programme had developed their own understanding of teaching and learning in a global context.

If such radical curricular change is not an option, a school can choose to adopt a specific type of global ethos – one associated with human rights or sustainability, for example. A global human rights framework could permeate school structures as well as curriculum content (Tarrow 1992). The Eco-Schools framework could be a school's contribution to global citizenship. In this case schools can apply for the international Eco-Schools awards. Case 4 gives a glimpse of the Eco-School option (sse Box 15.4).

Box 15.4 An Eco-School

Case 4: Fostering global citizenship by becoming an Eco-School

Eco-Schools is much more than an environmental management system for schools. It is a programme for promoting environmental awareness in a way that links to most, if not all, curriculum subjects. In particular, many cross-curricular issues such as citizenship, education for sustainable development, PSE, health education, social and environmental justice and the global dimension can be tackled through involvement in Eco-Schools. It is also an accredited award scheme that will raise the profile of your school in the wider community.

The Eco-Schools process is holistic. It works by involving the whole school – pupils, teachers and other staff, together with members of the local community – parents, the local authority, the media and local businesses. It encourages teamwork and helps create a shared understanding of what it takes to run a school in a way that respects and enhances the environment.

(Eco-Schools Scotland website)

One grammar school in Scotland which had been awarded the Eco-Schools Green Flag proved that it had the following: the support of the head teacher and senior management team; the involvement of pupils in democratic decision-making process and action at all stages; the active involvement of staff and the wider school community; and the willingness to take action to instigate long-term, sustainable change. The school also acted as an advisory school working with others in the area trying to foster a global/sustainable development ethos.

Classroom practice

There are various issues which relate to good practice in global citizenship, not least the need for all teachers to have some understanding of what such education actually looks like. Chapter 2 highlighted the need for global education to involve the head and the heart (cognitive and affective), the personal and political (values clarification and political literacy), and stressed the need for a more critical approach to global education. With this understanding in mind, the next section focuses upon curricular and pedagogic issues associated with classroom practice.

Curriculum issues

Mick Waters, Director of Curriculum at the Qualifications and Curriculum Authority in London, argues that:

> ... it's the job of everybody ... everybody in our schools, to try and develop a world-class curriculum for children that fits them for the future and [to] make sure it fits every single child we meet ... I know that people try to do that and I know that people across the country are working really hard within the constraints of a thing called the national curriculum to try and make things happen. And my challenge is to work with people across the system, to help them to help it to happen for children, rather than simply send publications saying what should happen.
>
> (Waters 2005)

As Waters hints, the national curriculum can appear as something of a hurdle in relation to the global dimension. The study by Davies *et al.* (2005) of global citizenship in the West Midlands found that 'both teachers and pupils feel constrained by the National Curriculum apparatus. Teachers are concerned about exams; pupils feel they never have time to do anything in depth' (2005: 4). However, despite what may sometimes feel like constraints, much of the success in implementing the global dimension depends upon what happens behind the closed door of the classroom.

Oxfam's (2006a) curriculum for global citizenship (see Chapter 2) provides one useful framework of the appropriate knowledge, skills, values and attitudes which need to permeate all subjects. Oxfam's website details skills such as the 'ability to challenge injustice and inequalities', and values and attitudes such as 'empathy and a sense of common humanity' and 'value and respect for diversity'. Its suggestions for global 'knowledge and understanding' include some of the following for Key Stages 3 and 4: basic rights and responsibilities; relationship between conflict and peace; cause of poverty; power relationships North/South; and lifestyles for a sustainable world. Taken with the subject booklets provided by the Development Education Association this framework can be appropriately applied to national curriculum subjects.

The global dimension of citizenship has received much publicity ranging from *Times Educational Supplement* magazines to NGO recommendations (DEA 2001) and student textbooks (Algarra 2002). Case 5 is an example of an activity that can raise issues which are central to global citizenship (see Box 15.5).

Box 15.5 Fair trade

Case 5: Fair trade

Children at a Yorkshire school took part in a Chocolate Trade Game from Christian Aid to learn more about the relationships between cocoa farmers, chocolate companies, supermarkets and consumers. It raised many issues around fair trade, sustainable development and conflict resolution. It was a fun activity and made children aware of the importance of being a global citizen. One of the children wrote to the head teacher after taking part in the game, asking why the school was not more committed to fair trade products and as a result more are now being used.

(Global Dimension website)

Citizenship is not the only place for developing global awareness, however, especially as the global element of Citizenship is less than 10 per cent of the recommended programme (DfEE 1999). Some subject associations such as the Geographical Association and the Association for Science Teaching offer support for developing the global dimension. Teachers may wish to reflect upon the issues associated with, and methods of developing, a particular aspect of the curriculum that they feel confident with and know to be closely linked to other global issues. The practice of 'story-telling' is a much used device in global education and can be used in English or Languages, for example. Stories from around the world which encourage students to think about the links between the personal, local and global can be incorporated into the curriculum.

Choosing a topic or issue that is global in outlook and raises global concerns can be problematic for teachers. In particular, if a critical global education is to be delivered, the issue of perspective is an important one. For example, Case 6 includes the Peace Pledge Union's perspective on a global perspective in history (see Box 15.6).

Successful classroom practice will also depend upon the incorporation of a suitable pedagogy as the following section explores.

Box 15.6 Learning peace through history

Case 6: Learning peace through history

War is studied in History lessons – in fact probably too much – and the focus is usually on the events that took place – battles, sinking of ships, declarations of war and declarations of peace. Visits to war cemeteries, battlefields and war museums tend to focus on sorrow, heroism and sacrifice. The really challenging questions of why, who was responsible and how can we avoid the same terrible mistakes in the future, generally do not surface in the study of war in History lessons.

(Peace Pledge Union website)

Pedagogical issues and teacher–pupil relationships

Global education is often associated with a pupil-centred, empowering pedagogy which emphasises skills of critical thinking, communication, co-operation and conflict resolution. Oxfam states that 'education for global citizenship encourages children and young people to explore, develop and express their own values and opinions, whilst listening to and respecting other people's points of view' (2006a: 2). To achieve this, a variety of participatory teaching and learning methodologies such as 'discussion and debate, role-play, ranking exercises, and communities of enquiry' (ibid.) are recommended. Photo-packs and resources such as *Change the World in Eight Steps* (Oxfam 2005c) or *Young Lives, Global Goals* (Save the Children 2005) model teaching approaches that harness the active and affective dimensions of global education.

A variety of resources exist which incorporate an interactive, pupil-empowering pedagogy. *Get Global!* (Action Aid 2003) focuses upon just such processes and learning activities:

Get Global! … is based on the belief that skills associated with being an active global citizen, e.g. communication, enquiry and critical thinking, are essential for dealing with the demands of an increasingly globalised and interdependent world. The methodology underpinning Get Global! is based on learning methods known as participatory rural appraisal techniques … developed in less economically developed countries … They use a range of participatory learning styles and visual tools, such as graphics, to understand and assess people's roles in the community and how they can effect change.

(Action Aid 2003: 3)

This resource introduces a range of teaching tools and methods for addressing global issues, including issue trees, research mind-maps, internet searches and why-why-why chains (Action Aid website). In secondary schools these pupil-empowering, competence-based pedagogies can sometimes feel daunting to teachers faced with large groups of teenagers. There are also those who believe that global education can be taught effectively through more didactic methods (Marshall 2005a).

A popular way of bringing global education into the classroom is the inclusion of outside speakers. At the time of writing, organisations such as Action Aid, People and Planet, and Water Aid offer a speaker service for schools. Case 7 highlights some of the benefits of this activity (see Box 15.7).

Box 15.7 Outside speakers

Case 7: A visitor in the school

As part of a topic on water, the head of geography in a school in West Sussex invited a volunteer speaker from Water Aid to come into Year 9 geography lessons to give a general talk about the organisation and its key concerns. The speaker discussed issues of water availability and sanitation in African countries such as Ethiopia and Tanzania, having been to these countries and describing this experience. The talk involved some student participation and lots of good visual aids. Afterwards students talked about the lesson very positively, explaining how it brought to life some of the issues they were studying in geography.

With older age-groups, for example Years 10–13, an outside visitor or powerpoint presentation supplied by an NGO can facilitate an interesting discussion, illustrating how global education can effectively raise interdisciplinary topics and knowledge in the classroom. Outside speaker visits work best when students are given a preparation session prior to the visit and are encouraged to reflect upon the experience afterwards.

Other pedagogical issues are raised by the particular dynamics of the classroom. Teachers constantly work with a particular ethnic, socio-cultural and gender mix of students. Some global issues bring these dynamics to the fore – for example, if you are discussing the role of women in the global economy in economics or the issue of international racism in a racially mixed PSHE class. Gaine (2005), for example, has explored the particular dilemmas for classroom practice when addressing intercultural and racist issues in all-white mono-cultural schools.

Although it may be a challenge to measure the impact of global citizenship teaching and learning, global education does present interesting opportunities for students and staff to critically reflect upon their own learning and development throughout the course of a topic or lesson. A global education portfolio or web-log of some kind can facilitate this sort of reflection.

Resources

Three broad categories of resource for global citizenship can be identified.

* Textbooks and teaching packs, for example, *Young Lives, Global Goals: teaching about poverty, children and the UN Millennium Development Goals* (Save the Children 2005), *Under the UN Flag: assemblies for citizenship in secondary schools* (UNICEF 2005), *The Changing Face of Slavery* (Anti-Slavery International 2001), *Citizenship in Focus: global concerns* (Foster 2000).
* Internet and multi-media resources, for example, Oxfam's Cool Planet website (2006b) or the United Nations' Cyber School Bus (website) or the Global Eye website run by Worldaware.
* Human resources and advice, for example, LEAs and schools, NGOs, the DEA, DfID, the British Council, DfES or UNESCO, *Developing the Global Dimension in the School Curriculum* (DfES 2005), *Putting the World into World-Class Education* (DfES 2004), *Education for Sustainable Development and Global Citizenship* (ACCAC 2002), *International Outlook: Educating Young Scots about the World* (SEED 2001), *Education for Global Citizenship: A Guide for Schools* (Oxfam 2006).

Of course the vigilant teacher and school will not draw upon these resources uncritically, and the checklist for analysing classroom resources cited in Pike and Selby (1988: 268–9) is still extremely relevant for checking bias.

As the references in this chapter show, the internet is a vital source of information in global education. The teaching and learning issues associated with this learning tool have been subject to much debate, but, so far, little research has been carried out on the impact of the internet upon global citizenship learning. However, the importance of publicising activities and projects on websites seems self-evident. Students may also find ways to incorporate web-blogs or online discussions in their global activities.

Access to the internet raises a range of issues for teachers – not least the fact that students are exposed to facts and opinions about controversial global issues. For example, Davies *et al.* (2005) highlight the fact that:

> Many teachers ... lack confidence and feel under-prepared in tackling controversial global issues, in terms both of knowledge and methods. They fear children would be anxious if war were discussed, that ethnic tensions in the class would be heightened, or that they should not present their own views.
>
> (Davies *et al.* 2005: 4)

Fortunately there is much advice available for teachers who are addressing controversial issues (much of which is summarised in Chapter 5). Citizenship related resources and websites such as CitizEd and Channel 4 are also useful for classroom teachers. Indeed there is a wide range of resources for supporting global citizenship in schools as this chapter has shown.

Concluding comments

This chapter has highlighted some of the dimensions of 'good' global citizenship practice in secondary schools. It is likely however that no global school will look the same as another because each is composed of staff and students with different interests, cultural backgrounds and international experiences. Therefore, whether a school is launching, developing or embedding the global dimension, the curricular and pedagogical challenges will vary. The maintenance of a global ethos may, in some cases, prove to be demanding as teachers may have to sustain global education in a climate where schools are faced with competing initiatives and policies. This chapter has suggested some of the ways in which teachers can draw upon outside resources and advice to ensure good, sustainable practice.

The final case study is taken from a keynote lecture given by Waters (2005) at the British Council's Education and Training National Conference (see Box 15.8). This is an example of a school which has chosen to focus on teachers' international experience and fostering a notion of internationalism. Other schools might choose to work more with their local global education organisations or focus upon a particular issue. Whatever the focus, there is some consensus (Davies *et al.* 2005) that, understandably, teachers and pupils require time and space to reflect creatively about what global citizenship means in the twenty-first century.

Box 15.8 A global school

Case 8: A global school

There is a school that really exploits internationalism for the adults, so the citizenship co-ordinator is in Indonesia, the science teachers are in South America, the humanities teachers are in New Zealand, the head teacher has been to China and the English and media teachers have been in America – and somebody stayed at school I presume. But it's a co-ordinated, planned, organised programme so all the children know who's where, why they're there and what they're going to get out of it at the end. The children are so proud of their adult staff for going places, doing things and showing things about their school to others. They have these amazing international evenings and when you talk to the children they talk about how much courage and confidence it gives them to take part in these evenings. There are 38 different languages in that school and they make use of every child's experience in so many ways. Food is the great leveller, you share food with people and you share a lot.

(Waters 2005)

Elsewhere I have talked about global education as a 'field' in the UK because of its heterogeneous nature (Marshall 2005a/b, 2006). This field is made up of different voices, ideologies and traditions, and it is a place where the meaning of global citizenship is constantly evolving. However, most global educators share a belief in global social justice, international interdependence and working towards a global citizenry ideal. A school that aspires to develop a holistic global outlook could do worse than begin by problematising and critically reflecting upon these concepts.

Bibliography

100 Great Black Britons. Online. Available http://www.100greatblackbritons.com (accessed 2 May 2006).

Academy of American Poets. Online. Available//www.poets.org (accessed 5 May 2006).

Action Aid (2003) *Get Global! a skills-based approach to active global citizenship for key stages three and four*, London: Action Aid.

Action Aid. Online. Available http://www.actionaid.org.uk (accessed 30 April 2006).

Advisory Group on Citizenship (1998) *Education for Citizenship and the Teaching of Democracy in Schools*, London: Qualifications and Curriculum Authority.

Alexander, T. (2001) *Citizenship Schools: a practical guide to education for citizenship and personal development*, London: Campaign for Learning.

Algarra, B. (2002) *Activate 3: enquiries into global citizenship*, Cheltenham: Nelson Thornes.

American Forum for Global Education. Online. Available http://www.globaled.org (accessed 9 May 2006).

Amnesty International (2001) *Siniko – Towards a human rights culture in Africa*, London: Amnesty International.

Amnesty International (2005) *Junior Urgent Action*, 'Help free 4 year old Ei Po Po', London: Amnesty International.

Amnesty International. Online. What can you do? Available http://www.amnesty.org.uk (accessed 3 July 2006).

Amos, M. (2001) *The Protection of Human Rights in the United Kingdom*, CEWC Newsletter, No. 1, London: Council for Education in World Citizenship.

Anderson, L. (1968) 'An examination of the structure and objectives of international education', *Social Education*, 32(7) (November): 639–47.

Anne Frank Center. Online. Available http://www.annefrank.com/ (accessed 4 June 2006).

Antidote (2003) *The Emotional Literacy Handbook: promoting whole-school strategies*, London: David Fulton.

Anti-Slavery International (2001) *The Changing Face of Slavery*, London: Anti-Slavery International.

Anti-Slavery International. Online. Available http://www.antislavery.org/ (accessed 30 April 2006).

Apple, M. (2001) *Educating the 'Right' Way: markets, standards, God, and inequality*, London: RoutledgeFalmer.

Argyle Primary School (2005) *Curriculum Content and Organisation*, Camden: Argyle Primary School.

Artlex. Online. Available http://www.artlex.com/ArtLex/ij/islamic.html (accessed 22 May 2006).

Ash, T.G. (2005) 'What we call Islam is a mirror in which we see ourselves', *The Guardian*, 15 September. Online. Available www.guardian.co.uk/comment/story/0,,1570236,00.html (accessed 25 November 2006).

Becker, J. (1975) *Guidelines for World Studies*, Indiana University: Mid-America Program for Global Perspectives in Education.

Bell, W. (1997) *Foundations of Futures Studies*, 2 vols, New Brunswick, NJ: Transaction Publishers.

Bemak, F. and Keys, S. (2000) *Violent and Aggressive Youth: intervention and prevention strategies for changing times*, Thousand Oaks, CA: Corwin Press.

Berkshire Family Historian. Online. Available http://www.berksfhs.org.uk/journal/Dec2002/BlackBritons.htm (accessed 22 May 2006).

Black History Month. Online. Available http//www.black-history-month.co.uk/ (accessed 22 May 2006).

Boulding, E. (1990) *Building a Global Civic Culture: education for an interdependent world*, Syracuse: Syracuse University Press.

British Council (2005) *Teachers' International Professional Development Programme*, London: British Council.

British Council (2006a) Online. Available http://www.britishcouncil.org (accessed 30 April 2006).

British Council (2006b) Online. Available http://www.britishcouncil.org/globalschools.htm (accessed 6 May 2006).

British and Foreign School Society. Online. Available http://bfss.org.uk/ (accessed 30 April 2006).

British Museum. Compass. Online. Available http://www.thebritishmuseum.ac.uk/compass (accessed 22 May 2006).

Brown, M. and Durie, D. (2000) *Local Citizen, Global Citizen*, London: Christian Aid.

Brown, M. and Jones, D. (eds) (2006) *Our World, Our Rights*, London: Amnesty International.

Brown, M., Markham, L. and Armistead, R. (2004) *Human Rights Trail Around York*, York: Centre for Global Education.

Brownlie, A. (2001) *Citizenship Education: the global dimension: guidance for key stages 3 and 4*, London: Development Education Association.

Brunstad, P.O. (2002) 'Longing for belonging: youth culture in Norway', in J. Gidley and S. Inayatullah (eds) *Youth Futures: comparative research and transformative visions*, Westport, CT: Praeger.

Buller, L. (2005) *A Faith Like Mine: a celebration of the world's religions through the eyes of children*, London: Dorling Kindersley.

Burney, I. (2005) *Oldham Journey Teachers Pack*, Oldham: Minority Ethnic Achievement Team.

Burns, R. and Aspeslagh, R. (eds) (1996) *Three Decades of Peace Education Around the World: an anthology*, New York: Garland Publishing.

Caesar, E. (2005) 'What we already know', *The Independent*, 31 December.

Callaghan, C. (2003) *The Journey: teachers' handbook*, Huddersfield: Primary Colours.

Carfree Cities www.carfree.com/.

Carrington, B. and Troyna, B. (eds) (1988) *Children and Controversial Issues*, Lewes: The Falmer Press.

Case, R. (1993) 'Key elements of a global perspective', *Social Education*, 57(6): 318–25.

Catholic Agency for Overseas Development (CAFOD). Global issues. Online. Available http://www.cafod.org.uk/resources/secondary_schools/globalisation/global_citizenship_ks3_background (accessed 14 April 2006).

Catling, S. (2000) 'Making sense of the media: the need for research', *Primary Geographer*, 42 (October): 24–6.

Catling, S. (2003) 'Curriculum contested: primary geography and social justice', *Geography*, 88(3): 164–210.

Centre for Citizenship and Human Rights Education, University of Leeds. Online. Available http://www.education.ac.uk/research/cchre/ (accessed 8 May 2006).

Centre for Cross Curricular Initiatives (2004) *Teaching for a Sustainable Future*, London: South Bank University.

Channel 4. Online. Available http://www.channel4.come/learning (accessed 30 April 2006).

CitizEd. Online. Available http://www.citiz.ed.info/ (accessed 8 May 2006).

Citizenship Foundation, London. Online. Available http://www.citizenshipfoundation.org.uk (accessed 8 May 2006).

Citizenship Pieces. Online. Available http://www.citizenship-pieces.org.uk (accessed 5 May 2006).

Claire, H. (2001) *Not Aliens: primary school children and the PSHE/Citizenship Curriculum*, Stoke-on-Trent: Trentham.

Claire, H. (2002) '"Why didn't you fight Ruby?" Teaching citizenship through history in key stage 1', *Education 3–13*, 30(2): 24–32

Claire, H. (ed.) (2004) *Teaching Citizenship in Primary Schools*, Exeter: Learning Matters.

Claire, H. (2006a) 'Education for cultural diversity and social justice', in J. Arthur, T. Grainger and D. Wray (eds) *Learning to Teach in the Primary School*, London: RoutledgeFalmer.

Claire, H. (2006b) *Teacher's Activity Book for Black Britons: from Romans to the Second World War*, video and DVD plus pack, London: BBC Active/Pearson.

Clarke, P. (2001) Teaching controversial issues: a four step classroom strategy for clear thinking on controversial issues. Online. Available http://www.bctf/Social/GlobalEd/GlobalClassroom/ClarkePat/TchgControversialIssues.pdf (accessed 5 May 2006).

Clough, N. and Holden, C. (2002) *Education for Citizenship: ideas into action. A practical guide for teachers of pupils aged 7–14,* London: RoutledgeFalmer.

Cogan, J. and Derricott, R. (2000) *Citizenship for the 21st Century: an international perspective on education*, London: Kogan Page.

Comic Relief. Online. Available http://www.comicrelief.com (accessed 4 June 2006).

Commission on British Muslims and Islamophobia (1997) *Islamophobia: a challenge for us all*, London: Runnymede Trust.

Commission on British Muslims and Islamophobia (2004) *Islamophobia: issues, challenges and action*, Stoke-on-Trent: Trentham Books.

Commission on Citizenship (1990) *Encouraging Citizenship: report of the Commission on Citizenship*, London: HMSO.

Commission on the Future of Multi-ethnic Britain (2002) *The Future of Multi-ethnic Britain*, (Parekh Report) London: Profile Books.

Commission for Racial Equality (2002) *Statutory Code of Practice on the Duty to Promote Race Equality*, London: Commission for Race Equality.

Communication Initiative. Online. Available http://www.comminit.com/strategicthinking/pdsmakingwaves/sld-1905.html (accessed 14 April 2006).

Council for Education in World Citizenship (CEWC) (2001) 'Human Rights in the UK', Council for Education in World Citizenship Newsletter No.1, London: CEWC.

Council for Education in World Citizenship (CEWC). Online. Available http://www.cewc. org (accessed 30 April 2006).

Crick Report (1998) *Education for Citizenship and the Teaching of Democracy in Schools*, London: Qualifications and Curriculum Authority.

Daffé, J., Kay, Y., Moore, J. and Nickolay, S. (2005) *Integrating Global and Anti-Racist Perspectives in the Primary Curriculum*, Nottingham: City of Nottingham Education Department.

Dalrymple, H. (n.d.) *Fair Trade School Handbook: a small but useful guide to help you become a fair trade school*, Leeds: Leeds Development Education Centre.

Davies, L. (2004) *Education and Conflict: complexity and chaos*, London: RoutledgeFalmer.

Davies, L. (2005) 'Rebuilding a civic culture post-conflict', *London Review of Education*, 2(3): 229–44.

Davies, L. and Leoni, J. (2006) 'Conflict resolution in schools', in F. Leach and M. Dunne (eds) *Conflict and Reconciliation: education in the 21st century*, Oxford: Peter Lang.

Davies, L., Harber, C. and Yamashita, H. (2005) *Global Citizenship Education: the needs of teachers and learners*, Birmingham: Centre for International Education and Research.

Davies, L., Williams, C, and Yamashita, H. (2006) *Inspiring Schools: taking up the challenge of pupil participation*, Birmingham: Centre for International Education and Research.

DEED (2005) *To Begin at the Beginning: bringing a global dimension to the early years*, Bournemouth: Development Education East Dorset.

Department for Education and Employment (DfEE) (1999) *The National Curriculum*, London: DfEE.

Department for Education and Skills (DfES) (2003) *Excellence and Enjoyment: a strategy for primary schools*, London: DfES.

Department for Education and Skills (DfES (2004) *Putting the World into World-Class Education*, London: DfES.

Department for Education and Skills (DfES) (2005a) *Developing a Global Dimension in the School Curriculum*, London: DfES.

Department for Education and Skills (DfES) (2005b) *Every Child Matters: change for children*, London: DfES.

Department for Education and Skills (DFES) (2006a) Racist bullying and other bullying. Online. Available http://www.teachernet.gov.uk/racistbullying (accessed 6 May 2006).

Department for Education and Skills (DfES) (2006b) Ethnic minority achievement. Online. Available http://www.standards.dfes.gov.uk/ethnicminorities/ (accessed 22 May 2006).

Department for Education and Skills (DfES) (2006c) The Standards Site. Online. Available http://www.standards.dfes.gov.uk/schemes2/citizenship/cit17/?view=get (accessed 6 May 2006).

Department for Education and Skills (DfES) (2006d) Global gateway. Online. Available http://www.globalgateway.org.uk (accessed 6 May 2006).

Department for Education and Skills (DfES) (2006e) The DfES sustainable development action plan 2005/06. Online. Available http://www.dfes.gov.uk (accessed 5 June 2006).

Department for Environment, Food and Rural Affairs (DEFRA) (2006) Key facts about global atmosphere. Online. Available http://www.defra.gov.uk/environment/statistics/globatmos/ kf/gakf07.htm (accessed 6 May 2006).

Department of the Environment, Transport and Regions (DETR) (1999) *Sustainable Development Education Panel First Annual Report 1998*, London: DEFRA.

Department for International Development (DfID)/Action Aid (2000a) *Learning Global Lessons: 50 non-fiction literacy hours*, Chard: Action Aid.

Department for International Development (DfID) (2000b) *Viewing the World: a study of television coverage of developing countries*, London: DfID.

Department for International Development (DfID) (2004) *School Children and Development Issues: a research study among 11–16 year olds*, London: DfID.

Department for International Development (DfID) (2006a) Global dimension. Online. Available http://www.globaldimension.org.uk (accessed 8 May 2006).

Department for International Development (DfID) (2006b) Enabling effective support: responding to the challenges of the global society. Online. Available http://www.dfid.gov.uk (accessed 9 May 2006).

Department for International Development (DfID) (2006c) Online. Available http://www.dfid.gov.uk (accessed 4 June 2006).

Development Education Association (2001) *Citizenship Education: the global dimension (Guidance for key stages 3 and 4)*, London: Development Education Association.

Development Education Association (2003a) *Global Perspectives and Teachers in Training*, London: Development Education Association.

Development Education Association (2003b) *Science: the global dimension (key stages 3 and 4)*, London: Development Education Association.

Development Education Association (2004) *Geography: the global dimension (key stage 3)*, London: Development Education Association.

Development Education Association. What is development education? Online. Available http://www.dea.org.uk (accessed 8 May 2006).

Development Education Association A–Z. Online. Available http://www.dea.org.uk/dec/index.html (accessed 6 May 2006).

Development Education Journal. Online. Available http://www.dea.org.uk (accessed 8 May 2006).

Directgov (2004) UK tops foreign investment table. 7 July. Online. Available http://www.direct.gov.uk/Nl1/Newsroom/NewsroomArticles/fs/en?CONTENT_ID=4014698&chk=OAUj%2B/ (accessed 14 April 2006).

Disney, A. (2004) 'Children's developing images and representations of the school link environment', in S. Catling and F. Martin (eds) *Researching Primary Geography*, London: Register of Research in Primary Geography.

Divine Chocolate. Bean to bar: the full story. Online. Available http://www.divinechocolate.com/Templates/Internal.asp?NodeID=90307&strAreaColor=Ye (accessed 6 May 2006).

Donaldson, M. (1978) *Children's Minds*, London: Fontana.

Donnellan, C. (2005) *The Globalisation Issue*, Cambridge: Independence Educational Publishers.

Dower, N. (2003) *An Introduction to Global Citizenship*, Edinburgh: Edinburgh University Press.

Eckersley, R. (1999) 'Dreams and expectations: young people's expected and preferred futures and their significance for education', *Futures*, 31(1): 73–90.

Ecological Footprint (2005) Ecological footprint of nations 2005 update. Online. Available http://www.ecologicalfootprint.org (accessed 8 June 2006).

Eco-Schools. Online. Available http://www.eco-schools.org (accessed 30 April 2006).

Eco-Schools Scotland. Online. Available http://www.ecoschoolsscotland.org (accessed 30 April 2006).

Education Action International Online. Available http://www.education-action.org (accessed 30 April 2006).

Egan, K. (1989) *Teaching as Storytelling*, Chicago, IL: University of Chicago Press.

Ellwood, W. (2001) *The No-Nonsense Guide to Globalization*, Rotherham: New Internationalist.

English, E., Hargreaves, L. and Hislam, J. (2002) 'Pedagogical dilemmas in the National Literacy Strategy: primary teachers' perceptions, reflections and classroom behaviour', *Cambridge Journal of Education*, 32(1): 9–26.

E-pals. Online. Available http://www.epals.com (accessed 30 April 2006).

Ethical Consumer. Online. Available http://www.ethicalconsumer.org/ (accessed 4 June 2006).

Ethnic Minority Attainment. Online. Available http://www.emaonline.org.uk (accessed 22 May 2006).

Fair Trade (2004) *Time for Change: fair-trade school handbook*, London: Fairtrade Foundation.

Fair Trade Foundation. Online. Available http://www.fair-trade.org.uk/ (accessed 8 May 2006).

Feuerverger, G. (2001) *Oasis of Dreams: teaching and learning peace in a Jewish-Palestinian village in Israel*, New York: RoutledgeFalmer.

Fiehn, J. (2005) *Agree to Disagree: citizenship and controversial issues*, London: Learning and Skills Development Agency.

Filipovic, Z. (1993) *Zlata's Diary: a child's life in Sarajevo*, London: Penguin.

Fisher, A. (2001) *Critical Thinking: an introduction*, Cambridge: Cambridge University Press.

Fisher, S. and Hicks, D. (1985) *World Studies 8–13: a teacher's handbook*, Edinburgh: Oliver and Boyd.

Fisher, S., Abdi, D., Ludin, J., Smith, R. and Williams, S. (2000) *Working with Conflict: skills and strategies for action*, London: Zed Books.

Foster, S. (2000) *Citizenship in Focus: global concerns*, London: Collins.

Frank, A. (1997, new edn) *The Diary of Anne Frank*, London: Viking.

Frazer, E. (1999) 'The idea of political education', *Oxford Review of Education*, 25(1–2): 7–15.

Freire, P. (1994) *A Pedagogy of Hope*, London: Continuum.

Frontline. Online. Available http://www.pbs.org/wgbh/pages/frontline/teach/divided (accessed 4 June 2006).

Gaine, C. (1995) *Still No Problem Here*, Stoke-on-Trent: Trentham Books.

Gaine, C. (2005) *We're All White Thanks: the persisting myth about white schools*, Stoke-on-Trent: Trentham Books.

Gallagher, T. (2004) *Education in Divided Societies*, London: Palgrave Macmillan.

Galtung, J. (1976) 'Peace education: problems and conflicts', in M. Haavelsrud (ed) *Education for Peace: reflection and action*, Godalming: IPC Science and Technology Press.

Garlake, T. (2003) *The Challenge of Globalisation: a handbook for teachers of 11–16 year olds*, Oxford: Oxfam.

Garner, R. (2005) 'Conflicts boost interest in politics and religion', *The Independent*, 19 August.

Gaudelli, W. (2003) *World Class: teaching and learning in global times*, Mahwah, NJ: Lawrence Erlbaum Associates.

Get Global Project. Online. Available http://www.getglobal.org.uk (accessed 4 June 2006).

Gidley, J. and Inayatullah, S. (2002) *Youth Futures: comparative research and transformative visions*, Westport, CT: Praeger.

Gidley, J., Bateman, D. and Smith, C. (2004) *Futures in Education: Principles, Practice and Potential*, Hawthorn: Australian Foresight Institute. Available http://www.swin.edu.au/agse/courses/foresight/monographs.htm (accessed 6 May 2006).

GLADE/Centre for Global and Development Education. Online. Available http://www.glade.org (accessed 30 April 2006).

Global Dimension. Online. Available http://www.globaldimension.org.uk/ (accessed 6 May 2006).

Global Education Associates. Online. Available http://www.globaleduc.org (accessed 9 May 2006).

Global Eye (2005) Focus on … telecommunications, Issue 24, Autumn. Online. Available http://www.globaleye.org.uk (accessed 6 May 2006).

Global Eye. Online. Available http://www.globaleye.org (accessed 30 April 2006).

Global Footprints. Online. Available http://www.globalfootprints.org/isssues/footprint (accessed 5 June 2006).

Global Gateway. Online. Available http://www.globalgateway.org.uk/ (accessed 8 May 2006).

Global Teacher Project. Online. Available http://www.globalteacher.org.uk (accessed 9 May 2006).

Goldstein, T. and Selby, D. (2000) *Weaving Connections: educating for peace, social and environmental justice*, Toronto: Sumach Press.

GrameenPhone. Online. Available http://www.grameenphone.com/modules.php?name=Content&pa=showpage&pid=3 (accessed 6 May 2006).

Graves, J. (2002) 'Developing a global dimension in the curriculum', *The Curriculum Journal*, 13(3): 303–11.

Grove, P. and Grove, C. (2006) The history of the 'ethnic' restaurant in Britain, Menu Magazine. Online. Available http://www.menumagazine.co.uk/book/restauranthistory.html (accessed 14 April 2006).

Guardian, The (2006b) 'Good lives: the people making a difference', 29 March.

Hahn, C. (1998) *Becoming Political: comparative perspectives on citizenship education*, Albany, NY: State University of New York.

Halsted, J.M. and Pike, M.A. (2006) *Citizenship and Moral Education: values in action*, London: RoutledgeFalmer.

Hand, P. (2003) *First Steps to Rights: activities for children aged 3–7 years*, London: UNICEF UK.

Hands On: Ideas to Go. Online. Available http://www.tve.org/ho/ (accessed 6 May 2006).

Hanvey, R. (1976) *An Attainable Global Perspective*, New York: Centre for War/Peace Studies.

Harris, I. and Morrison, M. (2003) *Peace Education*, 2nd edn, Jefferson, NC: McFarland and Co.

HealthNet. Online. Available http://www.healthnet.org/healthnet.php (accessed 6 May 2006).

Heater, D. (1980) *World Studies: education for international understanding in Britain*, London: Harrap.

Heater, D. (2001) 'The history of citizenship education in England', *The Curriculum Journal*, 12(1): 103–23.

Heater, D. (2004) *A History of Education for Citizenship*, London: RoutledgeFalmer.

Held, D. (1996) *Models of Democracy*, Cambridge: Polity Press.

Hickman, L. (2005) *A Good Life: the guide to ethical living*, St Austell: Eden Project Books.

Hicks, D. (1983/4) 'An interview with Robin Richardson', *World Studies Journal*, 4(2): 27–35.

Hicks, D. (ed.) (1988) *Education for Peace: issues, principles and practice in the classroom*, London: Routledge.

Hicks, D. (1990) 'World Studies 8–13: a short history 1980–89', *Westminster Studies in Education*, 13: 61–80.

Hicks, D. (2001) *Citizenship for the Future: a practical classroom guide*, Godalming: World Wide Fund for Nature UK.

Hicks, D. (2003) 'A futures perspective: lessons from the school room', *Journal of Futures Studies*, 7(3): 55–64.

Hicks, D. (2006) *Lessons for the Future: the missing dimension in education*, Victoria, BC: Trafford Publishing.

Hicks, D. and Holden, C. (1995) *Visions of the Future: why we need to teach for tomorrow*, Stoke-on-Trent: Trentham Books.

Hicks, D. and Slaughter, R. (eds) (1998) *Futures Education: the World Yearbook of Education 1998*, London: Kogan Page.

Hicks, D. and Steiner, M. (eds) (1989) *Making Global Connections: a world studies workbook*, Edinburgh: Oliver and Boyd.

Hicks, D. and Townley, C. (eds) (1982) *Teaching World Studies: an introduction to global perspectives in the curriculum*, Harlow: Longman.

Higgins, S. and Baumfield, V. (2001) *Thinking Through Primary Teaching*, Cambridge: Chris Kington Publishing.

Hines, C. (2000) *Localisation: a global manifesto*, London: Earthscan.

Hirst, B. (2006) *The Impact of Global Dimension Teaching on Children's Achievement*, Manchester: North West Global Education Network, Manchester Development Education Project.

Holden, C. (2000) 'Ready for citizenship? A case study of approaches to social and moral education in two contrasting primary schools in the UK', *The School Field International Journal of Theory and Research in Education*, XI(1): 117–30.

Holden, C. (2004) 'Heaven help the teachers! Parents' perspectives on the introduction of education for citizenship', *Educational Review*, 56(3): 247–58.

Holden, C. and Hicks, D. (2006) 'Making global connections: the knowledge, understanding and motivation of trainee teachers', *Teaching and Teacher Education*, 23(3): 13–23.

Huckle, J. (1996) 'Globalisation, postmodernity and citizenship', in M. Steiner (ed.) *Developing the Global Teacher*, Stoke-on-Trent: Trentham.

Hudson, A. (2005) 'Citizenship education and students' identities: a school-based action research project', in A. Osler (ed.) *Teachers, Human Rights and Diversity*, Stoke on Trent: Trentham Books.

Humanities Education Centre. Online. Available http://www.globalfootprints.org (accessed 30 April 2006).

Hutchinson, F. (1996) *Educating Beyond Violent Futures*, London: Routledge.

Imran, M. and Miskell, E. (2003) *Citizenship and Muslim Perspectives: teachers sharing ideas*, London: Islamic Relief; Birmingham: Teachers in Development Education.

Inayatullah, S. (1993) 'From "who am I?" to "when am I?" Framing the shape and time of the future', *Futures*, 25: 235–53.

Independent, The (2005) 24 April.

India Resource Centre. Online. Available http://www.indiaresource.org/ (accessed 14 April 2006).

Inservice Training and Educational Development (INSTED). Online. Available http://www.insted.co.uk/ (accessed 22 May 2006).

Inter-Faith Network (2004) *Connect: different faiths, shared values*, London: Inter-Faith Network in association with TimeBank and National Youth Agency.

Intergovernmental Panel on Climate Change (IPCC). Online. Available http://www.ipcc.ch (accessed 5 June 2006).

International Baccalaureate Organisation (IBO). Online. Available http://www.ibo.org/ (accessed 30 April 2006).

International Labour Migration. Online. Available http://www.ilo.org/public/english/protective/migrant/ (accessed 14 April 2006).

Internet Usage Statistics. Online. Available http://www.internetworldstats.com/stats.htm/ (accessed 14 April 2006).

Isenhart, M. and Spangle, M. (2000) *Collaborative Approaches to Resolving Conflict*, London: Sage.

Janoski, T. (1998) *Citizenship and Civil Society*, New York: Cambridge University Press.

Jarvis, H. and Midwinter, C. (1999) *Talking Rights, Taking Responsibility: a speaking and listening resource for secondary English and Citizenship*, London: UNICEF.

Jews for Justice for Palestinians. Online. Available http://www.jfjfp.org/ (accessed 22 May 2006).

Jones, R. (1999) *Tackling Racism or Teaching it?* Stoke-on-Trent: Trentham

Journal of Futures Studies. Online. Available http://www2.tku.edu.tw/~tddx/jfs/ (accessed 8 May 2006).

Journal of Peace Education. Online. Available http://www.tandf.co.uk/journals/offer/pec_info.asp (accessed 8 May 2006).

Kawagley, A. and Barnhardt, R. (1999) 'Education indigenous to place: western science meets native reality', in G.A. Smith and D.R. Williams (eds) *Ecological Education in Action: on weaving education, culture, and the environment*, Albany, NY: State University of New York Press.

Kelly, A.V. (1995) *Democracy and Education*, London: Paul Chapman Publishing.

Kerr, D. (1999) *Re-examining Citizenship Education: the case of England*, Slough: National Foundation for Educational Research.

Kettle, M. (2004) 'We all have one thing in common – our differences', *The Guardian*, 19 October.

Kick It Out. Online. Available http://www.kickitout.org/ (accessed 22 May 2006).

Klein, N. (2001) *No Logo,* London: Flamingo.

Ladson-Billings, G. and Gillborn, D. (eds) (2004) *The RoutledgeFalmer Reading in Multicultural Education*, London, RoutledgeFalmer.

Lambert, D., Morgan, A. and Swift, D. (2004) *Geography: the global dimension*, London: Development Education Association.

Layard, R. (2005) *Happiness: lessons from a new science*, London: Penguin.

Leat, D. (1998) *Teaching Through Geography*, Cambridge: Chris Kington Publishing.

Leeds Development Education Centre (n.d.) *A Quick Guide to North South School Links*, Leeds: Leeds DEC.

Leeds Development Education Centre (2005) *Global School Guide*, Leeds: Leeds Development Education Centre.

Lees, S. (2000) 'Sexuality and citizenship education', in M. Arnot and J. Dillabough (eds) *Challenging Democracy: international perspectives on gender, education and citizenship*, London: RoutledgeFalmer.

Let's Talk 80:20 (2001) *Let's Talk: a review*, Bray, Ireland: 80:20 Educating and Acting for a Better World.

Letterbox Library. Online. Available http://www.letterboxlibrary.com/ (accessed 22 May 2006).

Link Schools Programme. Online. Available http://www.lcd.org.uk (accessed 30 April 2006).

Lippmann, W. (1922, reprinted 1997) *Public Opinion*, Somerset, NJ: Transaction Publishers.

Lister, I. (1987) 'Global and international approaches to political education', in C. Harber (ed.) *Political Education in Britain*, London: Falmer Press.

Lister, R. (1997) *Citizenship: feminist perspectives*, Basingstoke: Macmillan Press.

London South Bank University. Online. Available http://www.lsbu.ac.uk/ (accessed 8 May 2006).

Lorax's Save the Trees Game, The. Online. Available http://www.seussville.com/games/lorax/ (accessed 4 June 2006).

Lynas, M. (2004) *High Tide: how climate crisis is engulfing our planet*, London: Harper Perennial.

Maiteny, P. (2004) Unit 5: *Theories and Perspectives on Environment and Development*, London: London South Bank University

Make Poverty History. Online. Available http://www.makepovertyhistory.org/ (accessed 6 May 2006).

Manchester Development Education Project (2006a) Online. Available. http://www.dep.org. uk (accessed 8 May 2006).

Manchester Development Project (2006b) Online. Available http://www.dep.org.uk/cities/ CaseStudies/Manchester/OldhamLinking.htm (accessed 22 May 2006).

Maquila Solidarity Network. The labour behind the label. Online. Available http://www. maquilasolidarity.org/resources/garment/labour-label.htm#Introduction (accessed 14 April 2006).

Marshall, H. (2005a) 'The sociology of global education: power, pedagogy and practice', unpublished doctorate thesis, University of Cambridge.

Marshall, H. (2005b) 'Developing the global gaze in citizenship education: exploring the perspectives of global education NGO workers in England', *The International Journal of Citizenship and Teacher Education*, 1(2): 76–92. Online. Available http://www.citized.info/ ijcte (accessed 13 April 2006).

Marshall, H. (2006) 'The global education terminology debate: exploring some of the issues in the UK context', in M. Hayden, J. Levy and J. Thomson (eds) *A Handbook of Research in International Education*, London: Sage.

Marshall, T.H. (1950) *Citizenship and Social Class*, Cambridge: Cambridge University Press.

Martin, F. (1995) *Teaching Early Years Geography*, Cambridge: Chris Kington Publishing.

Martin, F. (2005) 'North–South linking as a controversial issue', *Prospero*, 14(4): 47–54.

Martin, F. (2006a) *Teaching Geography in Primary Schools: learning to live in the world*, Cambridge: Chris Kington Publishing.

Martin, H. (2006b) 'Eco-warriors take a learning journey', *Primary Geographer*, 60: 7–9, Summer.

Macpherson, W. (1999) *The Stephen Lawrence Inquiry*, London: The Stationery Office.

McDonalds. About McDonalds. Online. Available http://www.mcdonalds.com/corp/about. html/ (accessed 14 April 2006).

McKeown, R. and Hopkins, C. (2003) 'EE # ESD: defusing the worry', *Environmental Education Research*, 9: 117–28.

McRae, H. (2006) 'Can't get no satisfaction? Look towards Mexico (or Ireland)', *The Guardian*, 9 February.

Meighan, R. and Siraj-Blatchford, I. (2003) *A Sociology of Educating*, London: Continuum.

Merryfield, M. (1997) 'A framework for teacher education in global perspectives', in M. Merryfield, E. Jarchow and S. Pickert (eds) *Preparing Teachers to Teach Global Perspectives*, Thousand Oaks, CA: Corwin Press.

Monahan, J. (2006) 'Profit from experience', *Times Educational Supplement, Teacher*, 26 May.

MORI (1998) *Children's Knowledge of Global Issues: a research study among 11–16 year olds*, London: MORI.

Morris, M. and Schagen, I. (1995) *Green Attitudes or Learned Responses?*, Slough: National Foundation for Educational Research.

Muñoz, V. (2006) Statement issued on implementation of plan of action for human rights education. Online. Available http://www.ohchr.org (accessed 3 July 2006).

Muslim Council of Britain, The. Online. Available http://www.mcb.org.uk/aboutmcb.php (accessed 21 May 2006).

Muslim News. Online. Available http://www.muslimnews.co.uk/ (accessed 5 May 2006).

Myers, N. and Kent, J. (2005) *The New Gaia Atlas of Planet Management*, London: Gaia Books.

Nakaseke Telecentre. Online. Available at http://www.comminit.com/strategicthinking/pdsmakingwaves/sld-1905.html (accessed 6 May 2006).

Nesbitt, E. (2004) *Intercultural Education: ethnographic and religious approaches*, Brighton: Academic Press.

Nesbitt, W. (1971) *Interpreting the Newspaper in the Classroom: foreign news and world news*, New York: Foreign Policy Asssociation.

North West Global Education Network. Online. Available www.globaldimensionnw.org.uk (accessed 4 June 2006).

Nussbaum, M. (1997) *Cultivating Humanity: a classical defense of reform in liberal education*, Cambridge, MA: Harvard University Press.

Observer, The (2004) 'Football's new world order', 6 June.

Office of Public Sector Information. Race Relations Amendment Act. Online. Available http://www.opsi.gov.uk/acts/acts2000/20000034.htm (accessed 24 May 2006).

Office for Standards in Education (OFSTED). Taking the first steps towards an education for sustainable development. Online. Available http://www.ofsted.gov.uk/publications (accessed 5 June 2006).

Office of the UN High Commissioner for Human Rights (2006) Speech by Eleanor Roosevelt on 10th anniversary of the Universal Declaration of Human Rights, cited in 'Teaching Human Rights: practical activities for primary and secondary schools'. Online. Available http://www.ohchr.org/english/about/publications/docs/abc-ch1.pdf (accessed 3 July 2006).

Oppenheimer, P. (2006) *Paul's Journey*, London: National Union of Teachers and the Holocaust Educational Trust.

Origination. Online. Available http://www.channel4.com/culture/microsites/O/origination/ (accessed 22 May 2006).

Orr, D. (2005) 'Greening the campus: the next phase', keynote lecture at fourth Greening of the Campus Conference, Ball State University, Indiana, September.

Oscarsson, V. (1996) 'Young people's views of the future', in A. Osler, H.F. Rathenow and H. Starkey (eds) *Teaching for Citizenship in Europe*, Stoke-on-Trent: Trentham.

Osler, A. (2005) 'Education for democratic citizenship: new challenges in a globalised world', in A. Osler and H. Starkey (2005) *Citizenship and Language Learning: international perspectives*, Stoke-on-Trent: Trentham.

Osler, A. and Starkey, H. (2003) 'Learning for cosmopolitan citizenship: theoretical debates and young people's experiences', *Educational Review*, 55(3): 243–54.

Osler, A. and Starkey, H. (2005) *Changing Citizenship: democracy and inclusion in education*, Maidenhead: Open University Press.

Osler, A. and Vincent, K. (2002) *Citizenship and the Challenge of Global Education*, Stoke-on-Trent: Trentham Books.

Oulton, C., Day, V., Dillon, J. and Grace, M. (2004a) 'Controversial issues – teachers' attitudes and practice in the context of citizenship education', *Oxford Review of Education*, 30(4): 489–507.

Oulton, C., Dillon, J. and Grace, M. (2004b) 'Reconceptualising the teaching of controversial issues', *International Journal of Science Education*, 26(4): 411–23.

Ouseley, H. (2004) 'Forget this phoney debate, we need to confront racism', *The Guardian*, 10 April.

Oxfam (1997) *A Curriculum for Global Citizenship*, Oxford: Oxfam.

Oxfam (2005a) *Making Sense of World Conflicts: activities and source materials for teaching English, Citizenship and PSHE*, Oxford: Oxfam.

Oxfam (2005b) Oxfam Briefing Note. *Who will be left to cheer the end of illegal US cotton subsidies?* 3 March, Oxford: Oxfam.

Oxfam (2005c) *Change the World in Eight Steps: a set of posters and activities for 7–14 year olds investigating the UN Millennium Development Goals*, Oxford: Oxfam.

Oxfam (2006a) *Education for Global Citizenship: a guide for schools*, Oxford: Oxfam.

Oxfam (2006b). Online. Available http://www.oxfam.org.uk/coolplanet/ (accessed 8 May 2006).

Oxfam (2006c) Iraq: war and peace. Online. Available http://www.oxfam.org.uk/coolplanet/teachers/iraq/index.htm (accessed 5 May 2006).

Oxfam (2006d) Milking it: small farmers and international trade. Online. Available http://www.oxfam.org.uk/coolplanet/milkingit (accessed 4 June 2006).

Oxfam (2006e) Change the world in 8 steps. Online. Available http://www.oxfam.org.uk/coolplanet/teachers/mdg (accessed 4 June 2006).

Oxfam (2006f) The coffee chain game. Online. Available http://www.oxfam.org.uk/coolplanet/teachers/coffee (accessed 4 June 2006).

Oxfam (2006g) *Teaching Controversial Issues*, Oxford: Oxfam GB.

Page, J. (2000) *Reframing the Early Childhood Curriculum: educational imperatives for the future*, London: RoutledgeFalmer.

Palmer, J. (1998) *Environmental Education in the 21st Century*, London: Routledge.

Parekh, B. (2006) 'Europe, liberalism and "the Muslim question"', in T. Modood, A. Triandafyllidou and R. Zapata-Barrero (eds) *Multiculturalism, Muslims and Citizenship: a European approach*, London: RoutledgeFalmer.

Peace Child International (2002) *Rescue Mission Planet Earth*, Buntingford: Peace Child International.

Peace Child International. Online. Available http://www.peacechild.org (accessed 5 May 2006).

Peace Education Commission of International Peace Research Association. Online. Available http://www.human.mie-u.ac.jp/-peace/about-ipra (accessed 8 May 2006).

Peace Pledge Union. Online. Available http://www.ppu.org.uk/learn (accessed 30 April 2006).

People and Planet. Online. Available http://www.peopleandplanet.org (accessed 30 April 2006).

Perry, W.G. (1999) *Forms of Educational and Intellectual Development in the College Years*, San Francisco, CA: Jossey-Bass Publishers.

Persona Dolls. Portsmouth Ethnic Minority Achievement Service. Online. Available http://www.blss.portsmouth.sch.uk/earlyears/eypdolls.html (accessed 5 May 2006).

Philo, G. and Berry, M. (2004) *Bad News from Israel*, London: Pluto Press.

Pickering, S. (2006) 'Sustainability through global partnerships', unpublished paper presented at Worcestershire Education Partnerships Network Spring Conference.

Pike, G. (2000) 'Global education and national identity: in pursuit of meaning', *Theory into Practice*, 39(2): 64–74.

Pike, G. and Selby, D. (1988) *Global Teacher, Global Learner*, London: Hodder and Stoughton.

Pike, G. and Selby, D. (1999/2000) *In the Global Classroom*, 2 vols, Toronto: Pippin Press.

Porritt, J. (2005) *Capitalism as if the World Matters*, London: Earthscan.

Q News. Online. Available http://www.q-news.com/ (accessed 5 May 2006).

Quaker Peace Education Project. Online. Available http://www.peacemakers.org.uk (accessed 5 May 2006).

Qualifications and Curriculum Authority (QCA) (1998) *Education for Citizenship and the Teaching of Democracy in Schools*, London: QCA.

Qualifications and Curriculum Authority (QCA) (1999) *The National Curriculum: handbook for primary teachers in England*, London: QCA and DfEE.

Qualifications and Curriculum Authority (QCA)/Department for Education and Employment (DfEE) (1999) *The National Curriculum: handbook for secondary teachers in England*, London: QCA/DfEE.

Qualifications and Curriculum Authority (QCA) (2002) *Citizenship: a scheme of work for key stage 3*, London: QCA.

Qualifications and Curriculum Authority (QCA) (2006a) Education for sustainable development. Online. Available http://www.nc.uk.net/esd (accessed 8 May 2006).

Qualification, and Curriculum Authority (QCA) (2006b) Innovating with history. Online. Available http://www.qca.org.uk/history/innovating/wider_curriculum.htm (accessed 22 May 2006).

Qualifications and Curriculum Authority (QCA) (2006c) Education for sustainable development. Online. Available http://www.qca.org.uk/ (accessed 22 May 2006).

Qualifications, Curriculum and Assessment Authority for Wales (ACCAC) (2002) *Education for Sustainable Development and Global Citizenship*, Birmingham: ACCAC Publications.

Quarrie, J. (ed.) (1992) *UN Conference on Environment and Development: Agenda 21*, London: Regency Press.

Race Equality Teaching (2006) Trentham Books. Online. Available http://www.trentham-books.co.uk (accessed 8 May 2006).

Reading International Solidarity Centre (RISC) (2004) *Choc-a-lot: a chocolate flavoured resource to explore global trade in cocoa*, Reading: RISC.

Real World Coalition (1996) *The Politics of the Real World*, London: Earthscan.

Richardson, R. (1976) *Learning for Change in World Society*, London: World Studies Project.

Richardson, R. (1986) 'The hidden message of schoolbooks', *Journal of Moral Education*, 15(1): 26–42.

Richardson, R. (1990) *Daring to be a Teacher*, Stoke-on-Trent: Trentham Books.

Richardson, R. (2004) *Here, There and Everywhere: belonging, identity and equality in schools*, Stoke on Trent: Trentham Books.

Richardson, R. and Miles, B. (2003) *Equality Stories: recognition, respect and raising achievement*, Stoke-on-Trent: Trentham Books.

Richardson, R. and Wood, A. (2000) *Inclusive Schools, Inclusive Society: race and identity on the agenda*, Stoke-on-Trent: Trentham Books.

Robbins, M., Francis, L. and Elliott, E. (2003) 'Attitudes towards education for global citizenship among student teachers', *Research in Education*, 69: 93–8.

Roche, C. (1996) 'Operationality in turbulence: the need for change', in D. Eade (ed.) *Development in States of War*, Oxford: Oxfam.

Roddick, A. (2001) *Take It Personally: how globalization affects you and powerful ways to challenge it*, London: Element Books.

Rokeach, M. (1960) *The Open and Closed Mind*, New York: Basic Books.

Rubin, A. (2002) 'Reflections upon the late-modern transition as seen in the images of the future held by young Finns', in J. Gidley and S. Inayatullah (eds) *Youth Futures: comparative research and transformative visions*, Westport, CT: Praeger.

Rudduck, J. and Flutter, J. (2000) 'Pupil participation and pupil perspective: carving a new order of experience', *Cambridge Journal of Education*, 30(1): 75–89.

Runnymede Trust. Online. Available http://www.runnymedetrust.org/ (accessed 8 May 2006).

SAPERE. Online. Newsletter 2005. Online. Available http://www.sapere.org.uk (accessed 4 June 2006).

Sardar, Z. (2004) 'What does it mean to be a British Muslim?', in R. Bechler (ed.) *What is British?*, London: British Council.

Save the Children (2000) *Partners in Rights: creative activities exploring rights and citizenship for 7–11 year olds*, London: Save the Children Fund.

Save the Children (2005) *Young Lives, Global Lives*, London: Save the Children.

Save the Children. Online. Available http://www.savethechildren.org (accessed 30 April 2006).

Schlosser, E. (2006a) 'Stuff the kids', *The Guardian*, 24 April.

Science Museum. Online. Available http://www.sciencemuseum.org.uk/learning/blackhistory month.asp (accessed 22 May 2006).

Scottish Education Executive Department (2001) *International Outlook: educating young Scots about the world*, Edinburgh: Scottish Executive Education Department.

Scottish Executive (2001) *The Global Dimension in the Curriculum*, Dundee: Learning and Teaching Scotland.

Scruton, R. (1985) *World Studies: education or indoctrination?*, London: Institute for Defence and Strategic Studies.

Selby, D. (1995) *Earthkind: a teachers' handbook on humane education*, Stoke-on-Trent: Trentham Books.

Selby, D. (2000) 'The signature of the whole', in E. O'Sullivan, A. Morrell and M. O'Connor (eds) *Expanding the Boundaries of Transformative Learning*, New York: Palgrave.

Send my Friend to School. Online. Available http://www.sendmyfriend.org/ (accessed 4 June 2006).

Shallcross, T. and Robinson, J. (2006) *Global Citizenship and Environmental Justice*, Amsterdam: Rodopi.

Shelley Primary School (2006) 'School brochure', West Sussex: Shelley Primary School.

Short, C. (1999) Keynote speech at Secondary Heads Association Conference, April.

Siemens AG. Online. Available http://www.siemens.com/ (accessed 14 April 2006).

Siraj-Blatchford, I. and Clarke, P. (2000) *Supporting Identity, Diversity and Language in the Early Years*, Buckingham: Open University Press.

Slaughter, R. (2005) *The Knowledge Base of Futures Studies*, Brisbane: Foresight International. Online. Available http://www.foresightinternational.com.au (accessed 8 May 2006).

Smith, A. and Robinson, A. (1996) *Education for Mutual Understanding: the statutory years*, Coleraine: University of Ulster.

Smith, J. and Armstrong, S. (2002) *If the World Were a Village*, London: A.C. Black.

Steiner, M. (1992) *Learning from Experience: world studies in the primary curriculum*, Stoke-on-Trent: Trentham Books.

Steiner, M. (1996) *Developing the Global Teacher: theory and practice in initial teacher education*, Stoke-on-Trent: Trentham Books.

Sterling, S. (2001) *Sustainable Education: re-visioning learning and change*, Dartington: Green Books.

Sterling, S. (2006) *Education for Sustainable Change*, Unit 7 Study Guide of the Education for Sustainability Programme, London: South Bank University.

Stewart, S. (1998) *Conflict Resolution: a foundation guide*, Winchester: Waterside Press.

Stradling R., Noctor, M. and Baines, B. (1984) *Teaching Controversial Issues*, London: Arnold.

Sustainable Development Education Panel (1998) *First Annual Report 1998*, London: Department of Environment, Transport and the Regions.

Sustainable Development Education Panel. Online. Available http://www.defra.gov.uk/environment/sustainable/educpanel/index.htm (accessed 5 June 2006).

Symons, G. (ed.) (2004) *Global Perspectives in Teacher Training*, London: Development Education Association.

Tarrow, N. (1992) 'Human rights education: alternative conceptions', in J. Lynch, C. Modgil and S. Modgil (eds) *Cultural Diversity and the Schools, Vol. 4: Human Rights, Education and Global Responsibilities*, London: Falmer Press.

TeacherNet. Sustainable schools. Online. Available http://www.teachernet.gov.uk/wholeschool/sd/susschools (accessed 5 June 2006).

Teachers in Development Education (TIDE) (2001) *Globalisation: what's it all about?* Birmingham: TIDE.

Teachers in Development Education (TIDE) (2002) *Start with a Story: supporting young children's exploration of issues*, Birmingham: Teachers in Development Education.

Teachers in Development Education (TIDE) (2005) *Climate Change – Local and Global: an enquiry approach*, Birmingham: TIDE.

Teachers in Development Education (TIDE) (2006a) Online. Available http://www.tidec.org (accessed 8 May 2006).

Teachers in Development Education (TIDE (2006b) 'School partnerships as a stimulus to curriculum enrichment and global learning', Teachers in Development Education Conference, 4 April.

Teachers International Professional Development Programme. Online. Available http://www.teachernet.gov.uk/tipd (accessed 30 April 2006).

TeachGlobal. Online. Available http://teachandlearn.net/teachglobal (accessed 14 June 2006).

Telquel (2002) Online. Available http://www.telquel-online.com (accessed 3 July 2006).

Temple, G. (2006) 'Thinking about linking', *Times Educational Supplement*, 31 March 2006. Online. Available http://www.tes.co.uk/search/story/?story_id=2216564 (accessed 25 November 2006).

Theodore, D. (2004) *Coming Unstuck: guidance and activities for teaching about racism with 10 to 11-year-olds*, Hampshire: County Council Education Department.

Thomas, G. (2001) *Human Traffic: skills, employers and international volunteering*, London: Demos.

Times, The (2006) 'Sorry miss, you must try harder', *Times2*, 18 April.

Times Educational Supplement, The (2004) 'No jam tomorrow?', *Teacher*, 23 January. Online. Available http://www.tes.co.uk/search/story/?story_id=389573 (accessed 25 November 2006).

Times Educational Supplement, The (2005) 'Global citizenship', 10 June.

Times Educational Supplement, The (2006) *Teacher*, 31 March.

Toffler, A. (ed.) (1974) *Learning for Tomorrow: the role of the future in education*, New York: Vintage Books.

Torney-Purta, J., Lehmann, R., Oswald, H. and Schulz, W. (eds) (1999) *Civic Education Across Countries: twenty four national case studies*, Amsterdam: International Association for Evaluation of Educational Achievement.

Training and Development Agency for Schools (TDA). Multiverse. Online. Available http://www.multiverse.ac.uk (accessed 22 May 2006).

Tye, K.A. (1999) *Global Education: a worldwide movement*, Orange, CA: Interdependence Press.

UK One World Linking Association. Online. Available http://www.ukowla.org.uk/Toolkit/equality.pdf (accessed 22 May 2006).

UN Cyber School Bus. Online. Available http://www.un.org/Pubs/CyberSchoolBus (accessed 30 April 2006).

UNESCO Associated Schools Project Network. Online. Available http://portal.unesco.org/education (accessed 25 November 2006).

UNICEF (1995) *Children Working for Peace*, London: UNICEF and Oxford; Oxford Development Education Centre.

UNICEF (2004) *How Do We Make Peace?* London: UNICEF.

UNICEF (2005) *Under the United Nations Flag: assemblies for citizenship in secondary school*, London: UNICEF.

UNICEF (2006a) Rights Respecting School Award. Online. Available http://www.unicef.org.uk/tz/teacher_support/rrs_award.asp (accessed 5 May 2006).

UNICEF (2006b) Convention on the Rights of the Child. Online. Available http://www.unicef.org.crc/ (accessed 6 May 2006).

UNICEF (2006c) Teacher zone. Online. Available http://www.unicef.org.uk/tz (accessed 3 July 2006).

UNICEF (2006d) Robbie Williams – more precious than gold. Online. Available http://www.endchildexploitation.org.uk (accessed 3 July 2006).

United Nations (1993) *The Nairobi Forward-Looking Strategies for the Advancement of Women*, DPI/926–41761, New York: United Nations.

United Nations Association (2006). Online. Available http://www.una-org/ (accessed 30 April 2006).

UN Millennium Development Goals. Online. Available http://www.un.org/millenniumgoals/ (accessed 4 June 2006).

Voluntary Service Overseas. Online. Available http://www.vso.org.uk/ (accessed 30 April 2006).

Wade, R. (2006) 'Partners for change', in S. Inman and M. Rogers (eds) *Building a Sustainable Future: challenges for initial teacher training*, Godalming: World Wide Fund for Nature UK.

Walker, M. (2005) 'Rainbow nation or new racism? Theorising race and identity formation in South African higher education', *Race, Ethnicity and Education*, 8(2): 129–46.

Ward, S. (ed.) (2004) *Education Studies: a student's guide*, London: RoutledgeFalmer.

Water Aid. Online. Available http://www.wateraid.org.uk (accessed 30 April 2006).

Waters, M. (2005) 'Making it happen', keynote lecture at Add the World to Your Class: creating international opportunities for schools, British Council Education and Training National Conference. Online. Available http://www.britishcouncil.org/learning-addtheworld (accessed 13 April 2006).

Waters, P. (2003) *On the Right Track*, York: (no publisher given).

Webster, K. (2004) *Rethink, Refuse, Reduce … education for sustainability in a changing world*, Preston Montford: Field Studies Council.

Wellington, J. (ed.) (1986) *Controversial Issues in the Curriculum*, Oxford: Blackwell.

Wellington, J. (2003) 'Science education for citizenship and a sustainable future', *Pastoral Care*, September: 13–18.

West Midlands Commission on Global Citizenship (2002) *Whose Citizenship? Exploring identity, democracy and participation in a global context*, Birmingham: Development Education Centre.

Whitworth, L. (2004) 'Religious education and citizenship education', in H. Claire (ed.) *Teaching Citizenship in Primary Schools*, Exeter: Learning Matters.

Wicks, S. (2004) *On the Right Track: what matters to young people in the UK?*, London: Save the Children.

Wiegand, P. (1992) *Places in the Primary School: knowledge and understanding of places at key stages 1 and 2*, London: Falmer Press.

Wikipedia. Anti-globalization. Online. Available http://www.wikipedia.org/wiki/Anti-globalisation (accessed 6 May 2006).

Wood, D. (1988) *How Children Think and Learn*, Oxford: Blackwell.

Wood, E.A. (2005) 'Young children's voices and perspectives in research: methodological and ethical considerations', *International Journal of Equity and Innovation in Early Childhood*, 3(2): 64–76.

World Commission on Environment and Development (WCED) (1987) Brundtland Report. Online. Available http://www.are.admin.ch/are/en/nachhaltig/international_uno/unterseite02330/ (accessed 25 November 2006).

World Education Centre (2004) *Embedding Education for Global Citizenship and Sustainable Development in Initial Teacher Education and Training Courses. A three year joint project between the World Education Centre and School of Education, University of Wales, Bangor*, Bangor: University of Wales.

World Futures Studies Federation. Online. Available http://www.wfsf.org (accessed 8 May 2006).

World Studies Trust. Online. Available http://www.globalteacher.org.uk (accessed 8 May 2006).

World Tourism Organisation. Online. Available http://www.world-tourism.org/ (accessed 6 May 2006).

World Travel and Tourism Council. Online. Available http://www.wttc.org/2006TSA/pdf/World.pdf (accessed 14 April 2006).

Worldwatch Institute (1999) *Vital Signs: the trends that are shaping our future 1999– 2000*, London: Earthscan.

Worldwatch Institute (2005) *Vital Signs: the trends that are shaping our future*, London: Earthscan.

Worldwatch Institute (2006) *Vital Signs: the trends that are shaping our future*, London: Earthscan.

World Wide Fund for Nature (WWF) (2006a). Online. Available http://www.wwflearning.org.uk/wwflearning-home (accessed 6 May 2006).

World Wide Fund for Nature (WWF) (2006b). Online. Available http://www.wwf.org.uk/core/wildlife/wildlife.asp (accessed 6 May 2006).

Wright, D. (2002) 'Japanese youth: reviewing futures in the "no taboos" post-bubble millennium', in J. Gidley and S. Inayatullah (eds) *Youth Futures: comparative research and transformative Visions*, Westport, CT: Praeger.

Young, M. and Commins, E. (2002) *Global Citizenship: the handbook for primary teaching*, Cambridge: Chris Kington.

Zephaniah, B. (2003) *We Are Britain*, London: Frances Lincoln.

Index